Clinical Neuropsychology and Technology

Thomas D. Parsons

Clinical Neuropsychology and Technology

What's New and How We Can Use It

Springer

Thomas D. Parsons
University of North Texas
Denton, TX
USA

ISBN 978-3-319-31073-2 ISBN 978-3-319-31075-6 (eBook)
DOI 10.1007/978-3-319-31075-6

Library of Congress Control Number: 2016934011

Printed on acid-free paper

This Springer imprint is published by Springer Nature
The registered company is Springer International Publishing AG Switzerland

I dedicate this book to Valerie Parsons...
her pure blue eyes reminded me that true
discovery consists not in simply seeking
novel landscapes, but in having new eyes.

Preface

> Perhaps it is because the profession of clinical neuropsychology is so young that any progress made in it may seem to be significant. However, it appears to the President of this Division that we are not actually making as much progress as we are inclined to believe and that this is true both in absolute terms and in comparison with the progress made in other clinical neurosciences.
>
> Dodrill (1997, p. 1)

As is apparent in Dodrill's presidential address to the American Psychological Associations's division on neuropsychology, I am not the first to stress the importance of technological progress for advancing neuropsychological assessments. What is striking about Dodrill's comments is that they are as true today as they were two decades ago. Advances in neuropsychological assessment are far behind progress made in other clinical neurosciences. The developments in neuroscience, computer science, and information technology have all the hallmarks of a broad technological revolution.

I began thinking about the importance of technology for neuropsychological assessment around the same time that Dodrill's presidential address was published. In 1998 I started graduate training in clinical psychology with an emphasis on neuropsychology. I had a background in computer science and electrical engineering from my time in the military and experience in computer networks and database programming. Throughout my neuropsychology training (graduate school, internship, and postdoctoral work), I was struck by the inefficiency of paper-and-pencil assessments and the fact that so many of the tests seemed to fall short of answering the referral questions I received while working in academic medical centers. Most of these tests were slightly modified tests that had been developed decades earlier. In addition to their lack of technological progress, the tests were theoretically questionable as they reflected early approaches to assessment found in non-clinical disciplines. A good deal of my training was in neurology departments, but most of the neuropsychological assessment tools revealed little correspondence to well-defined neuroanatomic systems. This seemed strange to me given that my work with researchers in neuroscience and computer science revealed many neural systems and modules that interconnected, with relative precision, neurocognitive processes to brain areas. When I compared these experiences with my work using neuropsychological assessment tools, I was frustrated by the imprecision and lack of sophistication of neuropsychological models of cognition. I felt then, and continue to believe, that technological upgrades to neuropsychological assessment tools would allow for clinical neuropsychological assessment data to better comport with functional neuroanatomic/neurocognitive systems.

My interest in computer science and advanced technologies led me to accept a position as a research scientist and assistant research professor position at the University of Southern California's Institute for Creative Technologies. During this time I was able to explore computerized methods for enhancing stimulus presentation, event logging, database development, and neuroinformatic approaches that could link behavioral responses to neurological models.

A few years ago I decided to make the transition into a more traditional tenure position where I would have increased opportunities to train the next generation of neuropsychologists in the application of advanced technologies for neuropsychological assessment. When preparing lectures I was once again struck by the absence of advances in computer science, information technology, and neuroinformatics in clinical neuropsychology. In other neuroscience subdisciplines evidence is readily apparent of advanced technologies, innovative research methods, novel data analytics, and collaborative knowledge bases. Unfortunately, clinical neuropsychology remains rather unchanged and there is little evidence of progress.

In November 2013 I received the early career award from the National Academy of Neuropsychology. At the same meeting, Dean Delis received the Distinguished Lifetime Contribution to Neuropsychology Award. Dr. Delis discussed the evolution of neuropsychological test development and the new frontiers in tablet-based testing. I remember my excitement when I realized that the distinguished lifetime achievement awardee and the early career awardee were both involved in advancing neuropsychological assessment with novel technologies. The following year, in February 2014, I presented two papers at the annual meeting of the International Neuropsychological Society, in Seattle, Washington. One paper was for a keynote symposium on ecologically valid methods of assessment in neuropsychology and the other paper was for a symposium on neuropsychology and technology in the twenty-first century. In addition to comparing paper-and-pencil, computer-automated, and simulation-based approaches to neuropsychological assessment these papers described the potential of virtual reality and information technology for enhancing clinical neuropsychology. Soon after, I began to structure these presentations into this text.

This book reviews currently available technologies that may be useful for neuropsychologists. In addition to enhanced technologies for administration and data capture, there is emphasis on the need for information technologies that can link outcome data to neuroinformatics and collaborative knowledgebases. I understand that this book is a rather ambitious first account of advances in technology for neuropsychological assessment. It is important to note that neuropsychologists need not view these advanced technologies as necessary replacements for current batteries. Instead, it is hoped that the tools described herein will offer neuropsychologists with additional tools that can be used judiciously with current batteries.

Denton, TX, USA Thomas D. Parsons

Acknowledgements

I wish to acknowledge the amazing people who helped me in making this book possible.

First, I wish to acknowledge my colleagues at the University of Southern California, and the University of North Texas. While at the University of Southern California's Institute for Creative Technologies, I had the great opportunity of working with Galen Buckwalter, Skip Rizzo, and Patrick Kenny. Their passion for virtual reality and neuropsychology shaped my development and proffered an impetus for my desire to update the tools used currently for neuropsychological assessment. At the University of North Texas, I have had a number of interesting interactions with my colleagues in Psychology. Additionally, I have benefitted from collaborative work with Ian Parberry in Computer Science and Lin Lin in Learning Technologies.

I also wish to acknowledge the first intellects who shaped my thinking. First, is Umberto Eco, in addition to Eco's semiotics (e.g., semiological guerrilla), his creation of the Abulafia computer in *Foucault's Pendulum* will always be my favorite technology for generating Aristotelian metaphors. I am also indebted to Jorge Luis Borges for his discussions of libraries, labyrinths, time, and infinity. Next, there is Ludwig Wittgenstein's brilliant early work in the *Tractatus Logico-Philosophicus*, and his later work in the *Philosophical Investigations*, wherein he discarded much of what he argued in the *Tractatus*!

There are also a number of students and postdoctoral fellows who both inspired me and diligently assisted with the research for the manuscript. Two graduate students stand out as exemplars of "why I do what I do" each day: Christopher Courtney from the University of Southern California and Timothy McMahan from the University of North Texas.

Finally, I must thank my best friend Valerie Parsons. Her encouragement and support have been invaluable. Also, our children, Tommy and Sophie: I am proud to have a bearcat and a bugaboo that are already fascinated by the brain and what it means to be a person. My family inspires and heals me. Dostoyevsky was correct that "The soul is healed by being with children."

Contents

About the Author

Thomas D. Parsons Ph.D., is a Clinical Neuropsychologist and Associate Professor of Psychology at the University of North Texas. Prior to joining the faculty at UNT, he was an Assistant Professor and Research Scientist at the University of Southern California's Institute for Creative Technologies. His work integrates neuropsychology and simulation technologies for novel assessment, modeling, and training of neurocognitive and affective processes. He is a leading scientist in this area and he has directed 17 funded projects during his career and he has been an investigator on an additional 13 funded projects. In addition to his patents for the eHarmony.com matching system, he has invented and validated virtual reality-based assessments of attention, spatial abilities, memory, and executive functions. He uses neural networks and machine learning to model mechanisms underlying reinforcement learning, decision making, working memory, and inhibitory control. He has over 100 publications in peer reviewed journals and book chapters. His contributions to neuropsychology were recognized when he received the 2013 National Academy of Neuropsychology Early Career Achievement award. In 2014, he was awarded the Fellow status in the National Academy of Neuropsychology.

Part I
Introduction

Chapter 1
Introduction

> *It would be strange, and embarrassing, if clinical psychologists, supposedly sophisticated methodologically and quantitatively trained, were to lag behind internal medicine, investment analysis, and factory operations control in accepting the computer revolution.*
>
> —Paul Meehl (1987)

> *There is one industry, however, that remains a glaring exception to the general rapid rate of technological progress that is ongoing in our society–the standardized-testing industry.*
>
> —Sternberg (1997)

Decades ago Paul Meehl (1987) called for clinical psychologists to embrace the technological advances prevalent in our society. Meehl's endorsement of technology for clinical psychology reflects the developments that were occurring during the 1980s for psychological testing (Bartram and Bayliss 1984; French and Beaumont 1987; Space 1981). In the 1980s, neuropsychologists also discussed the possibilities of computer-automated neuropsychological assessments and compared them to traditional approaches that involved paper-and-pencil testing (Adams 1986; Adams and Brown 1986; Adams and Heaton 1987; Long and Wagner 1986). An unfortunate limitation of progress beyond this period is that too great of emphasis was placed upon interpretive algorithms which led to questions about whether then-current programs could generate accurate clinical predictions (Anthony et al. 1980; Heaton et al. 1981). While it is unclear whether the computerized platforms during this period were adequate, it is clear that the use of computerized interpretation of clinical results from fixed batteries stalled progress in development of technologically advanced neuropsychological assessments (Russell 2011).

T.D. Parsons, *Clinical Neuropsychology and Technology*,
DOI 10.1007/978-3-319-31075-6_1

1 Sternberg's Call for Advances in Technology for Assessment of Intelligence

A decade after Meehl, Sternberg (1997) described the ways in which clinical psychologists have fallen short of meeting Meehl's challenge. This failure is apparent in the discrepancy between progress in cognitive assessment measures like the Wechsler scales and progress in other areas of technology. Sternberg used the example of the now-obsolete black-and-white televisions, vinyl records, rotary-dial telephones, and the first commercial computer made in the USA (i.e., UNIVAC I) to illustrate the lack of technological progress in the standardized-testing industry. According to Sternberg, currently used standardized tests differ little from tests that have been used throughout this century. For example, while the first edition of the Wechsler Adult Intelligence Scale appeared some years before UNIVAC, the Wechsler scales (and similar tests) have hardly changed at all (aside from primarily cosmetic changes) compared to computers. Although one may argue that innovation in the computer industry is different from innovation in the standardized-testing industry, there are still appropriate comparisons. For example, whereas millions of dollars spent on technology in the computer industry typically reflects increased processing speed and power, millions of dollars spent on innovation in the testing industry tends to reflect the move from multiple-choice items to fill-in-the-blank items. Sternberg also points out cognitive testing needs progress in ideas, not just new measures, for delivering old technologies. While clinical neuropsychology emphasizes its role as a science, its technology is not progressing in pace with other clinical neurosciences.

2 Dodrill's Call for Advances in Technology for Neuropsychological Assessment

At the same time Sternberg was describing the discrepancy between progress in cognitive assessment measures and progress in other areas of technology, Dodrill (1997) was contending that neuropsychologists had made much less progress than would be expected in both absolute terms and in comparison with the progress made in other clinical neurosciences. Dodrill points out that clinical neuropsychologists are using many of the same tests that they were using 30 years ago (in fact close to 50 years ago given the date of this publication). If neuroradiologists were this slow in technological development, then they would be limited to pneumo-encephalograms and radioisotope brain scans—procedures that are considered primeval by current neuroradiological standards. According to Dodrill, the advances in neuropsychological assessment (e.g., Weschler scales) have resulted in new tests that are by no means conceptually or substantively better than the old ones. The full scope of issues raised by Dodrill becomes more pronounced when he compares progress in clinical neuropsychology to that of other neurosciences. For example, clinical neuropsychologists have historically been called upon to identify focal brain lesions. When one compares clinical neuropsychology's progress with clinical neurology, it is apparent that while the difference may not have been that great prior the appearance of computerized tomographic (CT) scanning (in the 1970s), the advances since then (e.g., magnetic resonance imaging) has given clinical neurologists a dramatic edge.

3 From Lesion Localization to Assessment of Everyday Functioning

In addition to serving as an example of progress in neurology and the clinical neurosciences, neuroimaging reflects a technology that changed the way clinical neuropsychologists answered referral questions. By the 1990s, neuropsychologists were experiencing a shift in referrals from lesion localization to assessment of everyday functioning (Long 1996). With the advent and development of advanced technologies in the clinical neurosciences, there was decreased need for neuropsychological assessments to localize lesions and an increased need for neuropsychologists to describe behavioral manifestations of neurologic disorders. Clinical neuropsychologists were increasingly being asked to make prescriptive statements about everyday functioning (Sbordone and Long 1996).

Recently, scholars have been discussing the potential for a paradigm shift in clinical neuropsychology (Baxendale and Thompson 2010; Bilder 2011; Dodrill 1997, 1999; Green 2003; Parsons 2011; Perry 2009). The historical development of neuropsychology has resulted in a "normal science" that is informed by developments in psychology, neuroscience, neurology, psychiatry, and computer science. Each of these "informing disciplines" has gone through changes that challenge theory and praxes of neuropsychological assessment. These changes are what Kuhn (1962/1996) describes as paradigm shifts, in which new assumptions (paradigms/theories) require the reconstruction of prior assumptions and the reevaluation of prior facts. For psychology, the paradigmatic shifts are found in the move from mentalism (i.e., study of consciousness with introspection) to behaviorism (Watson 1912), and then cognition (Miller 2003) as now understood through connectionist frameworks (Bechtel and Abrahamsen 1990). Within the last decade, convergence between the social sciences and the neurosciences has resulted in social cognitive and affective neurosciences (Davidson and Sutton 1995; Lieberman 2010; Panksepp 1998). Further, in clinical psychology, shifting paradigms are seen in the incorporation of innovative technologies in treatment delivery (Dimeff et al. 2010). Neurorehabilitation has undergone a paradigm shift as a result of influences from basic and clinical research (Nadeau 2002; Barrett 2006; Mateer and Sohlberg 1988). For psychiatry (e.g., neuropsychopharmacology), the "paradigm shift" has been found in an understanding of psychiatric disorders and molecular biology models that account for gene/environment/development interaction (Meyer 1996). Likewise, neuroscience has seen a shift related to the understanding of communication between nerve cells in the brain—shift from predominant emphasis upon electrical impulses to an enhanced model of chemical transmission (Carlsson 2001). For neurology (and a number of related branches of neuroscience), a shift is found in new ways to visualize the details of brain function (Raichle 2009; Sakoglu et al. 2011). Finally, we are seeing shifts in computer science in the areas of social computing (Wang 2007), information systems (Merali and McKelvey 2006), neuroinformatics (Jagaroo 2009; Koslow 2000; Fornito and Bullmore 2014), and even the video game industry (de Freitas and Liarokapis 2011; Zackariasson and Wilson 2010).

4 Bilder's Neuropsychology 3.0: Evidence-Based Science and Practice

Recently, Bilder (2011) has argued that clinical neuropsychology is ready to embrace technological advances and experience a transformation of its concepts and methods. For Bilder, the theoretical formulations of neuropsychology are represented in three waves. In Neuropsychology 1.0 (1950–1979), clinical neuropsychologists focused on lesion localization and relied on interpretation without extensive normative data. In Neuropsychology 2.0 (1980–present), clinical neuropsychologists were impacted by technological advances in neuroimaging and as a result focused on characterizing cognitive strengths and weaknesses rather than differential diagnosis. For Neuropsychology 3.0 (a future possible Neuropsychology), Bilder emphasizes the need to leverage advances in neuroimaging that Dodrill discussed. Further, he calls on clinical neuropsychologists to incorporate findings from the human genome project, advances in psychometric theory, and information technologies. Bilder argues that a paradigm shift toward evidence-based science and praxes is possible if neuropsychologists understand the need for innovations in neuropsychological knowledgebases and the design of Web-based assessment methods.

5 Computerized Neuropsychological Assessment Devices

One area of technological advance in neuropsychological assessment is the advent of computer-automated neuropsychological assessment devices. These computer-automated neuropsychological assessments have been lauded for their potential to augment task administration (Parsey and Schmitter-Edgecombe 2013), scoring (Woo 2008), collect normative data (Bilder 2011), and in some cases interpret tests (Russell 1995, 2000). In addition to administration issues, advantages have been noted for complexity of stimulus presentation (Gur et al. 2001a, b; Schatz and Browndyke 2002) and logging of responses (Crook et al. 2009; Woo 2008). Bilder (2011) has argued that computerized neuropsychological assessments enable presentation of stimuli and collection of responses that clearly outperform a human examiner because these computerized assessments have enhanced timing precision and can rapidly implement of adaptive algorithms. The enhanced timing precision of the computer-automated assessment enables implementation of subtle task manipulations and trial-by-trial analysis methods found in cognitive neuroscience. Bilder argues that these offer greater sensitivity and specificity to individual differences in neural system function. Relatedly, there is increased interest in Internet-based assessment and the possibility for acquiring hundreds of thousands of participants in months. The longitudinal behavioral data garnered from Internet-based assessment offers potential for the development of repositories that can be stored with electronic medical records, genome sequences, and each patient's history.

6 Ecological Validity and Assessment of Everyday Functioning

While Bilder's arguments are very similar to the ones made in this book, they do not include a discussion of the need for ecological validity in neuropsychological assessments. An unfortunate limitation of most computer-automated neuropsychological measures is that they simply automate construct-driven paper-and-pencil assessments. The changing role for neuropsychologists has also resulted in increased emphasis upon the ecological validity of neuropsychological instruments (Franzen and Wilhelm 1996). An unfortunate limitation for neuropsychologists interested in assessing everyday functioning has been the lack of definitional specificity of the term "ecological validity" (Franzen and Wilhelm 1996). Early attempts to define ecological validity for neuropsychological assessment emphasized the functional and predictive relation between a patient's performance on a set of neuropsychological tests and the patient's behavior in everyday life. Hence, an ecologically valid neuropsychological measure has characteristics similar to a naturally occurring behavior and can predict everyday function (Sbordone 1996). Franzen and Wilhelm (1996) refined the definition of ecological validity for neuropsychological assessment via an emphasis upon verisimilitude and veridicality. By verisimilitude, they meant that the demands of a test and the testing conditions must resemble demands found in the everyday world of the patient. A test with verisimilitude resembles a task the patient performs in everyday life and links task demands to the prediction of real-world behavior (Spooner and Pachana 2006). By veridicality, they meant that performance on a test should predict some aspect of the patient's functioning on a day-to-day basis.

7 Construct-Driven Versus Function-Led Approaches

A refinement of the ecological validity discussion can be found in Burgess and colleagues' (2006) suggestion that neuropsychological assessments be developed to represent real-world "functions" and proffer results that are "generalizable" for prediction of the functional performance across a range of situations. According to Burgess and Colleagues (2006), a "function-led approach" to creating neuropsychological assessments will include neuropsychological models that proceed from directly observable everyday behaviors backward to examine the ways in which a sequence of actions leads to a given behavior in normal functioning; and the ways in which that behavior might become disrupted. As such, he calls for a new generation of neuropsychological tests that are "function led" rather than purely "construct driven." These neuropsychological assessments should meet the usual standards of reliability, but discussions of validity should include both sensitivity to brain dysfunction and generalizability to real-world function.

A number of function-led tests have been developed that assess cognitive functioning in real-world settings. For example, Shallice and Burgess (1991) developed the multiple errands test (MET) as a function-led assessment of multitasking in a hospital or community setting. However, there are a number of unfortunate limitations for such tests that are apparent in the obvious drawbacks to experiments conducted in real-life settings. Function-led neuropsychological assessments can be time-consuming, require transportation, involve consent from local businesses, costly, and difficult to replicate or standardize across settings. Further, data collection in these naturalistic observations tends to be limited.

8 Affective Neuroscience and Clinical Neuropsychology

A further issue for ecological validity is the need for assessments that take seriously the impact of affective arousal upon neurocognitive performance. While current approaches to neuropsychological assessment aid our understanding of cognitive conflict, everyday activities commonly come in the form of emotional distractors. Social and affective neuroscience studies have found that affective stimuli are particularly potent distracters that can reallocate processing resources and impair cognitive (e.g., attention) performance (Dolcos and McCarthy 2006; Pessoa 2008). Affective responses to emotional distractors may be understood as multimodal events in response to a stimulus that has particular significance for the participant, often signifying a potential threat or reward. Affective stimuli are particularly potent distracters that can reallocate processing resources and impact attentional performance (Dolcos and McCarthy 2006). Enhanced understanding of the effect of threatening stimuli upon executive functions has important implications for affective disorders (e.g., specific phobias, depression, and post-traumatic stress disorder) that are characterized by increased susceptibility to affective distraction (Ellis and Ashbrook 1988; Wang et al. 2008). Although cognitive-based understandings of brain–behavior relationships have grown in recent decades, the neuropsychological understandings of emotion remain poorly defined (Suchy 2011). Likewise, neuropsychological assessments often fail to assess the extent to which affective arousal may impair cognitive performance.

9 Virtual Environments for Enhanced Neuropsychological Assessments

Virtual environments (VE) are increasingly considered as potential aids in enhancing the ecological validity of neuropsychological assessments (Campbell et al. 2009; Renison et al. 2012). Given that VEs represent a special case of computerized neuropsychological assessment devices (Bauer et al. 2012; Schatz and Browndyke 2002), they have enhanced computational capacities for administration efficiency, stimulus presentation, automated logging of responses, and data analytic processing. Since VEs allow for precise presentation and control of dynamic perceptual stimuli, they can provide ecologically valid assessments that combine the veridical control and rigor of laboratory measures with a verisimilitude that reflects real-life situations (Parsons 2011). Additionally, the enhanced computation power allows for increased accuracy in the recording of neurobehavioral responses in a perceptual environment that systematically presents complex stimuli. Such simulation technology appears to be distinctively suited for the development of ecologically valid environments, in which three-dimensional objects are presented in a consistent and precise manner (Parsons 2011). VE-based neuropsychological assessments can provide a balance between naturalistic observation and the need for exacting control over key variables (Campbell et al. 2009; Parsons 2011). In summary, VE-based neuropsychological assessments allow for real-time measurement of multiple neurocognitive abilities in order to assess complex sets of skills and behaviors that may more closely resemble real-world functional abilities (Matheis et al. 2007).

10 Plan for This Book

In this book, I aim to discuss the evolution of technological adaptation in neuropsychological assessment. A common theme among neuropsychologists reflecting on the state of the discipline is that neuropsychologists have been slow to adjust to the impact of technology on their profession (Bigler 2013; Bilder 2011; Dodrill 1999). First, current neuropsychological assessment procedures represent a technology that has barely changed since the first scales were developed in the early 1900s (i.e., Binet and Simon's first scale in 1905 and Wechsler's first test in 1939). Although neuropsychologists are ardent to emphasize neuropsychology's role as a science, its technology is not progressing in pace with other science-based technologies. Instead, neuropsychological test developers tend to make cosmetic changes to paper-and-pencil assessments and emphasize improved psychometric properties (e.g., updated norms, improve subtest and composite reliability). An unfortunate limitation is that without the technological advances found in neuroinformatics and computer adaptive testing, updated neuropsychological test developers fail to account for back-compatibility issues that may invalidate clinical interpretations (Loring and Bauer 2010). A further issue is that while the historical purpose of clinical neuropsychology was differential diagnosis of brain pathology, technological advances in other clinical neurosciences (e.g., the development of neuroimaging) have changed the neuropsychologist's role to that of making ecologically valid predictions about the impact of a given patient's neurocognitive abilities and disabilities on everyday functioning. These reasons alone should prompt neuropsychologists to take seriously the need for technological progress for a progressive neuropsychology.

Throughout this book, there is an emphasis upon the importance of (1) enhancing ecological validity via a move from construct-driven assessments to tests that are representative of real-world functions—it is argued that this will proffer results that are generalizable for prediction of the functional performance across a range of situations; (2) the potential of computerized neuropsychological assessment devices (CNADs) to enhance: standardization of administration; accuracy of timing presentation and response latencies; ease of administration and data collection; and reliable and randomized presentation of stimuli for repeat administrations; and (3) novel technologies to allow for precise presentation and control of dynamic perceptual stimuli—provides ecologically valid assessments that combine the veridical control and rigor of laboratory measures with a verisimilitude that reflects real-life situations.

Following a discussion of ecological validity, Part II reviews "The Evolution of Neuropsychological Assessment" and focuses upon the three waves found in theoretical formulations of neuropsychological assessment. The organization of this section is as follows. In Chap. 3, "Neuropsychological Assessment 1.0," a brief overview will be given of the historical development of clinical neuropsychology's normal science and the current state that is leading to a shift in approaches. In Chap. 4, "Neuropsychological Assessment 2.0," current applications of computer-based neuropsychological assessments are described. In Chap. 5, "Neuropsychological Assessment 3.0," a discussion is proffered of the utility of simulation technology for ecologically valid neuropsychological assessments that make use of current technological advances.

In Part III, "Next Generation Neuropsychological Applications," there will be a discussion of novel technologies and approaches that allow the clinician to reach patients in novel approaches. In Chap. 6, "Teleneuropsychology: Coming out of the office," there will be a discussion of the ways in which electronic communications may be used to deliver health-related services from a distance, and its particular usefulness in bringing specialty services to underserved populations and/or remote areas. Chapter 7, explains about "Gamification of Neurocognitive Approaches to Rehabilitation."

In Part IV, "Conclusions," the book will conclude (Chap. 8) with a presentation of "Future Prospects for a Computational Neuropsychology." Herein, there will be a discussion of the importance of using technology to develop repositories for linking neuropsychological assessment results with data from neuroimaging, psychophysiology, and genetics.

Chapter 2
Ecological Validity

And it then becomes necessary to point out that there is something else–a 'truthlikeness' or 'verisimilitude'–with a calculus totally different from the calculus of probability with which it seems to have been confused.
—Karl Popper (p. 219)

Whilst traditional tests of executive function have been remarkably useful, we are now at the stage in the development of the field where one could create bespoke tests specifically intended for clinical applications rather than adapting procedures emerging from purely experimental investigations, as has been almost exclusively the case until recently.
—Burgess et al. (2006, p. 194)

Reason is and ought to be the slave of passions, and can never pretend to any other office save to serve and obey them.
—David Hume (1739/1978, p. 415)

1 Introduction

Over the past twenty years, neuropsychology has experienced a shift in assessment from lesion localization to assessment of everyday functioning (Hart and Hayden 1986; Heaton and Pendleton 1981; Long 1996; Manchester et al. 2004). Clinical neuropsychologists are increasingly being asked to make prescriptive statements about everyday functioning (Chaytor and Schmitter-Edgecombe 2003; Gioia and Isquith 2004; Olson et al. 2013; Rabin et al. 2007). This new role for neuropsychologists has resulted in increased emphasis upon the ecological validity of neuropsychological instruments (Chaytor et al. 2006). As a result, neuropsychologists have been experiencing a need to move beyond the limited generalizability of results found in many earlier developed neuropsychology batteries to measures that more closely approximate real-world function. A difficult issue facing neuropsychologists interested in assessment of real-world functioning is the question of what constitutes an ecologically valid assessment. In the psychology literature, the term "ecological validity" was

T.D. Parsons, *Clinical Neuropsychology and Technology*,
DOI 10.1007/978-3-319-31075-6_2

initially understood as the ability to generalize results of laboratory-based (i.e., controlled experiments) to events naturally occurring in the real world (Brunswick 1955). In cognitive psychology, this question was raised in Ulrich Neiser and Mahzarin Banaji's spirited exchange, which revolved around (1) Neisser's (1982) contention that the laboratory imposes an artificial situation that does not represent the everyday world; and (2) Banaji's rebuttal that the experimental setting should be kept "pure" and cleansed of the murky details that characterize ecologically valid settings (e.g., Banaji and Crowder 1989). In the 1990s, neuropsychologists developed a definition of ecological validity that was specific to neuropsychology (Sbordone 1996; Franzen and Wilhelm 1996) and a number of ecologically valid assessment tools were developed (Marcotte and Grant 2009; Tupper and Cicerone 1990, 1991).

In addition to these historical issues and emerging definitions for ecological validity in neuropsychological assessments, there is a growing desire for "ecological validity" to be need more than simple cosmetic changes to represent real-life situations. Instead, there is a more fundamental issue that the majority of neuropsychological assessments focus upon various aspects of veridical constructs and neglect the reality that real-life veridical decision making is merely a tool subordinate to adaptive decision making. New issues for ecological validity can be found in Goldberg's (2000) contrasting of veridical and agent-centered decision making; as well as Burgess et al.'s (2006) discussions of the need for "function-led approaches" to neuropsychological models and assessments. There is also a growing interest in the interplay of "cold" cognitive processing (linked to dorsal and lateral regions of the prefrontal cortex) of relatively abstract, context-free information, and "hot" cognitive processing (linked to the functioning of the orbitofrontal cortex) involved when emotionally laden information is present (Fonseca et al. 2012; Kerr and Zelazo 2004; Rossier and Sahakian 2013; McDonald 2013; Unsworth et al. 2005).

The plan of this chapter will be as follows: In Sect. 2, "The Everyday/Laboratory Research Conflict," there will be a review of Neiser and Banaji's debate about whether the laboratory imposes an artificial situation that does not represent the everyday world. In Sect. 3, "Early Attempts at a Neuropsychology-Specific Definition of Ecological Validity," the discussion will be extended to early attempts to offer a definition of ecological validity that was specific to neuropsychology. Section 4 builds on ideas from Burgess and colleagues (2006) and presents "Construct-Driven and Function-Led Approaches to Neuropsychological Assessment." Herein, the case of Burgess et al. (2006) is presented that argues for a "function-led approach" to models and assessments that proceed backward from a directly observable everyday behavior to measure the ways in which a set of actions lead to a given behavior in normal and disrupted processing. In Sect. 5, "Veridical and Actor-Centered Decision Making," the reader is presented with Goldberg's (2000) contention that existing neuropsychological procedures assess veridical, but not agent-centered, decision making, which limits the tests' ecological validity because most real-life decision making is agent-centered and adaptive, rather than veridical. In Section 6, "Importance of Affective States for Cognitive Processing," a final addition for improving our understanding of ecological validity is proffered that includes an enhancement of ecological validity via the inclusion of the interplay of "cold" cognitive processing of relatively abstract, context-free information, and "hot" cognitive processing involved when emotionally laden information.

2 The Everyday/Laboratory Research Conflict

The issue of ecological validity in psychological assessment has been expressed a number of times over the years via discussions of the limitations of generalizing sterile laboratory findings to the processes normally occurring in people's everyday lives. In 1978, Neisser proffered an opening address at the first International Conference on Practical Aspects of Memory, in which he argued for an ecologically valid approach to memory assessment (published in Neisser 1982). Neisser offered three main challenges to memory research: (1) the traditional approach has resulted in only few new discoveries; (2) the preoccupation with broad theoretical issues (e.g., mechanisms of forgetting) has resulted in a neglect of questions relevant to everyday life (e.g., the forgetting of appointments); and (3) the majority of the experiments were conducted in artificial settings and employed measures that have few counterparts in everyday life (e.g., unrelated wordlists). In Neisser's view, such research lacks "ecological validity." Hence, Neisser was arguing that the findings from many traditional cognitive assessments have not been demonstrated to generalize beyond the narrow laboratory context.

It is important to note, however, that an essential tension exists between persons striving for ecological validity and persons interested in maintaining experimental control. In 1989, Banaji and Crowder countered Neisser's arguments with the claim that the naturalistic study of memory has not been productive. They contended that the ecological approach to neurocognitive research is inconsequential and that scientific progress necessitates greater emphasis on experimental control. As Banaji and Crowder have challenged, if neurocognitive measures fail to establish internal validity, then one can conclude nothing from study findings. Following Banaji and Crowders's paper, a special issue of the American Psychologist (1991) was devoted to replies to the original article. A number of perspectives were presented related to the issue of whether memory capabilities that are called upon in the laboratory are similar to real-life tasks. From a neuropsychological perspective, these discussions would have been aided by then-current discussions in the neuropsychological literature on prospective memory (Meacham 1982) and the ways in which various environmental factors may define how memory deficits interact with other deficits (Schacter 1983). In addition to memory, there were other domains being discussed at that time from an ecological perspective: problem solving (Sinnott 1989); intelligence (Rogoff and Lave 1984; Sternberg and Wagner 1986); and categorization (Neisser 1987). In 1993, Barbara Wilson (1993) reflected on the Neisser and Banaji debate and called for a rapprochement (at least for neuropsychologists) that included a comprehensive range of neuropsychological assessments for evaluating the patient's current neuropsychological condition and potential for returning to everyday life in a community. While there was a great deal of controversy over whether cognitive assessment should emphasize standardized, laboratory-based methods, or more observational and naturalistic assessment practices (e.g., Banaji and Crowder 1989; Conway 1991; Neisser 1978), the debate has since subsided (deWall et al. 1994).

An issue that came up during the discussion of cognitive assessment of everyday functioning was the specificity of many of the skills needed for activities of daily living. Given the great variability among the skills needed for various daily activities, there may not be enough similarity available to allow for an adequate study of the skills (Tupper and Cicerone 1990, 1991). Williams (1988) suggested that neuropsychologists interested ecological validity need to define clusters of skills needed for a given task relative to whether the skill is used in many tasks across environments (i.e., generic) or used in new tasks in a limited number of environments (i.e., specific). According to Williams, this would allow for the use of traditional testing procedures for assessing skills that are used in many tasks across environments. However, functionally based test measures would need to be developed for skills used in new tasks in a limited number of environments. The work of Williams and others prompted a need for a more refined definition of ecological validity for the theory and praxes of clinical neuropsychology.

3 Early Attempts at a Neuropsychology-Specific Definition of Ecological Validity

The traditional approach to neuropsychological assessment included measures used for the purpose of diagnosing brain lesions or uncovering the behavioral consequences of those lesions (Lezak 1983). However, in the 1980s, a change in referral questions marked a shift from the "deficit measurement paradigm" described by Lezak to a new paradigm included emphasis upon functional competence (Chelune and Moehle 1986). The advent of neuroimaging changed the way clinical neuropsychologists answered referral questions. **Clinical neuropsychologists have experienced** a shift in assessment from lesion localization to assessment of everyday functioning (Long 1996). **With the advent and development of advanced technologies in the clinical neurosciences, there was decreased need for neuropsychological assessments to localize lesions and an increased need for neuropsychologists to describe behavioral manifestations of neurological disorders**. Clinical neuropsychologists were increasingly being asked to make prescriptive statements about everyday functioning (Sbordone and Long 1996). This new role for neuropsychologists resulted in increased emphasis upon the ecological validity of neuropsychological instruments (Franzen and Wilhelm 1996).

In his presidential address to the International Neuropsychology Society in 1981, Rourke (1982) described a gradual change in the practice of clinical neuropsychology from diagnostic assessments to more functional examinations. According to Rourke, the history of neuropsychology could be understood (at that point in time) as a three-stage continuum: (1) *static phase*, during which neuropsychologists focused more on relating performance on cognitive tests to well-documented lesions than to the cognitive nature of the tasks that were administered; (2) *cognitive phase*, during neuropsychologists began analyzing the cognitive task demands of various neuropsychological measures; and (3) *dynamic phase*, during which neuropsychologists began taking into consideration both brain development and individual differences. Support for Rourke's continuum is evidenced by the neuropsychologists in the 1980s that began to recognize the growing need for neuropsychological measures that could provide sufficient information concerning their effects on a functional level (Mapou 1988). This became especially important as neuropsychologists observed that brain imaging and other neurological techniques becoming more sophisticated. They reasoned that the advent and development of neuroimaging would result in a decrease in neuropsychological assessments for localizing lesions and an increase in use for behavioral manifestations of neurological disorders (Costa 1983). As a result, the content of neuropsychological batteries needed to be reevaluated and the clinical utility of the assessment was less determined by its sensitivity to the organic integrity of the brain. Instead, neuropsychological assessments should be evaluated based upon the extent to which each assessment provides information useful in the prediction of functional consequences (Mapou 1988). An unfortunate limitation of this period is that efforts to operationalize assessment models tended to focus on laboratory or clinical performance tests (Welsh and Pennington 1988; Welsh et al. 1991), with their inherent construct and measurement problems (Pennington et al. 1996; Rabbit 1997).

In the neuropsychological literature, the terms "ecological validity" and "everyday functions" can be found in increasing use during the 1990s (Tupper and Cicerone 1990, 1991). During that time, neuropsychologists were progressively aware of the importance of their findings for real-world activities (Sbordone and Long 1996). As a result, there were amplified discussions in the literature evaluating neuropsychological tests and assessment techniques. An unfortunate limitation for neuropsychologists interested in assessing everyday functioning was the lack of definitional specificity of the term "ecological validity" (Franzen and Wilhelm 1996). Early attempts to define ecological validity for neuropsychological assessment emphasized the functional and predictive relation between a patient's performance on a set of neuropsychological tests and the patient's behavior in everyday life. Hence, an ecologically valid neuropsychological measure has characteristics similar to a naturally occurring behavior and can predict everyday function (Sbordone 1996). Franzen and Wilhelm (1996) refined the definition of ecological validity for neuropsychological assessment via an emphasis upon two requirements: (1) *verisimilitude*: the demands of a test and the testing conditions resemble demands in the everyday world of the patient; and (2) *veridicality*: the performance on a test predicts some aspects of the patient's functioning on a day-to-day basis. According to Franzen and Wilhelm (1996), "verisimilitude" overlaps with face validity and describes the "topographical similarity" (i.e., theoretical relation) between the method by which the data were collected and the skills required for successful praxes in the natural environment of the patient

(Franzen 2000). In addition to the task demands of a given neuropsychological task, verisimilitude requires a consideration of the testing environment and methods. While a neuropsychologist may argue that the task demands of learning a recalling a list of words has "theoretical" similarity to the sorts of tasks that a patient might be required to perform in their everyday lives, the actual "praxes" of this task may be more representative of a laboratory experiment: words presented at a controlled rate, the task is performed free from distractions, and there are repeated opportunities to learn the list of words. Hence, the administrative controls that are in place to ensure reliability and internal validity may underestimate the implications of a patient's cognitive difficulties in everyday life and overestimate functional difficulties (e.g., patient may use compensatory strategies in their everyday world).

To require the verisimilitude component of ecological validity for a neuropsychological assessment means that the measure needs to resemble a task the patient performs in everyday life. Further, the test is developed while maintaining the relationship between task demands and the prediction of real-world behavior (Spooner and Pachana 2006). Early discussions of verisimilitude in neuropsychology emphasized that the technologies current to the time could not replicate the environment in which the behavior of interest would ultimately take place (Goldstein 1996). Further, most neuropsychological assessments in use today are yet to be validated with respect to real-world functioning (Rabin et al. 2007). There are a few examples of neuropsychological assessments that emphasize verisimilitude in approximating cognitive constructs: (1) *attention*, the Test of Everyday Attention (Robertson et al. 1996); (2) *executive function*, the Behavioral Assessment of the Dysexecutive Syndrome (Wilson et al. 1996); (3) *memory*: the Rivermead Behavioral Memory Test (Wilson et al. 1985); and (4) *prospective memory*, Cambridge Test of Prospective Memory (CAMPROMPT; Wilson et al. 2004). It is important to note that these "verisimilitude" assessments are somewhat conflicted in that while they focus on cognitive "constructs" (e.g., attention, executive function, memory), they are used for identifying "functional" abilities (Chaytor and Schmitter-Edgecombe 2003). Hence, an obvious question for the verisimilitude approach is whether the assessment of functional capacity can offer the neuropsychologist data relevant for understanding cognitive constructs disrupted relative to brain dysfunction.

Franzen and Wilhelm's (1996) second requirement for establishing an ecologically valid neuropsychological assessment is that it meets the requirements of "veridicality," or the degree to which performance on a test predicts some aspect of the patient's everyday functioning. An unfortunate limitation of most neuropsychological tests is that little is known about prediction of everyday behavior from neuropsychological tests. Further, such an analysis is complicated by the difficulties inherent in capturing an individual's functioning in a reliable and valid numerical fashion. A number of studies have correlated neuropsychological test data with the patient's vocational status (Bayless et al. 1989) and/or vocational functioning (Lysaker et al. 1995). Another approach has been to correlate neuropsychological test data with rating scales designed to assess aspects of daily functioning (Dunn et al. 1990). An unfortunate limitation of the veridicality approach is that direct parallels between the demands found on traditional neuropsychological assessments and functional performance are often not evident (Makatura et al. 1999; Wilson 1993; Wilson et al. 1989).

4 Construct-Driven and Function-Led Approaches to Neuropsychological Assessment

A recent development in the ecological validity discussion was introduced by Burgess and colleagues (2006) when they presented an analysis of neuropsychology's adaptation of outmoded conceptual and experimental frameworks. Burgess et al. proffer current construct-driven tests as examples of measures that fail to represent the actual functional capacities inherent in cognitive (e.g., executive) functions. They point out that cognitive construct measures such as the Stroop and Tower of London were not originally designed to be used as clinical measures (Burgess et al. 2006). Instead, these measures were found to be useful tools for cognitive assessment and normal populations and then later found their way into the clinical realm to aide in assessing constructs that are important to carrying out real-world activities. For example, if a patient's performance on the Stroop revealed difficulty inhibiting an automatic, over learned response, a neuropsychologist may be compelled to report caution relative to an aging patient's driving—safe driving of an automobile includes the ability to withhold an over learned behavior to press the brakes if a traffic light turns red when the driver is halfway through the intersection. An unfortunate limitation of this approach to predicting everyday functioning is that it forces the neuropsychologist to rely on measures designed for other purposes. Goldstein (1996) questioned this approach because it is difficult to ascertain the extent to which performance on measures of basic constructs translates to functional capacities within the varying environments found in the real world. A decade letter, Burgess et al. (2006) agree and argue that a further issue is that we need assessments that further our understanding about the ways in which the brain enables persons to interact with their environment and organize everyday activities. Instead of using the terms "verisimilitude" and "veridicality" when discussing "ecological validity," they use the term "representativeness" to discuss the extent to which a neuropsychological assessment corresponds in form and context to a real-world (encountered outside the laboratory) situation. They use the term "generalizability" to discuss the degree to which poor performance on a neuropsychological assessment will be predictive of poor performance on tasks outside the laboratory.

For example, one of the most widely used measures of executive function is the Wisconsin Card Sorting Test (WCST Heaton et al. 1993). The most extensive normative data are derived from an administration of the WCST that utilizes paper cards. The stimulus cards are administered by an experimenter on one side of a desk as he/she faces a participant on the other side of the desk. Participants are presented with a number of stimulus cards and instructed to match these stimulus cards to target cards. Although participants are not told how to match the cards, they are informed whether a particular match is correct or incorrect. It is important to note that the WCST (like many paper-and-pencil tests in use today) was not originally developed as a measure of executive functioning. Instead, the WCST was preceded by a number of sorting measures that were developed from observations of the effects of brain damage (e.g., Weigl 1927). Nevertheless, in a single study by Brenda Milner (1963), patients with dorsolateral prefrontal lesions were found to have greater difficulty on the WCST than patients with orbitofrontal or nonfrontal lesions. However, the majority of neuroimaging studies have found activation across frontal and nonfrontal brain regions and clinical studies have revealed that the WCST does not discriminate between frontal and nonfrontal lesions (Nyhus and Barcelo 2009; Stuss et al. 1983). Further, while data from the WCST do appear to provide some information relevant to the constructs of "set shifting" and "working memory," the data do not necessarily offer information that would allow a neuropsychologist to predict what situations in everyday life require the abilities that the WCST measures.

Burgess et al. (2006) suggest that future development of neuropsychological assessments should result in tests that are "representative" of real-world "functions" and proffer results that are "generalizable" for prediction of the functional performance across a range of situations. According to Burgess et al. (2006) a "function-led approach" to creating neuropsychological assessments will include neuropsychological models that proceed from directly observable everyday behaviors backward to examine the ways in which a sequence of actions leads to a given behavior in normal functioning; and the ways in which that behavior might become disrupted. As such, call for a new generation of neuropsychological tests that are "function led" rather than purely "construct driven." These neuropsychological assessments should meet the usual standards of reliability, but discussions of validity should include both sensitivity to brain dysfunction and generalizability to real-world function.

4.1 Function-Led Tests that Are Representative of Real-World Functions

A more ecological approach to neuropsychological assessment is to move from construct-driven assessments to tests that are "representative" of real-world "functions" and proffer results that are "generalizable" for prediction of the functional performance across a range of situations. According to Burgess et al. (2006), a "function-led approach" to creating neuropsychological assessments will include neuropsychological models that proceed from directly observable everyday behaviors backward to examine the ways in which a sequence of actions leads to a given behavior in normal functioning; and the ways in which that behavior might become disrupted. As such, he calls for a new generation of neuropsychological tests that are "function led" rather than purely "construct driven." These neuropsychological assessments should meet the usual standards of reliability, but discussions of validity should include both sensitivity to brain dysfunction and generalizability to real-world function. A number of investigators have argued that performance on traditional neuropsychological construct-driven tests (e.g., Wisconsin Card Sorting Test, Stroop) has little correspondence to activities of daily living (Bottari et al. 2009; Manchester et al. 2004; Sbordone 2008). According to Chan et al. (2008), most of these traditional construct-driven measures assess at the veridicality level and do not capture the complexity of response required in the many multistep tasks found in everyday activities.

4.2 Real-World Assessments Using the Multiple Errands Tasks: Potential and Limitations

A number of function-led tests have been developed that assess cognitive functioning in real-world settings. For example, Shallice and Burgess (1991) developed the multiple errands test (MET) as a function-led assessment of multitasking in a hospital or community setting. Participant performs a number of relatively simple but open-ended tasks (e.g., buying particular items, writing down specific information, traveling to a specific location) without breaking a series of arbitrary rules. The examiner observes the participant's performance and writes down the number and type of errors (e.g., rule breaks, omissions). The MET has been shown to have increased sensitivity (over construct-driven neuropsychological tests) to elicit and detect failures in attentional focus and task implementation. It has also been shown to be better at predicting behavioral difficulties in everyday life (Alderman et al. 2003). However, there are a number of unfortunate limitations for the traditional MET that are apparent in the obvious drawbacks to experiments conducted in real-life settings. Function-led neuropsychological assessments can be time-consuming, require transportation, involve consent from local businesses, costly, and difficult to replicate or standardize across settings (Logie et al. 2011; Rand et al. 2009). Further, there are times when function-led assessments in real-world settings are not feasible for participants with significant behavioral, psychiatric, or mobility difficulties (Knight and Alderman 2002).

In summary, early discussions of verisimilitude in neuropsychology emphasized that the technologies current to the time could not replicate the environment in which the behavior of interest would ultimately take place. Today, most neuropsychological assessments continue to represent outdated technologies and static stimuli that are yet to be validated with respect to real-world functioning. While much of the early discussion of ecological validity reflected an emphasis upon veridicality and verisimilitude, Burgess and colleagues (2006) have updated the discussion to include differentiating of construct-driven assessments from function-led neuropsychological assessments.

5 Veridical and Actor-Centered Decision Making

Over the past 30 years, there has been growing concern in the field of neuropsychology about the ecological validity of neuropsychological tests. While this concern often takes the prosaic form of elaborating the cognitive tasks with the surface features of real-life situations, little is done to adjust the assessments to measure real-world adaptive decision making. Goldberg and Podell (2000) contend that neuropsychological assessments need more than simple cosmetic changes to represent real-life situations. Instead, there is a more fundamental issue that the majority of neuropsychological assessments focus upon various aspects of veridical decision making and neglect the reality that real-life veridical decision making is merely a tool subordinate to adaptive decision making (Goldberg and Podell 1999). Given that many existing neuropsychological tests assess more narrow veridical than real-world adaptive (Goldberg (2012) also refers to this as "agent-centered") decision making, the neuropsychologist may not be collecting the data relevant to documentation of the full essence of the patients cognitive strengths and weaknesses.

The distinction made by Goldberg and colleagues (1999, 2000, 2005, 2009, 2012) includes a dichotomy between "veridical" and "agent-centered" cognition. By "veridical," Goldberg means that cognition is directed at solving problems characterized by agent-dependent choices that are fundamentally "true" and "false." These choices range from simple (e.g., 2 + 2 = ?) to complex (what day of the week will be September 11, 3001?). This agent-dependent decision making is contrasted with the sorts of agent-centered and "adaptive" decisions that occur in real life. This agent-centered decision ranges from simple (e.g., choosing from a restaurant menu) to decisions that will impact the agent's life (e.g., career decisions). For these agent-centered decisions, the dichotomous "true–false" metric does not apply because asserting that salad is an intrinsically correct choice and soup is an intrinsically false choice is self-refuting. Of course, this also holds for life decisions like the assertion that a doctoral degree in "clinical neuropsychology" is an intrinsically correct choice and one in "engineering" is an intrinsically false choice (Goldberg et al. 2012).

While this distinction is often underemphasized in clinical neuropsychology, it is central to understanding the nature of the patient's decision making. This is especially true when making decisions about a patient's competency for making cardinal decisions—such decisions are agent-centered, while veridical cognition serves a supportive role. Unfortunately, the vast majority of cognitive paradigms used in neuropsychological assessment are notoriously devoid of appropriate tools to study "agent-centered" cognition. Much of this is due to the traditional focus on assessment of veridical aspects of cognition in highly contrived, artificial, laboratory situations. This explains why many purported cognitive measures have notoriously poor ecological validity and why patients with prefrontal lesions have real-life problems even though they do well on neuropsychological tests purported to assess prefrontal functions (Sbordone 2010).

It is interesting to note that although cognitive neuroscience researchers have begun investigating various innovative paradigms that depart to various degrees from the traditional "veridicality" approaches (Lieberman and Eisenberger 2005; Nakao et al. 2009, 2010, 2012); Paulus and Frank 2003; Johnson et al. 2005; Volz et al. 2006), very little of these developments are found in emerging clinical neuropsychology approaches. Instead, neuropsychologists tend to cling to outmoded paradigms (e.g., Wisconsin Card Sorting Test; Stroop Test) that are veridical in nature. In order to correct this situation, Goldberg argues for the creation of a new generation of cognitive paradigms that are devoid of the "true–false" metric and based on subjective preference. Goldberg has developed the cognitive bias test (CBT) as a nonveridical agent-centered assessment (Goldberg et al. 1994a, b, 1997; Goldberg and Podell 1999; Podell et al. 1995). The CBT is an inherently ambiguous, multiple-choice task in which the patient is presented with cards that have geometric designs on them. Each geometric design is categorized along five binary dimensions, which allows for a comparison in dimensional similarity between any two cards. After the examiner presents the patient with a target card, two choice cards are presented simultaneously in a vertical alignment below the target card. The patient is asked to look at the target card and then choose one of the two choice cards that the patient likes best. The two choice cards are characterized by different degrees of dimensional similarity to the target card. As a result, the subject must select the choice card that is more different from, or similar to the target card. Following 60 trials, the patient's choice pattern is quantified. The CBT has two patterns of response: (1) The patient can respond in a highly context-dependent pattern in which the patient consistently chooses either the most different or the most similar choice card; or (2) The patient can respond in a context-invariant pattern in which the patient's choice is not based on a consistent comparison to the target (i.e., disregard for context), but rather some subjective dimensional, sensory preference.

The inherent ambiguity of the CBT allows for a novel approach to ecological validity that assesses actor-centered, adaptive decision making that is based on an agent's priorities. With the CBT, neuropsychologists have the first steps toward a future possible neuropsychological assessment that moves beyond a veridical, actor-independent decision making that requires a correct response intrinsic to the external situation. When contrasted with tests like the WCST that depend on veridical decision making, the CBT allows neuropsychologists to measure actor-centered decision making. Goldberg believes that the CBT better elucidates the functions of the frontal lobes and in a more ecologically valid way (Goldberg and Podell 1999, 2000).

6 Importance of Affective States for Cognitive Processing

Historically, much of psychology has been understood as comprising three related fields: cognition, affect, and motivation. Until recently, cognitive psychology has been the most extensively studied of the three, with affect and motivation being rather neglected. According to Baddeley (1981), the major reason for this is that cognition can be studied relatively easily in the laboratory whereas affect and motivation require assessment of real-world activities. In recent years, cognitive neuropsychology has witnessed a resurgence of interest in (1) going beyond the artificial situation of the laboratory to assessments that reflect the everyday world (Neisser 1982); and (2) bringing together studies of cognition, emotion, and conation (Masmoudi et al. 2012). In fact, research on emotions is increasingly found in the literature: affective neuroscience (Adolphs et al. 2002; Ledoux 1996), neuroscience of psychopathology (Kohler et al. 2010), and clinical neuropsychology (Stuss and Levine 2002).

While the discussion of laboratory versus real-world assessment was discussed in the 1980s (see above), the latter issue of bringing together studies of cognition, emotion, and conation is something that is increasingly being discussed in terms of affective neuroscience (Panksepp 1998). Although the terms "cognition," "motivation," and "emotion" as important drivers for theory development and praxes in behavioral neuroscience research, the term "cognition" has been increasingly overused and misused since the cognitive revolution. According to Cromwell and Panksepp (2011), this has resulted in deficient development of a usable shared definition for the term "cognition." They argue that this deficiency raises concerns about a possible misdirection of research within behavioral neuroscience. For Cromwell and Panksepp, the emphasis upon top-down (cortical → subcortical) perspectives tends to dominate the discussion in cognitive-guided research without concurrent noncognitive modes of bottom-up developmental thinking. They believe that this could hinder progress in understanding neurological and psychiatric disorders. As an alternative, they emphasize inclusion of bottom-up (subcortical → cortical) affective and motivational "state-control" perspectives. The affective neuroscience approach represents a more "embodied" organic view that accepts that cognitions are integrally linked to both our neurology as well as the environments in which we operate (Smith and Gasser 2005; Panksepp 2009, 2010).

The affective neuroscience critique that top-down perspectives tend to dominate the discussion in cognitive-guided research is readily applicable to the contemporary approach to neuropsychological assessment. Although cognitive-based understandings of brain–behavior relationships have grown in recent decades, the neuropsychological understandings of emotion remain poorly defined (Suchy 2011). While current approaches to neuropsychological assessment aide our understanding of cognitive conflict, everyday activities commonly come in the form of emotional distractors. Social and affective neuroscience studies have found that affective stimuli are particularly potent distracters that can reallocate processing resources and impair cognitive (e.g., attention) performance (Dolcos and McCarthy 2006; Pessoa 2008). Affective responses to emotional distractors may be understood as multimodal events in response to a stimulus that has particular significance for the participant, often signifying a potential threat or reward. Affective stimuli are particularly potent distracters that can reallocate processing resources and impact attentional performance (Dolcos and McCarthy 2006). Enhanced understanding of the effect of threatening stimuli upon executive functions has important implications for affective disorders (e.g., specific phobias, depression, and post-traumatic stress disorder) that are characterized by increased susceptibility to affective distraction (Ellis and Ashbrook 1988; Wang et al. 2008). As one precondition for a specific affective experience, emotion may include automatic and controlled recognition and evaluation of a stimulus. In addition to the appraisal of a stimulus, affective reactions are characterized by psychophysiological changes (e.g., alterations in skin conductance and heart rate; as well as behavioral approach or avoidance) and involve a number of subcomponents occurring in frontal subcortical circuits (Bonelli and Cummings 2007; Pessoa 2009; Ray and Zald 2012).

According to models of neurovisceral integration, autonomic, attentional, and affective systems are simultaneously engaged in the support of self-regulation (Critchley 2005; Thayer and Lane 2000, 2009). Working from a neurovisceral integration model, Capuana et al. (2014) examined whether increase in difficulty of an executive-control task increases would increase the need for cardiac autonomic regulation in maintaining effective cognitive control. Results indicate that pretask respiratory sinus arrhythmia predicted accuracy best on a Stroop task when errors resulted in financial loss. Greater respiratory sinus arrhythmia has also been found when participants have had to execute correct responses more quickly in the context of an emotional Stroop task (Mathewson et al. 2010). Several studies using the classical Stroop paradigm have found performance-related reductions in heart rate and respiratory sinus arrhythmia (e.g., Boutcher and Boutcher 2006; Delaney and Brodie 2000; Waldstein et al. 1997; Wright et al. 2007). Another psychophysiological metric that has been found to increase as workload increases is skin conductance. During the Stroop task, incongruent stimuli, associated with a higher degree of task difficulty than congruent stimuli, has been found to elicit larger skin conductance responses (Kobayashi et al. 2007). Increased task difficulty using an n-back task also results in increased skin conductance levels (Mehler et al. 2009). Additionally, numerous studies using various cognitive tasks have evidenced increased heart rate associated with increased cognitive workload (e.g., Carroll et al. 1986; Kennedy and Scholey 2000; Mehler et al. 2009; Sloan et al. 1991). An increase in respiratory rate has been consistently associated with increased cognitive demand (e.g., Backs and Selijos 1994; Brookings et al. 1996; Mehler et al. 2009).

Models of affective–cognitive interactions reveal two cortical–subcortical networks that play vital and dissociable roles in human emotion and cognition (Dolcos and McCarthy 2006). In a functional connectivity magnetic resonance imaging study, Seeley et al. (2007) identified these two cortical–subcortical networks as follows: (1) an "executive-control network" that links dorsolateral frontal and parietal neocortices; and (2) a "salience network" anchored by dorsal anterior cingulate (dACC) and orbital frontoinsular cortices with robust connectivity to subcortical and limbic structures. The "executive-control network" reflects brain regions and processes associated with active maintenance of goal-relevant behavior. The "salience network" includes brain regions and processes typically associated with affective processing. While the executive-control network is frequently coactivated with the salience network in tasks of attention, working memory, and response selection, the salience network also activates in response to threats.

Increased arousal may impact the processing of salient information and enhance the contrast between stimuli with different levels of salience (Critchley 2005).

The distinction of cognitive processes in this dual pathway approach has similarities to a neuropsychological subdivision of cognitive control (Zelazo et al. 2003). Zelazo et al. (2003) differentiate between "cold" cognitive control (the executive dysfunction pathway) and "hot" affective aspects of cognitive control (the motivational dysfunction pathway). In a similar fashion, Nigg (2000, 2001) distinguishes between behavioral inhibition (i.e., response inhibition) and motivational inhibition (i.e., personality and motivation). In Sonuga-Barke's (2003) neuropsychological research, these different aspects of inhibition have been shown to be related to different brain networks. The distinction between "cold" cognitive reasoning and "hot" affective processing has been studied in decision neuroscience. While "cold" cognitive processing tends to be relatively logic-based and free from much affective arousal, "hot" affective processing occurs in the face of reward and punishment, self-regulation, and decision making involving personal interpretation (Ardila 2008; Brock et al. 2009; Chan et al. 2008; Grafman and Litvan 1999; Happaney et al. 2004; Seguin et al. 2007). A number of studies have found that impairments in either the "cold" or "hot" cognitive functions may be related to deficits in everyday functioning (e.g., independence at home, ability to work, school attendance, and social relations (Goel et al. 1997; Grafman et al. 1996; Green 1996; Green et al. 2000; see Chan et al. 2008 for review).

The idea of "hot" decision making is consistent with the somatic marker hypothesis (Bechara 2004; Bechara and Damasio 2005; Bechara et al. 1997, 1998; Damasio 1996). Damasio (1994, 1996) suggested a somatic marker hypothesis approach to decision making, in which the experience of an emotion (e.g., "gut feeling" and "hunch") results in a "somatic marker" that guides decision making. According to Damasio (1994), the somatic marker is hypothesized to play a role in "hot" decision making in that it assists the "cold" decision making process by biasing the available response selections in a complex decision making task. According to the somatic marker hypothesis, when persons are faced with decisions, they experience somatic sensations (i.e., somatic markers) that occur in advance of real consequences of possible different alternatives (Bechara et al. 1997). These somatic markers act as affective catalysts for decision making, in which distinct alternatives are evaluated via somatic sensations that guide adaptive decision making (Damasio 1996). The ventromedial prefrontal cortex (VMPFC) and its limbic system connections are considered key structures in the somatic marker hypothesis and the decision making process (Bechara et al. 1997, 1998). However, the neuropsychological assessment of the VMPFC remains somewhat enigmatic as patients tend to have both an appearance of normality on most neuropsychological tests and also problems in their everyday lives (Zald and Andreotti 2010).

The somatic marker hypothesis was originally proposed to account for a subgroup of patients with VMPFC (i.e., orbitofrontal) lesions who appeared to have intact cognitive processing, but had lost the capacity to make appropriate life decisions. According to Damasio (1994), they had lost the ability to weigh the positive and negative features of decision-based outcomes. The Iowa gambling task

(IGT; Bechara et al. 1994; Bechara 2007) was developed to assess these patients and is increasingly being accepted as a neuropsychological measure of affect-based decision making (Bowman et al. 2005). The IGT is a computerized assessment of reward-related decision making that measures temporal foresight and risky decision making (Bechara et al. 1994; Bechara 2007). During IGT assessment, the patient is instructed to choose cards from four decks (A–D). Selection of each card results in on-screen feedback regarding either a “gain” or “loss” of currency. In the four decks, there are two advantageous (C and D) decks that result in money gained ($250 every 10 cards) and low monetary loss during the trial. The other two decks (A and B) are disadvantageous and involve greater wins (around $100 each card) than C and D (around $50) but also incur greater losses, meaning that one loses $250 every 10 cards in Decks A and B. The primary dependent variables derived from the IGT are total score and net score ([C + D]–[A + B]) and block score ([C + D]–[A + B]) for each segment or block of 20 cards, frequency of deck choices, and spared or impaired performance according to a cutoff point of −10 (Bechara et al. 2000) especially in brain-damaged subjects.

Neuroimaging studies of persons performing the IGT have revealed activation in the orbitofrontal cortex (Ernst et al. 2002; Grant et al. 1999; Windmann et al. 2006), which appears to be significant for signaling the anticipated rewards/punishments of an action and for adaptive learning (Schoenbaum et al. 2011). Evidence for the somatic marker hypothesis’s role in hot decision making over IGT trials can be found in the demonstration of an anticipatory electrodermal response in healthy controls to card selection (Bechara et al. 1996, 1997). For example, prior to selecting a card from a risky deck, a healthy control will show a physiological reaction indicating that the participant is experiencing bodily the anticipated risk. Further, studies have shown that damage to vmPFC (part of the orbitofrontal cortex) and the amygdala prevents the use of somatic (affective) signals for advantageous decision making (Bechara et al. 1996, 1998; Bechara et al. 2000). It is noteworthy that there are different roles played by the ventromedial prefrontal cortex (vmPFC) and amygdala in decision making. While vmPFC patients were able to generate electrodermal responses when they received a reward or a punishment, amygdala patients failed to do so (Bechara et al. 1999). These findings have been supported in other that have found positive correlations between the development of anticipatory skin conductance responses and better performance on a similar gambling task (Crone et al. 2004; Carter and Pasqualini 2004).

It is important to note that alternative explanations of Bechara’s findings have been posited. Tomb et al. (2002) suggested that the anticipatory responses are related to the belief that the risky choice will probably produce a large reward—higher immediate short-term benefits of the risky decks ($100 versus $50). According to Tomb et al. (2002), the anticipatory SCR effect is unrelated to any long-term somatic marker mechanism. Nevertheless, Tomb et al.’s (2002) account does not readily explain deficient performance in ventromedial PFC patients. While these patients fail to develop an anticipatory response to the decks with immediate short-term benefits, they also prefer these decks throughout the task (Clark and Manes 2004).

While the IGT may have potential for assessment of "hot" affective processing (Baddeley 2011), there have been failures to replicate the initial studies (Hinson et al. 2002, 2003). Whereas data from Bechara et al.'s (1998) early studies suggested normal performance of patients with dorsolateral prefrontal lesions, a number of later studies indicate significant effects of lesions that include either dorsolateral or dorsomedial prefrontal cortex regions (Manes et al. 2002: Clark et al. 2003). Further, researchers have argued that the IGT is deficient for understandings the affective impact of emotional stimuli upon cognitive processing because (1) the observed effects on the IGT may simply be cognitive (not affective) demands placed resulting from such a complex decision task (Hinson et al. 2002, 2003); and (2) the IGT is more of a learning task (Baddeley 2011), whereas a true assessment of affective impact upon cognitive processing requires a measure of the capacity to evaluate existing valences (i.e., positive, negative, and neutral). In a similar manner, Fellows and Farah (2005) have suggested that an elemental deficit in reversal learning (instead of deficit in decision making) may better explain the VMPFC lesion patients' selections of disadvantageous and risky cards on the IGT. Evidence for this is indicated by improved performance when the initial bias favoring the disadvantageous decks is removed by reordering the cards. Hence, while insensitivity to risk is often used to explain poor performance on the IGT, the learning and explicit reversal components of the IGT may better explain into what the IGT it is actually tapping. Further, like other cognitive measures, the IGT was created to assess the construct of decision making in a laboratory setting, but it remains to be seen whether a relation between performance on the IGT and real-world decision making exists (Buelow and Suhr 2009).

7 Conclusions

In summary, the past twenty years in neuropsychology we have seen a shift in assessment from lesion localization to assessment of everyday functioning. Clinical neuropsychologists are increasingly being asked to make prescriptive statements about everyday functioning. This new role for neuropsychologists has resulted in increased emphasis upon the ecological validity of neuropsychological instruments. As a result, neuropsychologists have been experiencing a need to move beyond the limited generalizability of results found in many earlier developed neuropsychology batteries to measures that more closely approximate real-world function. However, neuropsychologists have been slow to establish tests that will address assessment of everyday functioning. Part of the delay has resulted from a lack of clear consensus on what constitutes an ecologically valid assessment.

In addition to these historical issues and emerging definitions for ecological validity in neuropsychological assessments, there is a growing desire for "ecological validity" to be need more than simple cosmetic changes to represent real-life situations. Instead, there is a more fundamental issue that the majority of neuropsychological assessments focus upon various aspects of veridical constructs and neglect the reality that real-life veridical decision making is merely a tool subordinate to adaptive decision making. A recent focusing of the discussion by Burgess and colleagues (2006) emphasizes the need for "function-led approaches" to neuropsychological models and assessments. While these approaches have been gaining in popularity, there are a number of unfortunate limitations that are apparent in the obvious drawbacks to experiments conducted in real-life settings. Function-led neuropsychological assessments can be time-consuming, require transportation, involve consent from local businesses, costly, and difficult to replicate or standardize across settings. Further, there are times when function-led assessments in real-world settings are not feasible for participants with significant behavioral, psychiatric, or mobility difficulties. There is also a growing interest in the interplay of "cold" cognitive processing (linked to dorsal and lateral regions of the prefrontal cortex) of relatively abstract, context-free information, and "hot" cognitive processing (linked to the functioning of the orbitofrontal cortex) involved when emotionally laden information is present. Unfortunately, very little has been done to include affective components into the neuropsychological assessment.

In the chapters that follow, **there will be review of these issues for each of three waves found in theoretical formulations of neuropsychological assessment**. Throughout, there will be emphasis upon the ways in which both paper-and-pencil and computer-automated neuropsychological assessments reflect "construct-driven" and "function-led" approaches to neuropsychological assessment. A preference is emphasized for "function-led" approaches to models and assessments that proceed backward from a directly observable everyday behavior to measure the ways in which a set of actions lead to a given behavior in normal and disrupted processing. Further, there is discussion of the potential for improving our understanding of ecological validity via the inclusion of the interplay of "cold" cognitive processing of relatively abstract, context-free information, and "hot" cognitive processing involved when emotionally laden information.

Part II
Evolution of Neuropsychological Assessment

Chapter 3
Neuropsychological Assessment 1.0

Progress, far from consisting in change, depends on retentiveness. When change is absolute there remains no being to improve and no direction is set for possible improvement: and when experience is not retained, as among savages, infancy is perpetual. Those who cannot remember the past are condemned to repeat it.

—Santayana (1905, p. 284)

1 Historical Development of Neuropsychological Assessment 1.0

Examination of neuropsychological assessment's developmental history provides us with the lens through which we may consider current advances and facilitates our understanding of the current theoretical bases for various approaches (Barr 2008). It also serves as a reminder that corrective changes in the discipline involve "retaining" those successful underpinnings that solidified the discipline so that in our progress, we do not repeat past mistakes. Bilder (2011) has suggested that while the field of neuropsychology has experienced two distinctive periods (e.g., Neuropsychology 1.0 and 2.0), it is beginning third phase of Neuropsychology 3.0. According to Bilder, Neuropsychology 1.0 emerged in the 1950s and involved clinical assessments that were primarily qualitative and lacking in extensive normative data. Neuropsychology 2.0 involves a period from 1980 to the present and includes a greater emphasis upon classical psychometrics, standardization, and empirically supported batteries. Neuropsychology 3.0 is understood as an emerging phase with opportunities for incorporating novel computerized assessment approaches, formalizing neuropsychological concepts and measures into cognitive ontologies, and establishing collaborative neuropsychological knowledgebases.

While Bilder's delineation of neuropsychology's progress into three phases is helpful, the suggested timeline misses some of the nuances of technological development and adoption that will be discussed in this and subsequent chapters. This chapter discusses the development of the neuropsychological assessment

T.D. Parsons, *Clinical Neuropsychology and Technology*,
DOI 10.1007/978-3-319-31075-6_3

approaches from simple extensions of either physiological psychology or neurological examinations to contemporary development of the flexible test battery. Ultimately, this will involve a discussion of the technologies used by neuropsychologists during a period referred to as Neuropsychological Assessment 1.0. While Bilder chose to emphasize the advent of quantitative batteries as marker for the end neuropsychology's first phase, herein the emphasis is upon the changing "access to" and "adoption of" technologies for neuropsychological assessment. The plan of this chapter will be as follows: After a brief summary of neuropsychology's "prehistory," there will be discussion of neuropsychological assessment following nineteenth-century medicine and physiology. Here, there will be a development of qualitative approaches and neuropsychological assessments as extensions of the neurological examination. Next, there will be a discussion of the ways in which the neuropsychological assessment in 1.0 developed into the quantitative batteries that continue to be used today. Again, Neuropsychological Assessment 1.0 as conceived herein reflects both standardization and technological shifts as opposed to psychometric rigor alone.

2 Neuropsychology's Prehistory

While neuropsychological assessment is a relatively new discipline, the study of brain–behavior relations goes back much further and there is evidence that the ancient Egyptians were interested in assessing language and memory (Boller and Forbes 1998). For example, the Edwin Smith Surgical Papyrus written by Imhotep approximately in the seventeenth-century BC (Wilkens 1964) is the first noted cortical "localization" of function after brain injury (Stuss and Levine 2002). The Edwin Smith Surgical Papyrus includes 27 head injury cases (48 cases of physical injury in total). In classical Greece (e.g., Plato, Aristotle, Hippocratic writers), one finds an interest in brain–behavior relations. Hippocratic writers emphasized brain–behavior relations in descriptions of their patients. The Romans also were interested in the study of brain–behavior relations. Galen is considered by many to be the first experimental physiologist. He described major brain structures and emphasized the importance of direct observation. Unfortunate for Galen was the fact that Roman authorities forbade dissection of human bodies. As a result, his understandings were primarily limited to that gleaned from dissected and vivisection of animals. These descriptive approaches were passed into the Arabic world and preserved until the Renaissance.

Following the Renaissance, there was a shift from knowledge gleaned from dissection of animals to a period emphasizing practical human anatomy. As a result, understanding of human brain anatomy became progressively more sophisticated and accurate. By the eighteenth century, Franz Joseph Gall had started writing about the idea that the brain has specific functions that are localized to particular brain areas. According to phrenology, bulges on the skull conceal areas of particular brain development that reflect areas responsible for specific psychological functions. While some may argue that phrenology's description of anatomical localization of function within the brain qualifies it as the first manifestation of a neuropsychological theory (see for example Miller 1996), the essential points of Gall's doctrine (with the exception of his emphasis upon the cortex) have been shown to fail as a neuropsychological theory and its hypotheses both about brain development and its reflection in scalp topography were ultimately to be dismissed (see Heeschen 1994 for a discussion).

2.1 Diagram-Makers and Nineteenth-Century Medicine

A better place to look for the theoretical foundations of current neuropsychological assessments is in nineteenth-century medicine and physiology (see Meyer 1961). During the nineteenth century, a number of factors came together to form the basis of modern neuropsychology: localization of rationality in brain cortex; mapping of sensorimotor pathways; grouping of psychological processes into associated faculties; and relation between brain damage and loss of cognitive abilities. In the last quarter of the nineteenth century, a number of researchers known as "diagram-makers" proposed a new technological approach that used various schematic models depicting how a cognitive process (e.g., language) is represented in the brain (see Jacyna 2004a, b). While phrenology had been discredited as pseudoscience, cognitive (e.g., language) disturbances were studied mainly based on the localization of the cerebral lesions (see Cubelli 2005 for review).

Much of what is now considered part of neuropsychological assessment originated from attempts of late nineteenth-century and early twentieth-century physicians to improve the evaluation of the cognitive capacities of persons with brain disease. The assessment of cognitive dysfunction following acquired cerebral lesions is associated with the clinical descriptions by Paul Broca (1865) and the discovery of the left hemisphere dominance for language. Broca was able to demonstrate that language is a localizable function that can be damaged separately from other cognitive processes. In 1874, Wernicke developed a diagrammatic model of the sensory and motor language linked by a transmission pathway. While patients with Broca's aphasia are nonfluent, patients with sensory aphasia are fluent. In addition to providing evidence for a second form of aphasia that utilized a speech-language module, Wernicke was the first to posit an information processing network. According to Wernicke, the posterior portion of the superior temporal lobe (decodes speech sounds) is connected to Broca's area in the frontal lobes (area that programs speech sounds). Cubelli (2005) has argued that the neuropsychological importance of Broca's studies is primarily methodological in that he showed that a specific neurocognitive disorder could be systematically associated with focal brain damage.

According to Cubelli, Wernicke's (1874) work was more theoretically relevant to the development of neuropsychology in that Wernicke proposed a neuropsychological model that included psychological (i.e., levels of processing underlying oral repetition), neurological (i.e., cortical and subcortical pathways associated with each processing stage), and clinical (i.e., symptoms following circumscribed brain lesions) descriptions of persons performing a simple task of oral repetition. The result of Wernicke's multilevel formulation is a template for the development of future neuropsychological models.

3 Neuropsychological Assessment and Localization

3.1 Kurt Goldstein: A Holistic Approach to Neuropsychology

Neuropsychological assessment was practiced almost exclusively by neurologists until the latter half of the twentieth century (Boller 1998). As such, the neuropsychological examination has historically been characterized as both a refinement and an extension of the neurological examination (Benton 1985). In the early part of the twentieth century, a holistic approach emerged that included both cognitive neuropsychologists (e.g., Lashley (1929) and Hebb (1949) and neurologists like Wernicke's student, Kurt Goldstein (1939). Goldstein took a holistic approach to the brain, in which he postulated that function in a damaged area could be compensated through the capacity of other areas (compare to Lashley's mass-action-equipotentiality). Goldstein's understanding of the patient came less from focus upon on a specific deficit and more from the study of all aspects and simultaneous functioning.

Goldstein indicated that his emphasis was on working with patients rather than on experimental research in the laboratory designed to address theoretical questions (Goldstein and Scheerer 1941). Much of his research program was directed toward facilitating patients with discovery of a novel organization for their lives. Influence for this approach can be found in Goldstein's interest in the work of the phenomenological philosopher Edmund Husserl (Goldstein and Scheerer 1941; Gurwitsch 1949), which distinguishes between "sensuous congruency" and "equality" of experience. For Husserl, sensuous congruency is based on one's actual experience of the qualitative uniformity of the perceived objects. By equality, Husserl goes beyond purely perceptual experiences and associates the perceived object with further mental processing. These ideas correspond with Goldstein's distinction between "concrete" and "abstract" attitude. For Goldstein, the "concrete" attitude represents an overpowering of the patient by the actual experience, which is constrained to the immediate experiential features. By "abstract" attitude, Goldstein is emphasizing a patient's ability to disengage from the concrete experience and structure their impressions of the perceptual field.

3.1.1 Goldstein, Gelb, and "Case Schn"

Goldstein's holistic approach to neuropsychology was no doubt influenced via his work with the psychologist Adhémar Gelb who designed the cognitive tests for injured soldiers returning from the Great War (Teuber 1966). Goldstein and Gelb's 24-year-old patient "Case Schn" (i.e., Johann Schneider) had substantial brain damage including lesions in the left parietal–occipital junction (Marotta and Behrmann 2004). Patient Schneider displayed a number of cognitive impairments, including alexia, form agnosia, tactile agnosia, acalculia, loss of visual imagery and movement vision, loss of body schema, and loss of abstract reasoning (Goldenberg 2003). According to Goldstein and Gelb, patient Schn was unable to organize local feature elements into larger, more coherent "wholes." When blindfolded patient Schn was instructed to grasp his own nose in an experimental setting, he was unable to perform the task. However, in his everyday life, patient Schn had no visible difficulties in executing habitual actions such as finding a handkerchief in his pocket and putting it to his nose (Goldstein 1923). Goldstein (1931/1971) accounted for the dissociation between patient Schn's different responses to the motor tasks via the introduction of a distinction between "abstract attitude" (isolated, arbitrary movements performed on request) and "concrete attitude" (habitual movements).

3.1.2 Gelb and Goldstein's Sorting Task

Gelb and Goldstein (1920) developed a sorting task in the examination of a patient Th. who suffered from color amnesia. This test was based on the Holmgren test for color blindness. In the first condition of this test, the patient was asked to select one string from a collection of colored strings and then select those strings that were similar to the first one. In the second condition of the test, the examiner presented three strings. While the left and middle string matched in color, the right and middle string matched in brightness. The examiner instructed the patient to indicate which string matched the middle one. In a third condition of the test, the examiner presented two rows of six strings. One row varied from light to dark red. In a second row, the strings had the same clarity, but varied in color. The examiner instructed the patient to select the strings that matched each other. In a fourth condition of the test, the examiner instructed the patient to formulate the reason for her or his responses. Goldstein observed that patients performed the task very differently than healthy participants. His patients tended to take a "concrete" attitude and look at individual objects. Contrariwise, his healthy participants maintained the ability of "abstract attitude" in which features may be abstracted and concepts may be chosen to structure and organized perceptions. It is important to note that there were no quantitative scoring procedures during this time. Goldstein believed that the specific attitude could not be expressed in a single test score. Instead, the examiner had to observe how the patient performed the tasks.

3.1.3 Weigl–Goldstein–Scheerer–Color Form Sorting Test

Over the years, Goldstein refined his assessment of the loss of abstract attitude and the ability to formulate concepts following brain injury to assess deficits in abstract behavior (Goldstein and Scheerer 1941). A variant was developed by Weigl, the Gelb–Goldstein–Weigl–Scheerer Sorting Test that consisted of a set of common objects used in daily life activities. The patient was instructed to sort these in different groups. For example, the patient was to sort the objects according to color, material, or usage. Subsequently, the patient was assessed on ability to set shift and was assessed on her or his ability to sort the items according to a new criterion (Weigl 1942). In the Weigl–Goldstein–Scheerer–Color Form Sorting Test, the patient was assessed on her or his ability to sort geometrical objects (e.g., squares, triangles, and circles) that consisted of the colors red, green, blue, and yellow according to the form or color. Following his emigration to the USA, Goldstein continued to use this task in his clinical work (Bolles and Goldstein 1938).

In summary, Goldstein's work on abstract reasoning and categorical thinking has had a noteworthy impact upon neuropsychology (Goldstein 1990). Goldstein's "abstract attitude" refers to something that is lost in a patient following brain injury, as suggested by the tendency to focus on physical (i.e., concrete attitudes) and not conceptual (abstract) properties of their environments (Goldstein and Scheerer 1941). Goldstein's formulation of abstract versus concrete attitudes laid the foundation for the ways in which abstractions play an important role in automatic and controlled processing. He was one of the first neurologists to explore higher executive functions in everyday life, such as the abilities to establish and maintain particular cognitive sets, shift cognitive sets, and abstract from the properties in a test situation the needed rules for decision making (Goldstein 1936).

3.2 *Lev Vygotsky and Alexander Luria: Russian Neuropsychology*

Like Goldstein, Russian psychologists and neuropsychologists were interested in a qualitative understanding of the individual. In particular, Lev Vygotsky was interested in concept formation (see Hanfmann 1968). Vygotsky's test was made up of 22 wooden blocks that consisted of five different colors, six forms, two heights, and two sizes of the ground surface. Further, four cards that included nonsense words (lag, fik, mur, and sev) were located in the four corners of a board. The examiner explained to the participant that the set of objects consisted of four types of blocks, each with its own name. The examiner instructed the patient to discover which block belonged to which name. Vygotsky and Goldstein were both interested in the higher cognitive functions. For Vygotsky, these were described as "higher psychic functions," and for Goldstein, they were described as abstract attitude (Hanfmann 1968). In Vygotsky's student, Alexander Luria, we find a program of research that facilitated the subsequent differentiation and integration of basic and clinical research in neuropsychology (Christensen 1975). Luria obtained an Ed.D (doctor pedagogicheskikh nauk) in 1936 and an MD in 1943 at the Moscow Medical Institute. Luria was influenced by Vygotsky's cultural–historical approach to cognitive functioning, in which perceptual, attentional, and memory processing are converted into socially structured cognitive functions through learning. As a result, Luria, like Goldstein and Vygotsky, investigated the symbolic operations underlying the highest mental functions (Akhutina 2003).

The work of A.R. Luria is a good example of a neuropsychological evaluation derived from a neurological approach. In Luria's clinical evaluations, he employed a clinical–theoretical approach that primarily involved a qualitative approach (Luria 1966/1980). According to Luria, performance on a neuropsychological assessment reveals patterns or "functional systems" of interacting neurological areas that are responsible for a given behavior. Each neurological area of the brain participates in numerous such functional systems. Luria aimed to show that the cognitive sequelae of a brain injury reflect an interruption to the execution of any functional system that includes the injured areas(s). A great strength of Luria's flexible methodology is that it developed from his clinical experiences with thousands of patient evaluations (Luria and Majovski 1977; Majovski and Jacques 1980). As is often the case, the greatest strength of a clinical neuropsychology approach can be that it also involves a weakness. The most significant flaw in the original Luria battery is a lack of standard administration and scoring that has precluded an assessment of its validity. However, there have been attempts to overcome these deficiencies by developing an objective form, combining Luria's procedures with the advantages of a standard test battery (i.e., Luria-Nebraska Neuropsychological Battery, also known as LNNB; Golden et al. 1980).

3.3 Physiological and Comparative Psychology (Twentieth Century)

In the twentieth century, neuropsychology moved beyond the naive localization theory of the diagram-makers, which has been largely abandoned by most neuropsychologists (Goldstein 1990). The physiological and comparative psychology of the twentieth century provided impetus for this shift and the actual term "neuropsychology" emerged in the work of Lashley, Hebb, and Osler (Bruce 1985). Lashley's (1929, 1950) mass-action-equipotentiality-function doctrine resulted from research findings suggested that learning deficits were proportional to the quantity of cortex removed, independent of the location. For Lashley, the efficiency of any complex brain function is reduced in proportion to the amount of damage the brain as a whole has sustained. It is important to note that Lashly was not a naïve equipotentialist. Instead, he advocated a far more complex and integrative form of neural processing (Hebb 1963). Lashley's work found support in Donald Hebb. The two worked together at the University of Chicago. Hebb extended Lashley's ideas and provided an early integration of the existing literature in support of the regional localization doctrine. He also proffered descriptions of neural network assemblies and their functional relationships that incorporated elements of both localizationistic and mass-action doctrine into the analysis of the behavioral consequences of brain lesions (Meier 1992; further development of this synthesis can be attributed to Luria 1966). Hebb's behavior–cognition integration helped to counterbalance strict behaviorism and stimulated the rise of physiological psychology and psychobiology. Hebb's formulations gave "mental events" a neural basis and opened the door to a future possible cognitive neuropsychology (Hebb 1981).

3.3.1 Brenda Milner: Neuropsychology at McGill University

Eventually, Hebb teamed up with Wilder Penfield at McGill University for their pioneering research into the effects of removal of prefrontal or the anterior/mesial temporal tissue for intractable focal seizure disorders (Hebb and Penfield 1940). During this time, a number of influential proto-neuropsychologists visited Hebb and Penfield. For example, Henry Hacaen's time there had a profound influence on his future development and he named his laboratory "Groupe de Neuropsychologie et de Neurolinguistique" in the 1960s (Boller 1998). While at McGill, Hebb took on Brenda Milner as a PhD candidate in psychophysiology. Milner was also able to work with Penfield to study the behavior of epileptic patients treated with focal ablation of brain tissue. Milner is considered a pioneer in clinical neuropsychology and is noted for convincing her colleagues of the importance of collecting data on the cognitive capacities of patients undergoing unilateral cerebral excisions. In her early studies, she contrasted the effects of left and right temporal lobectomy, which lead to the establishment of research into hemispheric specialization (Berlucchi et al. 1997; Jones-Gotman et al. 1997).

Like Goldstein (see above), Milner used a sorting task to investigate the effect of different brain lesions on frontal lobe functioning. Milner used the Wisconsin Card Sorting Test (WCST). The WCST was developed by Grant and Berg (1948) as an extension of the Weigl-Goldstein card-sorting task. Of note, the WCST had the advantage of tapping into both quantitative and qualitative aspects of abstract reasoning, concept formation, and response strategies to changing contextual contingencies. This original WCST consisted of a set of 60 response cards. Each card had one to four duplicate patterns (e.g., stars, crosses, triangles, and circles) and was all in the same color (e.g., red, yellow, green, or blue). Participants were instructed to place each card under one of four key cards and to infer the sorting principle following feedback (correct, incorrect) from the examiner. The examiner scored each response in terms of errors, latency, degree of perseveration, and capacity to shift (Eling et al. 2008). Milner introduced the WCST as a neuropsychological assessment, and it has become a standard clinical tool for the diagnosis of executive dysfunction (Milner 1963).

Milner's (1963) study of eighteen patients with epileptogenic foci in the dorsolateral prefrontal cortex (dPFC) found that they committed more perseverative errors than patients with orbitofrontal cortex (OFC), temporal, or parietal damage. No significant differences were found across clinical groups for nonperseverative errors. According to Milner, the fewer number of achieved categories in patients with dPFC was due to their perseverative tendencies instead of their tendency to be distracted (i.e., to nonperseverative errors). Although these seminal findings and interpretations has had a huge impact on expected patterns of neuropsychological performance for patients with prefrontal lesions, many neuropsychologists now question the anatomical specificity of predicted from performance on the paper-and-pencil WCST. To a large extent, this a result of theoretically ill-posed approaches to localize the brain region ultimately responsible for correct WCST performance (Nyhus and Barceló 2009). Further, in its original paper-and-pencil format, the traditional WCST has been argued to be ill-suited to proffer accurate descriptions of the type and severity of cognitive deficits or for localizing lesions responsible for those deficits (Mountain and Snow 1993). This points to the need for caution when building cognitive models from these older experimental designs. Specifically, they lacked precision in spatial and temporal sampling of brain activations and may have limited the formulation of integrative formal models of prefrontal executive functions.

3.4 Summary

In summary, a review of the early years of neuropsychological assessment reveals an emphasis upon extending the neurological examination. During this time, clinicians were able to establish a sense of "normal" performance and tended to assign anything below that threshold as being a pathological deficit. An unfortunate limitation to this dichotomous approach is that it allowed little sense of normal variability. To remedy this, some clinics developed local quantitative procedures, but these usually had no real empirical standardization and no clear generalizable clinical use (Benton 1967). Further, some clinicians diagnosed "organicity" (meaning brain pathology of some kind) based on "pathognomonic" signs discovered in a patient's response to a test. A major problem for the neuropsychological assessment as extension of neurological examination is the lack of any standardized method of giving or scoring the assessment's procedures. In many cases, the description of administrative procedures is vague. Moreover, neuropsychologists taking this approach at times changed procedures for individual patients. Even when administrative procedures are clear, scoring procedures are not. Scoring is determined by the personal assessment of the clinician based on experience and knowledge rather than on any normative data. Despite these major problems, this approach clearly possesses a high degree of face validity as well as a strong theoretical foundation. Neuropsychologists have made great strides in proper standardization, scoring, and validation. As such, the revised neurological examination (i.e., neuropsychological assessment) has become a major tool of both clinical and experimental neuropsychology.

4 Development of the Quantitative Test Battery

4.1 Alfred Binet and Psychometric Assessment of Intellectual Ability

While much of early neuropsychology represents an extension of the neurological examination, many of the current approaches to neuropsychological assessment reflect the work of Binet and the Stanford-Binet test of psychometric intelligence. Binet's work reflects a careful development of objective procedures that had clear and precise criteria for establishing performance. Binet's scales also offered a new level of standardization, in which measures were normed on samples of various ages. Binet's transformative method was a precursor to the development of a psychometrically oriented battery approach. As a result of these areas of improvement, Binet's scales proffered a move away from the dichotomous classification found in neurologically oriented neuropsychological assessments (Rourke and Brown 1986).

An important factor in the development of clinical neuropsychology is the establishment of standardized assessment measures capable of identifying the neurocognitive effects of brain dysfunction. Standardized assessment in neuropsychology is largely due to its historic development from Alfred Binet's (Binet and Henri 1896, 1898; Binet and Simon 1905, 1908) tests of intelligence and the USA's entry into the World War I in 1917 (Anastasi and Urbina 1997). During this time, Robert Yerkes, Arthur Otis, and the American Psychological Association developed a group administered version of the Stanford-Binet (i.e., Army Alpha), and a novel group administered assessment composed of nonverbal tasks (i.e., Army Beta). Yerkes (1917) preferred a point-scale methodology (i.e., tests selected based upon specified functions) over Binet's age-scale approach (i.e., tasks fluctuate with age and developmental level). Ultimately, the Army group administered measures reflecting an amalgamation of Yerkes's point-scale approach and Binet's task-specific approach to measure cognitive performance. Further, a performance scale developed by David Wechsler was included in an Army battery (Yoakum and Yerkes 1920) that was made up of subtests developed primarily by Binet and World War I psychologists.

4.2 David Weschler: World Wars and Weschler Scales

A major shift in testing occurred when Wechsler applied testing procedures (i.e., group and individual) developed for normal functioning persons to the construction of a clinical test battery. Following World War I, Wechsler assembled the 1939 Wechsler-Bellevue battery, which included both verbal and performance Scales.

Wechsler selected 11 different subtests to form this initial battery. In addition to tests (Comprehension, Arithmetic, Digit Span, Similarities, and Vocabulary) from the 1937 revision of the Stanford-Binet, his battery included Picture Arrangement from the Army Group Examinations, Koh's Block Design (Block Design), Army Alpha (Information, Comprehension), Army Beta (Digit Symbol-Coding), Healy Picture Completion (Picture Completion), and the Pintner-Paterson Test (Object Assembly). Two unfortunate limitations were found in the Wechsler-Bellevue: (1) the reliability of the subtests and (2) the size and representativeness of the normative sample. As a result, the battery was revised in 1955 to form the Wechsler Adult Intelligence Scale (WAIS) in 1955, and in 1981, another revised edition (WAIS-R) was published. In 1997, the Wechsler Adult Intelligence Scale-III (WAIS-III) became available. Finally, in 2008, the WAIS IV was published.

By the 1940s, a number of specialized neurocognitive tests were available to clinicians for assessing the mental capacities of persons with brain disease (Conkey 1939; Shipley 1940; Benton and Howell 1941; Goldstein and Scheerer 1941; Wells and Ruesch 1941; Hunt 1943). During this time, Weschler also developed the Wechsler Memory Scale (WMS; Wechsler 1945, 1974 and revised in 1987; Wechsler Memory Scale-Revised; Wechsler 1987 and again in 1997; Wechsler Memory Scale-III; Wechsler 1997b). While the original Wechsler-Bellevue was developed for adults, Wechsler developed the Wechsler Intelligence Scale for Children (WISC) in 1949 (revised in 1974, 1991, 2003). In 1967, the Wechsler Preschool and Primary Scale of Intelligence (WPPSI) was published for the assessment of children between the ages of 4 and 6 years 6 months. The WPPSI was revised in 1989 (WPPSI-R; Wechsler 1989) and again in 2002 (WPPSI-III; Psychological Corporation 2002). The additive effects of these tests provided the foundation for today's neuropsychological assessment procedures (Halstead 1947; Reitan 1955; Lezak 1995; Spreen and Strauss 1998; Mitrushina et al. 1999; Heaton et al. 1991).

While commonly used by neuropsychologists, it is important to note that the Wechsler Adult Intelligence Scale (WAIS) and the Wechsler Memory Scale (WMS) were developed without the specific intention of using them as instruments to assess brain function and detect brain disorders, but extensive experience with these instruments has provided a basis for interpreting the tests in neurologic terms. Most current neuropsychological assessment approaches use several of the traditional tests in combination with newer techniques developed specifically to evaluate neurocognitive activities and provide insight into brain function in different disease states. Hence, the range of domains assessed by clinical neuropsychologists has expanded tremendously in recent decades to include areas beyond behavioral neurology and the traditional differentiation between organic and functional conditions in psychiatry. Although there are aspects of neuropsychological assessment that are similar to the conventional evaluation of the behavioral neurologist, neuropsychological measures have the advantage of standardization and psychometric rigor.

5 Ward Halstead: Establishment of the Fixed Battery Neuropsychological Battery

While standardized intelligence tests such as the Wechsler and Binet scales had growing clinical utilization, a number of investigators were interested in developing quantitative clinical psychometric procedures beyond these standardized intelligence tests. One reason was the relative insensitivity of intelligence tests to the behavioral consequences of many brain lesions (e.g., prefrontal executive functions). The earliest adjunctive set of measures was the Halstead Neuropsychological Battery. It is interesting to note that the Halstead was not primarily interested in clinical application (Goldstein 1985; Reed 1985). Instead, his work was concerned with the distinguishing between intellectual components found in learned versus innate capacities. Halstead's distinction between these components is similar to Hebb's (1949) "Intelligence A" and "Intelligence B" and to Cattell's (1963) "crystallized" and "fluid" abilities. During this time, there was an increasing desire to establish an empirical base for a more scientific approach to neuropsychological assessment. Halstead's student, Ralph Reitan, introduced some modifications to the battery to develop a composite (i.e., Halstead Impairment Index) of outcomes defined by group differences on each of 10 subtests (Reitan 1964). Through a process of clinical and experimental evaluation, seven of the ten survived and were developed into the primary components of the HRB and Halstead Impairment Index. Reitan went on to supplement Halstead's seven tests with numerous other clinical procedures to enhance the clinical usefulness of evaluations. The HRB offered a battery of objective measures that could be used for diagnosis and categorization of brain damage. The Halstead–Reitan Battery was developed specifically to detect "organic" dysfunction and differentiate between patients with and without brain damage (e.g., to distinguish "organic" from "functional" disorders). Over the years, tests have been designed in concert with evolving information regarding the mediation of behavior by specific structures or circuits provide greater insight into the integrity or disintegration of neurologic function. Extensive experience with these instruments provides a basis for interpreting the tests in neurologic terms.

In addition to being one of the first battery approaches, the Halstead–Reitan Battery is commonly referred to today as a "fixed battery" approach because test selection is "fixed" irrespective of the patient's presenting problem. Hence, the Halstead–Reitan Battery represents a comprehensive battery of tests that are administered to each patient in a standardized manner. Advocates of the Halstead–Reitan Battery argue that fixed batteries facilitate the following: (1) comparison of test scores across patient groups and settings (Hom 2003); (2) inclusion of technicians in test administration (Russell 1995, 1998); and (3) development of datasets for research studies (Sweeney et al. 2007). While the HRB has become widely used in neuropsychological assessment (Hom 2003; Ross et al. 2013, 2014), there has been some debate related to the amount of administration time, cost, and potential for excessive testing sessions that may be difficult for patients to tolerate (Lezak 1995; Russell 1998).

6 Contemporary Development of the Flexible Test Battery

An alternative to the "fixed" battery neuropsychological assessment found in the HRB is the "flexible battery" approach, in which neuropsychologists take a hypothesis-driven approach. In the "flexible" battery, the referral question, presenting problem, and clinical interview are used for initial test selection. A limited set of measures are used to evaluate a broad range of cognitive functions and establish the patient's strengths and weaknesses. Following this initial assessment of strengths and weaknesses, the neuropsychologist will then select additional measures based on the patient's performance on the core battery and reported cognitive concerns. The "flexible" battery approach has emerged as the most widely used approach to neuropsychological assessment. In a recent survey of practicing neuropsychologists, Sweet et al. (2006) found that 76 % used a flexible battery and only 7 % used a standardized battery such as the HRB. In a related survey, Rabin et al. (2005) found that most neuropsychologists frequently used a flexible battery approach and only 15.5 % used the HRB. Recently, Bigler (2007) presented an argument in support of the use of flexible battery neuropsychological assessment in forensic neuropsychology. Through a review of the developments in neuropsychology that have occurred since the HRB was originally validated, Bigler (2007) offered evidence for the acceptability of a flexible battery. Further support for the flexible battery approach can be found in Larrabee's (2008) review of findings from studies comparing the validity of flexible batteries to fixed batteries. Larrabee (2008) concluded that flexible batteries are as valid as approaches relying on the HRB.

6.1 Arthur Benton: Iowa-Benton Flexible Battery Approach

An early precursor to the flexible battery approach can be found in the work of Arthur Benton (Benton 1964, 1969). Benton has had a great influence on the development of clinical neuropsychology and his work bridges behavioral neurology, cognitive psychology, neurolinguistics and aphasiology, developmental psychology, clinical psychology, and experimental/physiological psychology (Meier 1992). While a member of the neurology department at Iowa, Benton developed procedures for assessing visuospatial judgment, visuoconstructional praxis, facial recognition, auditory perception, serial digit learning, cerebral dominance, developmental learning disorders, and language behavior (Costa and Spreen 1985). Benton's flexible battery approach is a hypothesis-driven approach to standardized measurement of higher brain functions in patients with known or suspected brain disease. Benton's methods have now evolved into the Iowa-Benton method, in which quantitative measurements are considered key for assessing domains of cognition and behavior, in a time-efficient manner. According to Tranel (2009), the Iowa-Benton flexible battery approach maintains a close link to neuroanatomy and the findings from neuropsychological assessments are both informed by and inform findings from neuroimaging and physiological recordings.

6.2 *Edith Kaplan: Boston Process Approach*

Development of the flexible battery has resulted in what now called the "process" approach, which resulted from work by neuropsychologists in Australia (Walsh 1987), Denmark (Christensen 1979), and the USA (Kaplan 1988). The process approach extends early formulations of the flexible battery approach via increased emphasis upon standardization. For example, the qualitative information gleaned from analyses of behavior is quantified and subjected to psychometric analyses. As a result, the process approach allows for greater assessment of clinical limits in an operationally defined, repeatable, and quantifiable manner. The emphasis upon process analyses results from the belief that the resolution to problems presented via standardized assessment measures may be achieved by various processes, and each of these may be related to different brain structures. Hence, the ways in which a given patient responds are viewed as important as the patient's response itself.

While there has been a great deal of debate about whether the fixed or flexible battery approach is the best, most would agree that there are strengths found in including both qualitative and quantitative information (Rourke and Brown 1986). Over the years, various procedures have been developed to maximize the use of the battery of tests. Psychometrics have been applied to test results to maximize the value of the neuropsychological assessment battery approach by combining information, minimizing variability among groups, and grouping patients by behavioral characteristics (Bezeau and Graves 2001; Maroof 2012; Zakzanis 1998, 2001; Woods et al. 2003). According to Stuss (2002), factor analyses have allowed for the differentiation of assessment variables into functional representative groupings and provided a methods and systems for examining shared and independent variance to maximize brain–behavior understanding. Further, discriminant function analyses have been utilized for classification of patients into their proper groups for validation of the battery approach (Stuss and Trites 1977).

7 Conclusions

Over the course of the last several decades, clinical neuropsychology has gained recognition as a discipline with relevance to a number of diverse practice areas (e.g., neurology, neurosurgery, psychiatry, and family medicine) as well as neuroscience-specific research areas (e.g., behavior, learning, and individual differences). As a result, neuropsychologists tend to apply a working understanding of psychology, physiology, and neurology to assess, diagnose, and treat patients with neurological, medical, neurodevelopmental, psychiatric, and cognitive disorders. A typical neuropsychological assessment examines brain–behavior relations as they pertain to neurocognitive, affective, and behavioral expressions of central nervous system dysfunction. Neuropsychologists use specialized assessment procedures to measure deficits in cognitive functioning, personality, and sensory–motor functions, and connect the results to specific brain areas that have been affected. Current approaches to neuropsychological evaluation typically range from an ordinal scale (i.e., impaired/nonimpaired) for basic sensory and perceptual functioning to an integral scale (i.e., percentile relative to normative group) for more complex functions. The question of normal versus abnormal functioning of the central nervous system includes not only the assessment of the consequences of trauma and diseases to the central nervous system, but also the impact of psychiatric conditions in which central nervous system involvement is assumed but not well defined.

As mentioned above, much of what is now considered part of neuropsychological assessment originated from attempts of late nineteenth-century and early twentieth-century physicians to improve evaluation of the cognitive capacities of persons with brain disease. As such, during a period focusing on localization, neuropsychologists received referrals from neurosurgeons to psychometrically localize brain damage. As a result, developed measures were based upon a localization paradigm that focused upon double dissociation—two neocortical areas are functionally dissociated by two behavioral measures, and each measure is affected by a lesion in one neocortical area and not the other (Teuber 1955; Probram 1971). Given the importance of neuropsychological assessment for lesion localization, it became increasingly important that neuropsychological assessment has enhanced psychometric rigor. In addition to the reliability and validity issues mentioned above, this also includes issues of sensitivity and specificity. By sensitivity, neuropsychologists are referring to a test's ability to detect even the slightest expression of abnormalities in neurological (primarily central nervous system) function. Sensitivity is understood as a reflection of the neuropsychological test's ability to identify persons with a disorder. This is often referred to as true positive rate. By specificity, neuropsychologists are referring to the ability of a neuropsychological test to differentiate patients with a certain abnormality from those with other abnormalities or with no abnormality. This is often referred to as true negative rate. A score on any test can be a true positive, false positive, true negative, or false negative. For a score to be true positive, it must have high sensitivity to dysfunction, allowing dysfunctions to be detected. If a score on any test is false positive, it indicates sensitivity to dysfunction, but lacks specificity to a particular dysfunction. A score on any test can be a true negative if it has high specificity, allowing negative to be distinguished from others. If a score on any test is false negative, this indicates a lack of sensitivity, without regard to specificity of the test. For any evaluation, it is important to understand the rates of each of the four categories of results. The ability to identify brain dysfunction varies greatly among neuropsychological tests and is determined by the fidelity with which the neuropsychological test distinguishes normal from abnormal function and by the specific type of deficit that the patient exhibits. The WAIS, for example, has no memory subtests and is necessarily insensitive to memory-related deficits, whereas it has demonstrated sensitivity to disorders affecting visuospatial, calculation, and attentional abilities. In general, tests that are timed, requiring the patient to complete the test in a specified period, have greater sensitivity to diffuse or multifocal cerebral changes than untimed tests.

In summary, in a number of ways, clinical neuropsychology can be viewed as representing a synthesis of the best features of neurological, psychiatric, and psychological examination procedures, whereby the systematic neurological assessment of functional cortical and subcortical systems is combined with the precise scaling of psychometric measurement. Neuropsychological assessment allows the examiner to reduce the subjectivity in traditional neurological examinations by conducting assessments that lead to quantifiable standardized scores, thereby increasing the reliability of the assessment as well as allowing for a more sensitive baseline for comparisons across time. Further, availability of normative data and use of standardized administration procedures allow neuropsychological evaluation to be more sensitive than unstructured mental status testing in the detection of mild cognitive disturbances.

8 Changing Roles and Tools in Neuropsychological Assessment 1.0

It is important to note, however, that with the advent of neuroimaging, the need for neuropsychologists to localize brain damage has been greatly reduced. Unfortunately, many neuropsychologists continue to rely on "localization" as the chief basis for validating neuropsychological tests. As Ronald Ruff has contended, although neuroimaging caused the role of neuropsychology to shift from localization to documentation of neuropsychological deficits for prediction of real-world functioning, clinical neuropsychologists many times fail to develop ecologically oriented assessments and continue to use localizationist-developed test batteries (Ruff 2003).

Although today's neuropsychological assessment procedures are widely used, neuropsychologists have been slow to adjust to the impact of technology on their profession. Two essential limitations have resulted from this refusal of technological adaptation: First, current neuropsychological assessment procedures represent a technology that has barely changed since the first scales were developed in the early 1900s (i.e., Binet and Simon's first scale in 1905 and Wechsler's first test in 1939). In order for neuropsychologists to fully embrace the development of new batteries that take real-world functioning (i.e., ecological validity) seriously, there is a need for them to move beyond cosmetic changes to standardized tests to computerized measures. However, neuropsychologists have historically resisted embracing technological advances in computation. While neuropsychology emphasizes its role as a science, its technology is not progressing in pace with other science-based technologies. Second, while the historical purpose of clinical neuropsychology was differential diagnosis of brain pathology, technological advances in other clinical neurosciences (e.g., the development of neuroimaging) have changed the neuropsychologist's role to that of making ecologically valid predictions about the impact of a given patient's neurocognitive abilities and disabilities on everyday functioning.

Chapter 4
Neuropsychological Assessment 2.0: Computer-Automated Assessments

We must embrace neuropsychology as a scientific discipline to ensure that we will continue to be at the forefront in the study of brain–behavior relationships, as well as in the design and development of technologies to ameliorate disease conditions.
— Eric Zillmer: President's address (2004)

Since the 1980s, a number of neuropsychologists have written reviews expressing optimism and concerns that computer-automated neuropsychological (Adams 1986; Adams and Brown 1986; Kane and Kay 1992, 1997; Kane and Reeves 1997; Kay and Starbuck 1997; Larrabee and Crook 1991). On the positive side, computer-automated neuropsychological assessments have been lauded for their potential to augment task administration (Parsey and Schmitter-Edgecombe 2013), scoring (Woo 2008), collect normative data (Bilder 2011), and in some cases interpret tests (Russell 1995, 2000). In addition to administration issues, advantages have been noted for the complexity of stimulus presentation (Gur et al. 2001a; 2001b; Schatz and Browndyke 2002) and logging of responses (Crook et al. 2009; Woo 2008). There are also a number of concerns that have been raised. A notable concern is whether the patient's perception of the computer-generated stimuli and responses to the computerized administration is significantly different from traditional paper-and-pencil measures (Cernich et al. 2007; Hoskins et al. 2010; Williams and McCord 2006). Further, concerns involve the different levels of familiarity that patients will have to computer software and interfaces (e.g., mouse and keyboard; Iverson et al. 2009; Kapur 1988). These issues may result in a failure of computer-administered tests to deliver results that are identical (or even comparable) to a paper-and-pencil test administered by an examiner (Feldstein et al. 1999; French and Beaumont 1987; Ozonoff 1995). For example, there are two commercially available versions of the Wisconsin Card Sorting Test (WCST): a manual version (Heaton et al. 1993) and a computer version (Heaton and PAR 2003). While some of these differences may reflect cohort issues (e.g., persons with autism; Ozonoff 1995), studies have shown that the paper-and-pencil and computerized versions of the WCST are not equivalent (Feldstein et al. 1999; see Table 1 for advantages and disadvantages of computerized neuropsychological assessments).

T.D. Parsons, *Clinical Neuropsychology and Technology*,
DOI 10.1007/978-3-319-31075-6_4

Table 1 Computer-based neuropsychological assessments: advantages and disadvantages

Advantages	Disadvantages
Administration (stimulus presentation) • Enhanced control over administration and scoring • Increased accuracy of timing presentation • Automatic randomization of test trials • Alternate forms and adaptive testing protocols • Ability to set accurate basal and ceiling levels and subsequently discontinue the test • Ease of administering tests in different languages • Capacity to rapidly test a large number of persons • Reduced assessment times (adaptive testing) • Administer tests on portable devices (smartphones or handheld computers)	*Administration* • Errors can occur in test administration due to problematic hardware and software interactions • Do not allow for "testing the limits," • Do not allow for flexibility in evaluations • Do not provide structured encouragement
Logging and scoring (behavioral responses) • Increased accuracy of measurement/logging of response latency, strength, and variability • Ability to integrate and automate interpretive algorithms such as decision rules for determining impairment or statistically reliable • Ability to measure performance on time-sensitive tasks (e.g., reaction time)	*Logging and scoring* (behavioral responses) • Behavioral responses from computerized tests may not provide identical (or even similar) results as paper-and-pencil counterpart • May mask deficits that would otherwise be apparent in some populations (e.g., persons with autism may perform better when faced with a computer) • Computerized assessments may tap into cognitive functions at a level that is rarely demanded in real-life settings
Impact on participant • May increase openness and engagement of respondents • Decrease in examiner influence on responses • May increase accessibility and availability of neuropsychological services	*Impact on participant* • Computerized tests may not be experientially or psychometrically equivalent to paper-and-pencil counterparts (validity) • Negative attitudes (including anxiety) about computers persists, especially among individuals with limited exposure to technology, computerized administration may alter task performance • Understanding and assessing levels of effort and motivation can prove challenging
Normative database • Enhanced normative data collection and comparison • Ease of exporting responses for data analytic purposes • Automated data exporting for research purposes	*Normative database* • None noted

In a review of utilization rates of computerized tests and batteries among clinical neuropsychologists in the USA and Canada, Rabin et al. (2014) found that computerized testing barely registers in clinical practice. While the review lists a number of advantages of computer-based neuropsychological assessments, a number of concerns were also mentioned. In addition to questions about psychometric and experiential equivalency, Rabin et al. (2014) suggest that this may also reflect a lack of exposure to computerized assessment methods during training. They suggest that the realization of the potential benefits of computerized testing may involve heightened acquaintance to such measures at various levels of professional neuropsychological training. In sum, these studies point to the need for increased exposure and thorough validation of the computerized batteries (Bauer et al. 2012).

In a recent joint position paper of the American Academy of Clinical Neuropsychology and the National Academy of Neuropsychology, computer-based assessments were defined as "any instrument that utilizes a computer, digital tablet, handheld device, or other digital interface instead of a human examiner to administer, score, or interpret tests of brain function and related factors relevant to questions of neurologic health and illness" (Bauer et al. 2012, p. 2). It is laudable that the clinical neuropsychology community has endeavored to establish a consensus statement related to technological advances in neuropsychological assessment. However, there are some limitations of the definition. First, computer-based assessments are not always administered by a computer "instead of a human examiner to administer, score, or interpret tests." Further, the lumping together of so many disparate technologies and functions into one definition trivializes the complexities involved. According to the statement, computer-based assessments involve a host of devices (computer, digital tablet, handheld device, or other digital interface) for administration, scoring, or interpretation of tests of brain function. This lumping together is of great concern to any discipline that involves these various areas. Further, it ignores the important issues that result from such a simplification for ecologically valid assessments and the need for data capture for large neuropsychological databases.

Throughout this book, there is an emphasis upon the importance of (1) using technology to develop repositories for linking neuropsychological assessment results with data from neuroimaging, psychophysiology, and genetic; and (2) moving from construct-driven assessments to tests that are representatives of real-world functions and proffer results that are generalizable for prediction of the functional performance across a range of situations. The plan for this chapter is as follows: In Sect. 1, there will be a discussion of the historical development of computerized assessments. This will include early attempts at automation and interpretation, followed by a period of disillusionment, and finally resurgence for return-to-play decisions. Next, in Sect. 2, there will be a discussion of various application areas for computerized assessments. In Sect. 3, "common currency" assessments are presented. Finally, Sect. 4 closes the chapter with a discussion of the needs for ecologically valid assessments.

1 Historical Development of Computerized Assessments

1.1 Early Attempts at Automation

Early work with automated testing did not make full use of computers (Space 1981). For example, Gedye (1967, 1968) and Miller (1969) automated the pictorial paired-associate learning task using a teaching machine (the ts-512). In 1969, Elwood used a paper-tape-controlled and solenoid-operated console that used a microphone, rear-projection screen, push-button panel, tape recorder, and typewriter to administer the Wechsler Adult Intelligence Scale (WAIS). In the early 1970s, Studies using the automated system reported that the automated WAIS was as reliable as the standard version, and the two versions correlated very highly (Elwood 1972; Elwood and Griffin 1972). Microcomputers became popular in the 1970s and 1980s with the advent of increasingly powerful microprocessors. This introduction soon led to the development of computer-automated versions of classical paper-and-pencil and electromechanical neuropsychological assessments (Kane and Kay 1992). As a result, computers were increasingly employed during the 1980s and 1990s for neuropsychological test administration, scoring, and interpretation (Adams and Heaton 1987; Kane and Kay 1992, 1997). One of the earliest platforms for computerized assessment, scoring, and basic interpretation was called the neuropsychological key (Russell et al. 1970). According the Russell (2011), Carolyn Shelley programmed a decision-tree algorithm that placed the scoring and the preliminary interpretation of test results into an automated program. Following the initial computer automation, the period 1980s saw continued development of the neuropsychology key and establishment of the lateralization index (Russell 1984; Russell and Starkey 2001). Also during this period, Reitan developed the Neuropsychological Deficit Scale program to lateralize brain damage (Reitan 1991). In lieu of these advances, there were discussions about the importance of automated rules for statistical prediction that incorporate psychometric data, patient history, and results from clinical or neurological examinations (Garb and Schramke 1996).

Initial enthusiasm suggested that computerized administration, scoring, and interpretation could be integrated with computer technology (Kane and Kay 1992; Russell 1995). Although computer-based interpretation was increasingly used during this period (Russell 1995, 2000), concerns were raised regarding whether sophisticated algorithms can generate accurate clinical predictions (Adams 1986; Adams and Brown 1986; Adams and Heaton 1985, 1987; Adams et al. 1984; Anthony et al. 1980; Heaton and Adams 1987; Heaton et al. 1981; Long and Wagner 1986). In response to these publications on the inadequacy of computer interpretation, Russell (2011) has argued that these critiques are primarily review articles that were based on only two studies (the other publications were reviews citing these two studies). One of these studies was completed in Heaton's laboratory

(Anthony et al. 1980; Heaton et al. 1981) and the other was performed by Adams (Adams, et al. 1984). Russell also points out that these reviews overlooked studies that questioned their results. Results from a study that reanalyzed the Anthony et al. (1980) study found agreement between the original neuropsychological key study and the crossvalidation when both sensitivity and selectivity were considered (Goldstein and Shelly 1982). Russell (2011) also points to two studies by Wedding (1983a, b) that found the neuropsychology key to be almost as accurate as an experienced neuropsychologist (see also Garb 1989; Russell 1998). While it is unclear whether the computerized platforms during this period were adequate, it is clear that the use of computerized interpretation of clinical results from fixed batteries has dwindled over the years.

1.2 Computer Automations of Paper-and-Pencil Tests

Although there was some decrease in enthusiasm for fixed batteries during this period, interest in the development of computerized administration and scoring has continued. A quick literature review reveals that throughout the 1980s there was burgeoning interest in computerization (or at least quasi-computerization) of various assessment measures. For example, some assessments have been developed for computerized symptom validity testing (Allen et al. 2003). Examples of computerized neuropsychological measures used to distinguish between persons putting forth their best effort and those who are not include: Computerized Assessment of Response Bias (Green and Iverson 2001); Victoria Symptom Validity Test (Slick et al. 1997); and the Word Memory Test (Green 2003). Further, during this period neuropsychologists transferred a number of paper-and-pencil measures to the personal computer platform (see Bartram and Bayliss 1984). A few examples of computerized versions of traditional paper-and-pencil neuropsychological tests include: the Raven's Progressive Matrices (Calvert and Waterfall 1982; French and Beaumont 1990; Knights et al. 1973; Rock and Nolen 1982; Waterfall 1979); the Peabody Picture Vocabulary Test (Klinge and Rodziewicz 1976; Knights et al. 1973; Space 1975); the Category Test (Beaumont 1975; Choca and Morris 1992); the Hidden and Embedded Figures tests (Brinton and Rouleau 1969); and the Wisconsin Card Sorting Test (Fortuny and Heaton 1996; Heaton 1999). Further, research by Gilberstadt et al. (1976) looked at automated versions of the Shipley-Hartford Vocabulary Test, Raven's Matrices, and Digit Span and Digit Symbol subtests of the WAIS. Initial attempts at assessing the equivalence of these measures to traditional tests were made (Eckerman et al. 1985). Early studies tended to reveal significant test–retest reliabilities and no significant differences were found between manual and computer administrations (Bartum and Bayliss 1984; Mead and Drasgow 1993).

1.3 Computer Scoring of Paper-and-Pencil Tests

For much of the 1980s to early 2000s, the focus of many test developers has been upon slight revisions of the paper-and-pencil versions with computerized scoring. Scoring programs for various paper-and-pencil tests have been developed that allowed for automatic calculation of normative scores, generation of profiles, and reporting of interpretive statements: California Verbal Learning Test-Second Edition (Delis et al. 2000); Delis–Kaplan executive function system (Delis et al. 2001); Neuropsychological Assessment Battery (Stern and White 2003); Ruff Neurobehavioral Inventory (Ruff and Hibbard 2003); Wechsler Adult Intelligence Scale-Fourth Edition (Wechsler 2008); Wechsler Memory Scale-Fourth Edition (Wechsler 2009); and the Wisconsin Card Sorting Test (Heaton et al. 1993).

For example, while automated versions of the original WAIS were developed in 1969 (Elwood and Griffin 1972) and again in 1980 (Vincent 1980), these automations provided only rudimentary stimulus presentation and limited data recording. The technology used for administration of the Wechsler scales changed little between the 1980s and the early 2000s. Given the major advances in technology, it is interesting that for the past few decades, the most widely used neuropsychological tests (e.g., Wechsler scales in various manifestations: WAIS-R, WAIS III) progressed so little in terms of technological advances (Hartlage and Telzrow 1980; Guilmette et al. 1990; Lees-Haley et al. 1996). According to a 2005 study surveying assessment practices and test usage patterns among 747 North American, doctorate-level clinical neuropsychologists, the Wechsler Scales were the most frequently used tests in their neuropsychological assessments (Rabin et al. 2005). While the administration of the Wechsler scales changed very little during this time, software was developed that allowed for automatic calculation of normative scores, generation of profiles, and reporting of interpretive statements.

A recent development for traditional paper-and-pencil assessments is the establishment of the Q-Interactive platform that enables examiners to create batteries at both the battery (e.g., Wechsler Memory Scale—4th Edition, Delis-Kaplan Executive Function System) and subtest levels for administration on a portable iPad device and scored in real time (Daniel 2012, 2013). This automation of traditional paper-and-pencil tests uses two tablet PCs, one for the examiner and the other for the examinee. While the examinee's tablet does little more than replace the traditionally printed stimulus booklet, the examiner's tablet offers a number of advances over simply replacing examiner's manual: Scores item response times and accuracy shows the examinee's touch responses, implements administration rules (e.g., start and discontinue), and records examiner notes. While this approach offers an advance via a two-PC approach, it currently offers little else over other computer-automated neuropsychological assessments.

2 Application Areas of Computerized Assessments

2.1 Computer-Automated Batteries for Return-to-Capacity Decisions

2.1.1 Military Neuropsychology and Return-to-Duty Decisions

Military and sport neuropsychology fields have used computer-automated neuropsychological assessments since the 1980s to rapidly and efficiently measure neurocognitive functioning. Within the US military, computer-based neuropsychological assessments such as the Automated Neuropsychological Assessment Metrics (ANAM) have been used for both pre- and post-deployment assessment. The ANAM is a computer-based battery of tests designed to measure a participant's neuropsychological functioning. The ANAM was initially developed within the Department of Defense and the current version represents over 30 years of research linked to older standardized test batteries, including the Unified Tri-Service Cognitive Performance Assessment Battery (Reeves et al. 2007). With ongoing DoD support, ANAM has undergone several revisions and its use has spread from defense-related research to other academic research areas (Kane et al. 2007). The ANAM has been widely used to assess acquired brain injury with military populations (Ivins et al. 2009; Roebuck-Spencer et al. 2012; Vincent et al. 2008; Vincent et al. 2012). This data collection has led to a large database (N = 107,500 active duty service members ranging from 17 to 65 years of age) for normative validation (Vincent et al. 2012).

2.1.2 Sports Neuropsychology and Return-to-Play Decisions

Starting in the late 1990s, computer-automated neuropsychological assessments became a central component of sport-related concussion management (Ferrara et al. 2001; Meehan et al. 2012; Notebaert and Guskiewicz 2005; Randolph 2011; Resch et al. 2013). According to a recent study by Meehan et al. (2012), 93 % of athletic trainers used the Immediate Post-concussion Assessment and Cognitive Testing (ImPACT), followed by 2.8 % using CogSport/CogState (CogState 2011). Part of the allure of computer-based neuropsychological assessments is that groups of athletes can be baselined in a brief period of time and then athletic trainers can longitudinally track their cognitive deficits. Further, the portability of these computer-based assessments allows them be used on the field when (and where) injuries happen (Allen and Gfeller 2011; Broglio et al. 2007; Collie and Maruff 2003; Maerlender et al. 2010). Given the portability and automated administration, sports neuropsychologists are increasingly using computer-automated batteries, such as ImPact or Cogsport, to inform return-to-play decisions (Lovell 2002; Lovell et al. 2004; Schatz et al. 2006).

2.1.3 Immediate Post-concussion Assessment and Cognitive Testing (ImPACT) Test Battery

Immediate Post-Concussion Assessment and Cognitive Testing (ImPACT) is a computerized battery of tests that was specifically developed for identifying and managing concussion in athletes and is currently used by a large number of athletic organizations at various levels of athletic play (Iverson et al. 2003). The primary aim of ImPACT is to offer a computerized assessment and management tool for concussive injuries in an athletic environment (Schatz et al. 2006). Using ImPACT, the sports neuropsychologist is able to objectively evaluate the concussed athlete's post-injury condition and track recovery for return-to-play decisions (Schatz et al. 2006). The ImPACT collects basic demographic information, descriptive data, and various aspects of neurocognitive functioning: Word Memory; Design Memory; X's and O's; Symbol Match; Color Match; and Three Letters (see Table 2). The ImPACT includes a 22-item Post-Concussion Symptom Scale (Schatz et al. 2006).

Table 2 Computer-automated batteries for return-to-capacity decisions

	ANAM	CogSport	ImPACT
Platform	PC-Based	Web-based	PC or Web-based
Approximate time (min)	25–30	20	20
Change assessment	Reliable change indices	Simple difference method and effect sizes	Reliable change indices
Tests	• Simple reaction time (SRT) • Code substitution • Procedural reaction time • Mathematical processing • Matching to sample • Code substitution delayed	• Detection task • Identification task • One card learning • One back • Chase task • Groton maze learning	• Word memory • Design memory • X's and O's • Symbol match • Color match • Three letters
Psychometrics	• Test–retest reliability (1–16 weeks) did not meet minimum criterion for acceptable reliability • Validity values ranging from −0.01–0.65	• Test–retest reliability (10 min–4 weeks) did not meet minimum criteria for acceptable reliability. • Validity values ranged from 0.23–0.83	• Test–retest reliability (1 day–2 years) did not meet minimum criteria for acceptable reliability. • Validity values ranged from 0.20–0.88

Note RT = Reaction time. ImPACT = Immediate Post-Concussion Assessment and Cognitive Testing. ANAM = Automated Neuropsychological Assessment Metrics

2.1.4 CogSport/State/Axon Sports

The CogState neuropsychological assessment battery consists of tasks that utilize playing card stimuli and is presented on a laptop computer (Collie et al. 2002; Falleti et al. 2006). On each trial of each task, a single playing card is presented in the center of the computer monitor. The values, color, and suit of the playing cards are determined by the requirements of each task. Given the emphasis upon return-to-play decisions, the CogSport/Axon approach to the identification of concussion-related cognitive impairment has been validated using the baseline method (Collie et al. 2003). The normative method used for the CogSport/Axon battery to compare the rates of abnormal performance in noninjured and concussed athletes (Gardner et al. 2012). In a study designed to determine the sensitivity and specificity of the CogSport/Axon test battery, Louey et al. (2014) computed normative data and reliable change indices from a noninjured athlete sample (n = 260) and a recently concussed sample (n = 29). Results suggests that while the use of the normative method for CogSport identifies most cases of recent concussions, the baseline method is preferred for CogSport because it offers a more precise approach to assessing concussion-related cognitive impairments. The CogSport battery is made up of the following tests: Detection Task; Identification Task; One Card Learning; One Back; Chase Task; and Groton Maze Learning (see Table 2).

2.1.5 ANAM-Sports Medicine Battery

While the ANAM was initially developed as a more general cognitive/psychomotor assessment tool, its potential for assessment of specific neurocognitive disorders is now being explored. The ANAM platform allows for a flexible or fixed battery of tests (31 test modules) that are selected by the test administrator to run in an overarching, sequential manner (Vincent et al. 2008). Given the large normative database for return-to-duty following brain injury in military samples, the ANAM-sports medicine battery (ASMB) was developed. The ASMB was designed for assessment, monitoring, and management of sports-related concussions (Cernich et al. 2007). The ASMB is made up of the following tests: Simple Reaction Time (SRT); Code Substitution; Procedural Reaction Time; Mathematical Processing; Matching to Sample; and Code Substitution Delayed (see Table 3).

2.2 Computer-Automated Neuropsychological Assessment with Specific Patient Populations

Computerized neuropsychological assessments have been used with a number of different patient populations. Although computerized neuropsychological testing has yet to become a routine component of the assessment process, there is

Table 3 Computerized assessment of aging

Test	Hardware (Input)	Admin (min)	Domains	Strengths	Weaknesses
ANAM Levinson et al. (2005)	PC/laptop (Mouse/keyboard/ speech recognition optional)	20	• Attention • Memory • Concentration • Executive function • Reaction time • Motor speed • Language	Correctly classified 100 % of AD patients versus age-matched control	Patients often exhibited procedural confusion
CAMCI Saxton et al. (2009)	Tablet PC (Touch screen)	25	• Attention • Memory • Executive function • Processing speed	High sensitivity (86 %) and specificity (94 %) in MCI detection	Only one published study available, no data available in AD population
CANS-MCI Tornatore (2005)	PC/laptop (Touch screen)	25	• Memory • Executive function • Language	Strong correlation with conventional tests	Only one published study available, no longitudinal data available
CANTAB De Jager et al. (2002)	PC/laptop Also mobile = iPad (Touch screen)	Depends on subtests	• Attention • Working memory • Visuospatial memory	Early detection of memory deficits	Study data are available for only a small selection of subtests
CNS-VS Gualtieri (2005)	PC/laptop (keyboard)	30	• Attention • Memory • Psychomotor speed • Processing Speed • Cognitive Flexibility	Discrimination of normal control versus MCI, MCI versus mild AD	Lack of normative data for older age groups
CDR Wesnes et al. (2010)	PC/laptop (2-button answering device)	20–25	• Attention • Memory • Reaction time	Good psychometric properties. Measures of psychomotor speed showed possible sensitivity for detecting decline over 6 months	Adds little diagnostic value to basic clinical workup

(continued)

Table 3 (continued)

Test	Hardware (Input)	Admin (min)	Domains	Strengths	Weaknesses
CogState Lim et al. (2013)	PC/laptop/ tablet— Web-based (keyboard)	15–20	• Attention • Memory • Executive function • Language • Social cognition	High test–retest reliability and stability in all groups and adequate to detect AD-related cognitive impairment	Difficult to distinguish early MCI from healthy controls without several rounds of administration
MicroCog Elwood (2001)	PC/laptop (Set of keyboard keys)	30–45	• Attention • Memory • Reaction time • Spatial • Reasoning	Cognitive scoring significantly correlated with Full IQ component WAIS-III	Significant anxiety/ frustration in cognitively impaired subjects
Mindstreams Doninger et al. (2009)	PC/laptop— Web-based (keyboard)	45–60	• Attention • Memory • Executive function • Verbal Fluency • Visuospatial • Motor • Information processing	Effective in detection of MCI performed poorly compared to HC participants in all domains, with significant differences in memory ($p = 0.003$; $d = 0.96$) executive function ($p = 0.046$; $d = 0.64$), and overall battery performance ($p = 0.041$; $d = 0.63$).	Length of time required for completion

Note ANAM = Automated Neuropsychological Assessment Metrics. CAMCI = Computer Assessment of Mild Cognitive Impairment. CANS-MCI = Computer-administered Neuropsychological Screen for Mild Cognitive Impairment. CANTAB = Cambridge Neuropsychological Test Automated Battery. CNS-VS = Central Nervous System Vital Signs. CDR = Cognitive Drug Research

increasing interest in the potential benefits of incorporating computerized tests into neuropsychological assessment of patients with various clinical conditions. Some examples of studies using computerized neuropsychological assessment of patients include: attention deficit hyperactivity disorder (Nigg 2005; Sonuga-Barke et al. 2008); bipolar disorder (Sweeney et al. 2000); cardiovascular disease (Raymond et al. 2006); dementia (Cummings et al. 2012); epilepsy (Witt et al. 2013); multiple sclerosis (Settle et al. 2015); obsessive–compulsive disorder (Martoni et al. 2015);

schizophrenia (Gur et al. 2001; Irani et al. 2012; Nieuwenstein et al. 2001); and substance abuse (Di Sclafani et al. 2002; Lopez et al. 2001). While there is increasing interest in using computerized neuropsychological assessments, there is a large need for the validation of these computerized tests in specific patient populations before routine use.

2.2.1 Computerized Assessment of Aging

A number of reviews have emerged to discuss the literature on computerized neuropsychological assessment batteries that have been developed to provide cognitive screening of dementia (Canini et al. 2014; Cummings et al. 2012; de Oliveira and Brucki 2014; Dougherty et al. 2010; Inoue et al. 2009; Zygouris and Tsolaki 2015). These reviews suggest that computerized neuropsychological measures may add sensitivity to clinical trials and may be beneficial tracking cognitive performance among cognitively normal persons where cognitive changes will prompt a comprehensive neuropsychological assessment (Coley et al. 2011). Examples of computerized neuropsychological assessments such as the ANAM (Levinson et al. 2005); Cambridge Neuropsychological Test Automated Battery (CANTAB; De Jager et al. 2002; Égerházi et al. 2007; Soares and de Oliveira 2015), CogState (Fredrickson et al. 2010; Hammers et al. 2012; Lim et al. 2013), and Computer Assessment of Mild Cognitive Impairment (Saxton et al. 2009) have been used in studies with older adults. Findings suggest that computerized neuropsychological tests accurately assess cognition in older adults (Fazeli et al. 2013; Zygouris and Tsolaki 2015). Key advantages of computerized neuropsychological assessments with older adults include a high degree of standardization in both administration, scoring; and sensitivity to declines in psychomotor speed and reaction time. That said, the reviews also point to some potential concerns for using computerized neuropsychological assessments with an aging cohort. Some examples include: the lack of equivalence in participants' experience with computers, potential for large practice effects, and the need for psychometric validation of computerized assessments.

2.2.2 Computerized Assessment of Children

Computerized neuropsychological testing has long been applied for attention deficit hyperactivity disorder (ADHD). One of the most commonly used computer-based assessments in ADHD evaluations is the continuous performance test (Huang-Pollock et al. 2012; Nigg 2005; Sonuga-Barke et al. 2008; Willcutt et al. 2005). Another commonly used measure for children is the Cambridge Neuropsychological Test Automated Battery (CANTAB) because it is known to be sensitive to cognitive dysfunction across multiple domains of ADHD and to the amelioration of cognitive dysfunction through pharmacotherapy (Chamberlain et al. 2011). An advantage of the CANTAB is that it separates mnemonic and strategic components of working memory. There are several studies using the CANTAB to assess medication effects in ADHD (Bedard et al. 2002, 2004; McLean et al. 2004; Mehta et al. 2004). Further, the CANTAB has been used to investigate neuropsychological functioning in children with ADHD (Fried et al. 2012; Rhodes et al. 2005; Gau et al. 2009). A further use of computerized neurocognitive testing has been with evaluating young athletes for sports-related concussion. Although current empirical evidence for the development and utility of computerized neuropsychological testing for preadolescent students is limited, it is an emerging area in research (De Marco and Broshek 2014). The Multimodal Assessment of Cognition and Symptoms for Children is an emerging computerized neuropsychological assessment that was designed to assess cognitive abilities in children between the ages of 5 and 12 (Vaughan et al. 2014). The battery consists of six cognitive tests that produce the following composites: Response Speed, Learning & Memory, and Accuracy/Speed Efficiency. The battery also includes an assessment of performance validity. Results from a recent study found that there were no differences between individual versus group format among a sample of children aged 5 to 18. These findings suggest that computerized baseline assessment can be effectively administered across groups.

3 "Common Currency" Assessment Batteries

As can be seen from the review in this chapter thus far, there are many computerized neuropsychological assessment batteries that are used to gather information on aspects of cognitive functioning. While they all tend to have some overlap, there is an unfortunate lack of uniformity among the measures used to capture these cognitive constructs. A perhaps greater limitation to adoption for many neuropsychologists is that these computerized assessments are generally expensive. Further, each computerized assessment must be fully vetted and most are a long way off from having normative databases on homogenous nondiverse populations and most do not cover the lifespan. There is great need for computerized assessment tools that can address these issues and be used as a form of "common currency" across diverse study designs and populations (Gershon et al. 2013).

3.1 Penn Computerized Neurocognitive Battery

One freely available (to qualified examiners) computerized neuropsychological assessment battery is the Penn Computerized Neurocognitive Battery (CNB). The CNB includes a comprehensive battery assessing multiple cognitive domains: attention; working memory; abstraction and mental flexibility; memory (verbal, facial, object); language; visuospatial; and emotion processing. This battery has been administered to patients with schizophrenia, relatives of these patients and healthy controls (Gur et al. 2001a, b, 2007). Studies assessing the CNB have demonstrated good test–retest reliability and sensitivity to diagnosis (Gur et al. 2007). The CNB has also been associated with positive reliability and construct validity when compared to traditional paper-and-pencil batteries in healthy samples (Gur et al. 2001a) and in schizophrenia patients (Gur et al. 2001b). The availability of the CNB in the public domain and Web-based administration has yielded large-scale normative and disease-specific data on thousands of individuals (Moore et al. 2015).

3.2 NIH Toolbox

To provide a "common currency" battery that would be free to qualified neuropsychologists, the contract for the NIH Toolbox for the Assessment of Neurological and Behavioral Function was initiated by the NIH Blueprint for Neuroscience Research. The goal was to develop a set of computerized neuropsychological measures to enhance the collection of data in large cohort studies and to advance biomedical research. The NIH Toolbox was one of the initiatives of the NIH Blueprint for Neuroscience Research. It was developed to offer a validated battery to measure outcomes in longitudinal, epidemiological, and intervention studies across the life span (3–85 years of age). The set of measures in the NIH Toolbox includes the following: cognition, emotion, motor, and sensory function. The primary goal of the NIH Toolbox was to maximize the yield from large, expensive studies with minimal increment in subject burden and cost (Gershon et al. 2010).

A novel component of the NIH Toolbox is that it makes the use of two approaches that offer promise for strengthening the measurement of psychological constructs: item response theory (IRT) and computerized adaptive testing (CAT). The IRT approach offers an alternative to classical test theory by moving beyond scores that are relative to group-specific norms. In IRT, the probability of a particular item response is modeled to the respondent's position on the underlying construct of interest (Embretson and Reise 2013). This approach can be useful for providing item-level properties of each NIH Toolbox measure across the full range of each construct. The NIH Toolbox also uses CAT to shorten the length of time needed for an assessment. The CAT tests are, on average, half as long as paper-and-pencil measures with equal or better precision (Weiss 2004). The CAT approach offers the NIH Toolbox with enhanced efficiency, flexibility, and precision. It also provides an opportunity to assess more domains of interest without adversely affecting participant burden.

The NIH Toolbox also assesses affect and psychological well-being in adults ages 18 and older: positive affect; life satisfaction; and purpose (Salsman et al. 2013). Measures of positive affect assess activated emotion; high arousal (e.g., excitement, joy); and low arousal (e.g., contentment, peace). Assessing both affective valence and the activating nature of an emotion may offer an important distinction for improving our understanding about the relation between psychological well-being and physical health (Cohen and Pressman 2006). Ultimately, the NIH Toolbox offers a "common currency" for researchers and clinicians to select the optimal outcome measures for patient populations.

3.3 NIH Executive Abilities: Methods and Instruments for Neurobehavioral Evaluation and Research (EXAMINER)

The NIH Executive Abilities Methods and Instruments for Neurobehavioral Evaluation and Research (EXAMINER) is an NIH-sponsored project to develop a neuropsychological assessment battery that reliably and validly assesses executive functions for clinical investigations across a wide range of ages and disorders (Kramer et al. 2014). The NIH EXAMINER was part of a broader NIH effort to develop "common currency" assessment tools including: the Patient Reported Outcomes Measurement Information System (PROMIS) and the NIH Toolbox (Weintraub et al. 2013). The NIH EXAMINER project uses three separate approaches to conceptualize and measure executive functioning: (1) construct-driven parsing of executive ability into more discrete and measurable constructs (e.g., working memory, set shifting, fluency, and inhibition); (2) activities of daily living (e.g., decision making, social cognition); and informant-based rating scales. The NIH EXAMINER is made up of a series of both paper-and-pencil and computer-automated tasks that target working memory, inhibition, set shifting, fluency, insight, planning, social cognition, and behavior. In addition to individual test scores, the NIH EXAMINER yields composite scores based on item response theory.

In summary, "common currency" initiatives such as the Penn CNB, PROMIS, NIH Toolbox, and NIH EXAMINER are likely to illuminate understanding and permit researchers and clinicians to select the optimal outcome measures for their patient populations.

4 What About Ecologically Valid Computer-Based Assessments?

An unfortunate limitation of most computer-automated neuropsychological measures is that they simply automate construct-driven paper-and-pencil assessments. Two approaches have been taken to address this issue using computerized assessments. First, there is the assessment of the degree to which performance on a computerized assessment predicts some aspect of the participant's everyday functioning. Little is known about how well most computer-automated neuropsychological tests predict everyday behavior. One example is the use of CPTs to assess

ADHD symptoms. For example, commission errors (i.e., behavioral response that occurs when no response is required) are assumed to reflect impulsivity in everyday life. Omission errors (i.e., failure to respond to a target) are thought to reflect inattention behaviors. In a large epidemiological study, Epstein and colleagues (2006) examined the relationships between ADHD symptoms and specific CPT parameters. Contrary to predictions, they found that omission and commission errors had a nonspecific relationship to ADHD symptomatology. Omissions were related to hyperactivity symptoms, not inattention symptoms. Although commissions were related to impulsivity symptoms, they were also related to hyperactivity and inattention symptoms. Few studies have compared CPT tests with other more subjective behavioral questionnaires. In a study by Barkley and Murphey (2011), the Deficits in Executive Functioning Scale (DEFS) was used to assess executive functioning deficits in daily life. Findings suggested that the CPT scores were largely unrelated to the executive functioning scale ratings. In fact, of all the CPT scores, the CPT reaction time was the most closely related which only 7 % of the variance. Likewise, studies have used the CANTAB to explore the pattern of associations between self-assessed (e.g., Subjective Scale to Investigate Cognition in Schizophrenia) and objective neuropsychological performance (CANTAB) in a sample of outpatients with schizophrenia. Findings suggest that although outpatients with schizophrenia express some cognitive difficulties, the cognitive nature of these subjective complaints does not strictly correspond with objective performances. These results also suggest that theoretical constructs of cognitive functions do not always have ecological validity. The authors recommend that both objective performance and subjective cognitive complaints be taken into account in assessment of patient well-being (Prouteau et al. 2004).

Another approach to computer-automated assessment is to develop assessments that have topographical similarity (i.e., theoretical relation) between the stimuli used on the computer screen and the skills required for successful praxes in the natural environment of the patient. For example, the task demands of learning and recalling of pictures of objects has "theoretical" similarity to the sorts of tasks that a patient might be required to perform in their everyday lives. One example of this approach is The Psychologix Computer-Simulated Everyday Memory Battery, which incorporates video recordings and two-dimensional stimuli that are representative of real-world objects and settings. Crook and colleagues (Crook et al. 1979, 1980) have developed this computerized battery over the past 35 years (previously known as the Memory Assessment Clinics Battery). The battery includes the following tests: (1) Name–Face Association Test, in which patients watch video recordings of persons introducing themselves (and name the city that they are from) and then tested on both immediate and delayed recall; (2) Incidental Memory Test, which assesses the patient's recall of the name of the city that was provided during Name–Face Association test; (3) First–Last Names Test, which measures associate learning and recall of four to six paired first and last names over three to six trials; (4) Narrative Recall, in which patients watch a 6-min television news cast and then are assessed on their ability to answer 25 multiple-choice questions related to the news broadcast; (5) Selective Reminding, which draws from

Buschke's (1973) approach to evaluate learning and retention of 15 grocery items over five trials; (6) Misplaced Objects Test, in which the patient uses a touch screen to place common objects (e.g., cup, hat, and boots) in one of twelve boxes (each box represents a room in a house) on a grid; (7) Recognition of Faces, in which the patient must touch the monitor to select facial photographs; (8) Telephone Dialing Test, in which the patient dials 7- or 10-digit numbers by touching a graphic representation of a telephone dialing pad on a monitor; and (9) Reaction Time, in which the patient lifts his or her finger off a graphically rendered gas pedal or brake pedal in response to a red or green traffic light.

An unfortunate limitation of such approaches is the actual "praxes" of these task may be more representative of a laboratory experiment (i.e., objects presented at a controlled rate, performed free from distractions, and repeated opportunities to learn the list of words). Hence, the administrative controls that are in place to ensure reliability and internal validity may underestimate the implications of a patient's cognitive difficulties in everyday life and overestimate functional difficulties (e.g., patient may use compensatory strategies in their everyday world). A test with verisimilitude resembles a task the patient performs in everyday life and links task demands to the prediction of real-world behavior (Spooner and Pachana 2006).

Chapter 5
Neuropsychological Assessment 3.0

> *For a variety of reasons clinical neuropsychology has been slow to embrace techniques like computer and virtual-based methods that may have much greater application in detecting subtle impairments, including those associated with mTBI.*
>
> —Erin D. Bigler (2013)

Virtual environments (VEs) are increasingly considered as potential aids in enhancing the ecological validity of neuropsychological assessments (Campbell et al. 2009; Parsons 2011; Schultheis et al. 2002; Renison et al. 2012). Part of this increased interest is due to recent (past 10–15 years) enhancements in 3D rendering capabilities and shading that accelerated graphics considerably and allowed for greatly improved texture and shading in computer graphics. Earlier virtual reality equipment suffered a number of limitations, such as being large and unwieldy, difficulty in operation, and very expensive to develop and maintain. Over the past decade, researchers have steadily progressed in making VE hardware and software more reliable, cost-effective, and acceptable in terms of size and appearance (Bohil et al. 2011). The VEs of today are advanced computer interfaces that allow patients to become immersed within a computer-generated simulation of everyday activities.

Given that VEs represent a special case of computerized neuropsychological assessment devices (Bauer et al. 2012; Schatz and Browndyke 2002), they have enhanced computational capacities for administration efficiency, stimulus presentation, automated logging of responses, and data analytic processing. Since VEs allow for precise presentation and control of dynamic perceptual stimuli, they can provide ecologically valid assessments that combine the veridical control and rigor of laboratory measures with a verisimilitude that reflects real-life situations (Parsons 2011). Additionally, the enhanced computation power allows for increased accuracy in the recording of neurobehavioral responses in a perceptual environment that systematically presents complex stimuli. Such simulation technology appears to be distinctively suited for the development of ecologically valid environments, in which three-dimensional objects are presented in a consistent and precise manner (Schultheis et al. 2002). VE-based neuropsychological assessments can provide a balance between naturalistic observation and the need for exacting control over key

T.D. Parsons, *Clinical Neuropsychology and Technology*,
DOI 10.1007/978-3-319-31075-6_5

variables (Campbell et al. 2009; Parsons 2011). In summary, VE-based neuropsychological assessments allow for real-time measurement of multiple neurocognitive abilities in order to assess complex sets of skills and behaviors that may more closely resemble real-world functional abilities (Matheis et al. 2007).

The plan for this chapter is as follows: Sect. 1 will review issues regarding ecological validity that can be enhanced by virtual reality-based assessments. Section 2 evaluates construct-driven virtual reality assessments. Section 3 argues for function-led approaches to neuropsychological assessment. Section 4 gives an example of affect-sensitive virtual environments. Section 5 looks at virtual reality environments for memory assessment. The chapter concludes with a discussion of Neuropsychological Assessment 3.0.

1 What Constitutes an Ecologically Valid Assessment of Cognitive Functioning

A difficult issue facing neuropsychologists interested in adding virtual environments to their assessments of real-world functioning is the question of what constitutes an ecologically valid assessment of cognitive functioning. Early attempts to define ecological validity for neuropsychological assessment emphasized the functional and predictive relation between a patient's performance on a set of neuropsychological tests and the patient's behavior in everyday life. Franzen and Wilhelm (1996) refined the definition of ecological validity for neuropsychological assessment via an emphasis upon two requirements: (1) *Verisimilitude*: The demands of a test and the testing conditions resemble demands in the everyday world of the patient and (2) *Veridicality*: The performance on a test predicts some aspect of the patient's functioning on a day-to-day basis.

1.1 Construct-Driven Versus Function-Led Assessments

A recent development in the ecological validity discussion has been to discuss neuropsychology's adaptation of outmoded conceptual and experimental frameworks. Burgess et al. (2006) argue that most neuropsychological assessments in use today are construct-driven tests that fail to represent the actual functional capacities inherent in cognitive (e.g., executive) functions. By "construct-driven," these authors are referring to tests that aim to assess a hypothetical cognitive construct that can be inferred from research findings (e.g., correlation between two variables). Burgess et al. (2006) give the "working memory" and "general intelligence" as examples of constructs. They point out that cognitive construct measures like the Stroop and Tower of London were not originally designed to be used as clinical measures (Burgess et al. 2006). Instead, these measures were found to be useful tools for cognitive assessment and normal populations and then later found their way into the clinical realm to aid in assessing constructs that are important to carrying out real-world activities. For example, if a patient's performance on the Stroop revealed difficulty inhibiting an automatic, overlearned response, a neuropsychologist may be compelled to report caution relative to an aging patient's driving—safe driving of an automobile includes the ability to withhold an overlearned behavior to press the brakes if a traffic light turns red when the driver is halfway through the intersection. An unfortunate limitation of this approach to predicting everyday functioning is that it forces the neuropsychologist to rely on measures designed for other purposes. Goldstein (1996) questioned this approach because it is difficult to ascertain the extent to which performance on measures of basic constructs translates to functional capacities within the varying environments found in the real world. A decade later, Burgess et al. (2006) agree and argue that a further issue is that we need assessments that further our understanding about the ways in which the brain enables persons to interact with their environment and organize everyday activities. Instead of using the terms "verisimilitude" and "veridicality" when discussing "ecological validity," they use the term "representativeness" to discuss the extent to which a neuropsychological assessment corresponds in form and context to a real-world (encountered outside the laboratory) situation. They use the term "generalizability" to discuss the degree to which poor performance on a neuropsychological assessment will be predictive of poor performance on tasks outside the laboratory.

Another example can be found in one of the most widely used measures of executive function, the Wisconsin Card Sort Test (WCST). The most extensive normative data are derived from an administration of the WCST that utilizes paper cards. The stimulus cards are administered by an experimenter on one side of a desk as he/she faces a participant on the other side of the desk. Participants are presented with a number of stimulus cards and instructed to match these stimulus cards to target cards. Although participants are not told how to match the cards, they are informed whether a particular match is correct or incorrect. It is important to note that the WCST (like many paper-and-pencil tests in use today) was not originally developed as a measure of executive functioning. Instead, the WCST was preceded by a number of sorting measures that were developed from observations of the effects of brain damage. Nevertheless, in a single study by Brenda Milner (1963), patients with dorsolateral prefrontal lesions were found to have greater difficulty on the WCST than patients with orbitofrontal or nonfrontal lesions. However, the majority of neuroimaging studies have found activation across frontal and nonfrontal brain regions, and clinical studies have revealed that the WCST does not discriminate between frontal and nonfrontal lesions (Nyhus and Barcelo 2009; Stuss et al. 1983). Further, while data from the WCST do appear to provide some information relevant to the constructs of "set shifting" and "working memory," the data do not necessarily offer information that would allow a neuropsychologist to predict what situations in everyday life require the abilities that the WCST measures. Further, it has been shown that patients with frontal lobe pathology do not always differ from control subjects on the WCST (Stuss et al. 1983).

Burgess et al. (2006) suggest that future development of neuropsychological assessments should result in tests that are "representative" of real-world "functions" and proffer results that are "generalizable" for prediction of the functional performance across a range of situations. According to Burgess et al. (2006), a "function-led approach" to creating neuropsychological assessments will include neuropsychological models that proceed from directly observable everyday behaviors backward to examine the ways in which a sequence of actions leads to a given behavior in normal functioning and the ways in which that behavior might become disrupted. As such, call for a new generation of neuropsychological tests that are "function-led" rather than purely "construct-driven." These neuropsychological assessments should meet the usual standards of reliability, but discussions of validity should include both sensitivity to brain dysfunction and generalizability to real-world function.

1.2 Importance of Affective States for Cognitive Processing

In recent years, cognitive neuropsychology has witnessed a resurgence of interest in going beyond the artificial situation of the laboratory to assessments that reflect the everyday world and bringing together studies of cognitive and affective processing. Research on emotions is increasingly found in the literature. According to Cromwell and Panksepp (2011), there is a need for both top-down (cortical → subcortical) perspectives and concurrent noncognitive modes of bottom-up developmental thinking. They emphasize inclusion of bottom-up (subcortical → cortical) affective and motivational "state-control" perspectives. The affective neuroscience approach represents a more "embodied" organic view that accepts that cognitions are integrally linked to both our neurology and the environments in which we operate. The affective neuroscience critique that top-down perspectives tend to dominate the discussion in cognitive-guided research is readily applicable to the contemporary approach to neuropsychological assessment. Although cognitive-based understandings of brain–behavior relationships have grown in recent decades, the neuropsychological understandings of emotion remain poorly defined (Suchy 2011). There have been attempts to add affective components to assessments of decision making. For example, the Iowa gambling task (IGT) was developed as a computerized card sorting task of reward-related decision making that measures temporal foresight and risky decision making (Bechara 2007). Unfortunately, researchers have argued that the IGT is deficient for understanding the affective impact of emotional stimuli upon cognitive processing because (1) the observed effects on the IGT may simply be cognitive (not affective) demands placed resulting from such a complex decision task (Hinson et al. 2002, 2003) and (2) the IGT is more of a learning task (Baddeley 2011), whereas a true assessment of affective impact upon cognitive processing requires a measure of the capacity to evaluate existing valences (i.e., positive, negative, and neutral). In a similar manner, Fellows and Farah (2005) have suggested that an elemental deficit in reversal learning (instead of deficit in decision making) may better explain the VMPFC lesion patients' selections of disadvantageous and risky cards on the IGT. Evidence for this is indicated by improved performance when the initial bias favoring the disadvantageous decks is removed by reordering the cards. Hence, while insensitivity to risk is often used to explain poor performance on the IGT, the learning and explicit reversal components of the IGT may better explain into what the IGT it is actually tapping. Further, the IGT falls short of an ecologically valid assessment because it does not mimic real-world activities. Like other cognitive measures, the IGT was created to assess the construct of decision making in a laboratory setting, but it remains to be seen whether a relation between performance on the IGT and real-world decision making exists (Buelow and Suhr 2009).

2 Construct-Driven Virtual Environments

2.1 Virtual Reality Versions of the Wisconsin Card Sorting Test

Although VE-based neuropsychological assessments have been proposed as a potential answer to the requirements for generalizability of everyday functioning, many of the VEs that have been developed simply recreate construct-driven assessments in a simulated environment. For example, a number of early VE-based neuropsychological assessments were modeled off of the WCST (Elkind et al. 2001; Pugnetti et al. 1995, 1998). One of the first VEs modeled off of the WCST required patients to reach the exit of a virtual building through the use of environmental cues (e.g., categories of shape, color, and number of portholes) that aided in the correct selection of doors leading from room to room (Pugnetti et al. 1995, 1998). Similar to the WCST, after a fixed number of successful trials, the correct choice criteria (e.g., categories) were changed so that the patient had to shift cognitive set and devise a new choice strategy in order to pass into the next room. Pugnetti et al. (1998) compared neurologically impaired patients and non-impaired controls on both the VR task and the WCST. While the controls performed more successfully on both tests, weak correlations were found between the VR task and the WCST. As a result, there is question about whether the WCST and the VE-based assessment were measuring different functions. It is important to note that the Pugnetti version had a heavy reliance on navigating through a building and this may have confounded the results.

A more current VE-based neuropsychological assessment modeled off of the WCST did not have the potentially confounding effects of navigation. In the Virtual Reality Look for a Match Test (VRLFAM), Elkind et al. (2001) developed a beach scene, in which participants were asked to deliver frisbees, sodas, popsicles, and beach balls to umbrellas. Each umbrella had one of the four objects on it (differing in type, color, and number). As the participant delivered the objects, he/she received verbal feedback (e.g., "That's it" or "That's not what I want"). Following the WCST, the participant had 128 turns to twice match 10 times to color, 10 to object, and 10 times to number (in that order) to successfully complete the task. Results from comparison of healthy control performance on VRLFAM and the WCST indicated that all performance scales (with the exception of WCST perseverative errors) were directly related (Elkind 2001). An unfortunate limitation of modeling VE-based neuropsychological assessments off of the WCST is that the virtual analogues, like the original WCST, may not be able to differentiate between patients with frontal lobe pathology and control subjects (Stuss et al. 1983). Further, while data from the VE-based assessments, like the WCST, do appear to provide information relevant to the constructs of "set shifting" and "working memory," the VE assessments seem to do little to extend ecological validity.

2.2 *Virtual Classroom for Assessment of Attention*

Another paradigm borrowed from construct-driven assessments for the development of VE-based assessments can be found in the embedding of various construct-driven tasks (e.g., Stroop and Go/No-Go) into virtual environments. A number of virtual classroom environments have emerged that include construct-driven assessments (see Table 1 for review of virtual classrooms over the past 10 years). In these virtual classrooms, the participant is seated at one of the desks and is surrounded by desks, children, a teacher, and a whiteboard much like they would be in a real-world classroom. Various construct-driven tasks can be presented on the whiteboard in the front of the room, and the participant performs a task (e.g., Stroop or continuous performance tasks) with auditory (e.g., airplane passing overhead, a voice from the intercom, the bell ringing) and visual (e.g., children passing notes, a child raising his hand, the teacher answering the classroom door, principal entering the room) distractors in the background.

In a comparison of the traditional Stroop task with the ClinicaVR (Digital Media Works) version of a VR Classroom Stroop task, Lalonde et al. (2013) found that the VR Classroom Stroop was correlated with the traditional Stroop measure and was also reported to be more enjoyable than the traditional Stroop task. The ClinicaVR (Digital Media Works) VR Classroom also includes a CPT. In a clinical trial of the virtual classroom, Parsons et al. (2007) compared performance of ten children with attention deficit/hyperactivity disorder (ADHD) with ten typically developing children. In this study, children with ADHD performed differently from typically developing children in a number of different ways: (1) Children with ADHD made more commission and omission errors; (2) children with ADHD exhibited more overall body movement; and (3) children with ADHD were more impacted by distracting stimuli. Additionally, performance measures in the VR Classroom were significantly correlated with traditional measures and behavior checklists (Parsons et al. 2007). Thus, the virtual classroom was able to assess not only attentional abnormalities but also behavioral abnormalities concurrently. These results have

Table 1 Construct-driven test: virtual classroom continuous performance test (CPT)

Study sorted by year	Traditional tests	Sample design	Research outcomes
Parsons et al. (2007)	SWAN Behavior Checklist; Conners' CPT-II; Stroop task; TMT; Visual Attention and Verbal Fluency (NEPSY); DS, Coding B, and Vocabulary (WISC-III); BNT	ADHD (n = 10, children) Controls (n = 10, children)	• ADHD participants committed more omission and commission errors and were more impacted by distracters than control children • The VR classroom task was also found to be correlated with traditional assessments of ADHD
Gutierrez-Maldonado et al. (2009)	None given	ADHD (n = 10, children) Controls (n = 10, children)	• ADHD participants showed more progressive performance decline compared to control children • ADHD children were more negatively impacted by distracters in the VR classroom
Pollak et al. (2009a)	TOVA	ADHD (n = 37, children) Controls (n = 17, children)	• The VR classroom was more sensitive on reaction time and rate of omission errors than the TOVA • The VR classroom was able to distinguish children with and without ADHD on reaction time, variability of reaction time, and commission and omission errors
Pollak et al. (2010)	TOVA ADHD Rating Scale	Methylphenidate versus placebo ADHD (n = 27 children)	• All 3 measures were found to be sensitive to the effects of methylphenidate • Virtual classroom proved more sensitive on rate of omission errors compared to the TOVA • Virtual classroom was also rated as more enjoyable than TOVA • Medication and medication by test type were not significant

(continued)

Table 1 (continued)

Study sorted by year	Traditional tests	Sample design	Research outcomes
Adams et al. (2009)	BASC Vigil-CPT	ADHD (n = 18, children) Controls (n = 16, children)	• ADHD children performed worse than controls • Large effect sizes for virtual classroom (d = 0.91) and Vigil (d = 0.71) • Virtual classroom had greater specificity for identifying ADHD
Gilboa et al. (2011)	CPRS-R:L	NF1 (n = 29, children) Controls (n = 25, children)	• NF1 children had more attention deficits in the virtual classroom, as evidenced by more omission and commission errors • Attention deficits on the test were consistent with parent reports on the CPRS-R:L
Nolin et al. (2012)	Vigil-CPT	Concussion (n = 25, adolescents) Controls (n = 25, adolescents)	• Concussed adolescents had increased commission errors and left–right head movements • Concussed adolescents reported more simulator sickness following VR exposure
Bioulac et al. (2012)	CPT	ADHD (n = 20, children) Controls (n = 16, children)	• ADHD children showed decreased correct hits and increased reaction time throughout the study • ADHD children performed worse on the VR classroom and CPT tasks than controls
Iriarte et al. (2012)	None	Normative sample N = 1272 Spanish-speaking children	• Males were quicker at responding, but also had greater motor activity and deviation from focus • Girls had slower reaction time, but also had better performance on all tasks

(continued)

Table 1 (continued)

Study sorted by year	Traditional tests	Sample design	Research outcomes
Díaz-Orueta (2013)	CPT WISC-IV	ADHD (n = 57, children)	• Convergent validity of the virtual classroom test was established with the CPT • Significant correlations between the virtual classroom and CPT were observed on all variables • Virtual classroom was able to distinguish between children with and without ADHD
Lalonde et al. (2013)	CBCL, BRIEF, DKEFS Color–Word Interference Test, TMT, Verbal Fluency; Twenty Questions	Healthy participants (n = 38, adolescents)	• Virtual classroom was correlated with the traditional DKEFS Stroop task • Virtual classroom was rated more enjoyable than traditional measures

Note BASC = Behavioral Assessment System for Children; CPT = Continuous Performance Test; WISC-IV = Wechsler Intelligence Scale for Children—Fourth Edition; CPRS-R:L = Conners' Parent Rating Scales—Revised: Long Version; CBCL = Child Behavior Checklist; BRIEF = Behavior Rating Inventory of Executive Functioning; TMT = Trail Making Test; BNT = Boston Naming Test; NEPSY = NEuroPSYchological Assessment; TOVA = Test of Variables of Attention been replicated in other studies attempting to validate the VR Classroom for use with ADHD (Adams et al. 2009; Bioulac et al. 2012; Pollak et al. 2009, 2010; see Table 1).

Perhaps the best validated of these virtual classrooms is the AULA virtual reality test (Diaz-Orueta et al. 2013; Iriarte et al. 2012). The AULA has a normative sample comprised of 1272 participants (48.2 % female) with an age range from 6 to 16 years (M = 10.25, SD = 2.83). The AULA is significantly correlated with the traditional CPT and can distinguish between children with ADHD with and without pharmacological interventions. In comparison of the AULA Virtual Reality CPT with standard computerized tests, the AULA VR CPT was found to be more sensitive to reaction time and rate of omission errors than the TOVA and was also rated as more enjoyable than the TOVA computerized battery (see Table 1). In another recent study, Diaz-Oreta et al. (2013) analyzed the convergent validity between the AULA and the Conners' Continuous Performance Test (CPT). The AULA and CPT were administered correlatively with 57 children who had a diagnosis of ADHD. Convergent validity was indicated via the observed significant correlations between both tests in all the analyzed variables (omissions, commissions, reaction time, and variability of reaction time).

2.3 *Virtual Apartment for Assessment of Attention*

The classroom paradigm has been extended to a virtual apartment that superimposes construct-driven stimuli (e.g., Stroop and CPT) onto a large television set in the living room. In a preliminary study, Henry and colleagues (2012) with 71 healthy adult participants found that the VR-Apartment Stroop is capable of eliciting the Stroop effect with bimodal stimuli. Initial validation data also suggested that measures of the VR-Stroop significantly correlate with measures of the Elevator counting with distracters, the Continuous Performance Task (CPT-II), and the Stop-it task. Results from regression indicated that commission errors and variability of reaction times at the VR-Apartment Stroop were significantly predicted by scores of the Elevator task and the CPT-II. These preliminary results suggest that the VR-Apartment Stroop is an interesting measure of cognitive and motor inhibition for adults.

2.4 *Construct-Driven Driving Simulations*

Another area in which construct-driven assessments have been embedded into virtual environments is the driving simulator. Using a driving simulator, researchers can superimpose various stimuli (e.g., Stroop stimuli) to create dual-task assessments of cognitive constructs. Lengenfelder et al. (2002) developed a driving course in which participants drove a car with the dual-task requirement of correctly identifying a four-digit number presented during the driving course. Performance measures included driving speed and correct number of stimuli identification. Although results revealed no differences in speed management between the two groups, participants with a TBI had greater difficulty completing the secondary task than healthy controls. In a more current study, Cyr and colleagues (2009) used a similar driving simulator that included a dual-task performance assessment in patients with moderate and severe levels of TBI compared to healthy controls. The participants were required to adhere to standard safe driving practices while responding to dual-task stimuli (flashing symbols in the peripheral field of the simulated view) at random intervals. Results revealed that the dual-task simulation was a valid measure for predicting crash rate within the simulation for individuals with TBI.

3 Need for Function-Led Assessments

Burgess et al. (2006) suggest that future development of neuropsychological assessments should result in tests that are "representative" of real-world "functions" and proffer results that are "generalizable" for prediction of the functional performance across a range of situations. According to Burgess et al. (2006), a "function-led approach" to creating neuropsychological assessments will include neuropsychological models that proceed from directly observable everyday behaviors backward to examine the ways in which a sequence of actions leads to a given behavior in normal functioning and the ways in which that behavior might become disrupted. As such, he calls for a new generation of neuropsychological tests that are "function-led" rather than purely "construct-driven." These neuropsychological assessments should meet the usual standards of reliability, but discussions of validity should include both sensitivity to brain dysfunction and generalizability to real-world function.

A number of investigators have argued that performance on traditional tests of executive function (e.g., Wisconsin Card Sorting Test, Stroop Test) has little correspondence to activities of daily living. As such, neuropsychologists are left uncertain of the efficacy of these tests for predicting the way in which patients will manage in their everyday lives (Bottari et al. 2009; Manchester et al. 2004; Sbordone 2008). According to Chan et al. (2008), most of these traditional measures assess at the impairment level and do not capture the complexity of response required in the many multistep tasks found in everyday activities. It is important to note that a number of function-led tests of executive function have been developed to assess real-world planning (e.g., Zoo Map and Six Elements subtests of the Behavioral Assessment of the Dysexecutive Syndrome; Wilson et al. 1996) and self-regulation (e.g., the Revised Strategy Application Test, Levine et al. 2000; Sustained Attention to Response Test, Robertson et al. 1997; see Chan et al. 2008 for review).

3.1 Multiple Errands Paradigm for Function-Led Assessments

Shallice and Burgess (1991) developed the Multiple Errands Test (MET) as a function-led assessment of multitasking. The MET requires the patient to perform a number of relatively simple but open-ended tasks in a shopping context. Participants are required to achieve a number of simple tasks without breaking a series of arbitrary rules. The MET has been shown to have increased sensitivity (over traditional neuropsychological measures) to elicit and detect failures in executive function (e.g., distractibility and task implementation deficits). It has also been shown to be better at predicting behavioral difficulties in everyday life (Alderman et al. 2003). Further, the MET has been found to have strong inter-rater reliability (Dawson et al. 2009; Knight et al. 2002), and performance indices from the MET were able to significantly predict severity of everyday life executive problems in persons with TBI (Cuberos-Urbano et al. 2013).

Potential limitations for the MET are apparent in the obvious drawbacks to experiments conducted in real-life settings (e.g., Bailey et al. 2010). Logie et al. (2011) point out a number of limitations in the MET: (1) time-consuming; (2) transportation is required for participants; (3) consent from local businesses; (4) lack of experimental control; and (5) difficulty in adapting tasks for other clinical or research settings. McGeorge et al. (2001) modeled a Virtual Errands Test (VET) off of the original MET. However, the VET tasks were designed to be more vocationally oriented in format containing work-related as opposed to the shopping errands used in the MET. In a study involving five adult patients with brain injury and 5 unimpaired matched controls, participants completed both the real-live MET and the VET. Results revealed that performance was similar for real-world and VE tasks. In a larger study comparing 35 patients with prefrontal neurosurgical lesions to 35 controls matched for age and estimated IQ (Morris et al. 2002), the VE scenario was found to successfully differentiate between participants with brain injuries and controls. A limitation of these early VEs is that the graphics were unrealistic, and performance assessment involved video recording test sessions with subsequent manual scoring.

In the past decade, a number of virtual environments with enhanced graphics (and usability) have been developed to model the function-led approach found in the MET. In addition to the virtual environments for assessment of nonclinical populations (Logie et al. 2011), a number of virtual errand protocols have been developed to evaluate executive functions of clinical populations (see Table 2 for review of virtual errand protocols over the past 10 years). For example, virtual shopping scenarios (see Parsons et al. 2013 for review) offer an advanced computer interface that allows the clinician to immerse the patient within a computer-generated simulation that reflects activities of daily living. They involve a number of errands that must be completed in a real environment following certain rules that require problem solving. Since they allow for precise presentation and control of dynamic perceptual stimuli, they have the potential to provide ecologically valid assessments that combine the control of laboratory measures within simulations that reflect real-life situations.

A number of other function-led VEs are being modeled to reflect the multitasking demands found in the MET. The Multitasking in the City Test (MCT) is modeled after the MET and involves an errand-running task that takes place in a virtual city (Jovanovski et al. 2012a, b). The MCT can be distinguished from existing VR and real-life METs. For instance, MCT tasks are performed with less explicit rule constraints. This contrasts with the MET, in which participants must abide by certain rules (not traveling beyond a certain spatial boundary and not entering a shop other than to buy something). This difference was intentional in the MCT because the researchers aimed to investigate behaviors that are clearly not goal-directed. The MCT is made up of a virtual city that includes a post office, drug store, stationary store, coffee shop, grocery store, optometrist's office, doctor's office, restaurant/pub, bank, dry cleaners, pet store, and the participant's home. Although all buildings in the MCT VE can be entered freely, interaction within them is possible only for those buildings that must be entered as part of the task requirements. The MCT was used to compare a sample of post-stroke and traumatic brain injury (TBI) patients to an earlier sample of normal controls. Jovanovski et al. (2012b) found that although the patient sample developed adequate plans for executing the tasks, their performance of the tasks revealed a greater number of errors. The MCT was significantly correlated with a rating scale completed by significant others.

Virtual reality assessments modeled off of the MET have also been created and validated in samples with stroke or injury-related brain deficits. These protocols are often placed in living of work settings (see Table 2 for review of MET-based VEs from the past 10 years): virtual office tasks (Jansari et al. 2013; Lamberts et al. 2009; Montgomery et al. 2011); virtual apartment/home tasks (Saidel-Goley et al. 2012; Sweeney et al. 2010); virtual park (Buxbaum et al. 2012); virtual library task (Renison et al. 2012); virtual anticipating consequences ask (Cook et al. 2013); virtual street crossing (Avis et al. 2013; Clancy et al. 2006; Davis et al. 2013; Nagamatsu et al. 2011); and virtual kitchen (Cao et al. 2010) (Table 3).

An example of a recently developed virtual environment for function-led assessment is the virtual library task. Renison et al. (2012) aimed to investigate whether performance on a virtual library task was similar to performance of the same task in a real-world library. Findings revealed that scores on the virtual library task and the real-world library task were highly positively correlated, suggesting that performance on the virtual library task is similar to performance on the real-world library task. This finding is important because the virtual reality environment allows for automated logging of participant behaviors and it has greater clinical utility than assessment in real-world settings. Comparisons of persons with traumatic brain injury and normal controls supported the construct validity of the virtual library task as a measure of executive functioning. In fact, the virtual library task was found to be superior to traditional (e.g., WCST) tasks in differentiating between participants with TBI and healthy controls. For example, the WCST failed to significantly differentiate between the two groups. This is consistent with studies

Table 2 Function-led virtual reality errand tests for assessment of executive functioning

Study	Traditional tests	Design	Outcome
Carelli et al. (2008) Virtual Supermarket	MMSE	Within subjects (n = 20) Usability data for RCT	• Temporal and accuracy outcome measures were able to monitor differences in abilities • Results revealed need for more practice to ensure task learning • Large variance in performance time
Cipresso et al. (2013) Virtual Multiple Errands Test (VMET)	MMSE; DS; Short Story Recall; TMT A, B, FAB; Corsi's Span; Corsi's Block; phonemic fluency test; semantic fluency test; disyllabic word test; ToL; Token Test; Street Completion; STAI; BDI	OCD group (n = 15) Controls (n = 15)	• While performing routine tasks in the VMET, patients with OCD had more difficulties working with breaks in volition than normal controls
Josman et al. (2014) Virtual Action Planning Supermarket (VAP-S)	BADS, OTDL-R	Stroke (n = 24) Control (n = 24)	• Stroke participants showed a modest relationship between the BADS and number of purchases in the VAP-S • The VAP-S demonstrated decent predictive validity of IADL performance
Josman et al. (2009) Virtual Action Planning Supermarket (VAP-S)	BADS	Clinical (n = 30) Controls (n = 30)	• VAP-S was sensitive to differences in executive functioning between schizophrenia patients and controls
Law et al. (2012) Edinburgh Virtual Errands Test (EVET)	N/A	Healthy controls (n = 42)	• Participants were able to navigate the environment and perform tasks • Factor demand and factor plan were shown to have little effect on ability to complete tasks
Logie et al. (2011) Edinburgh Virtual Errands Test (EVET)	Word Recall Task, Working Memory Verbal Span, Working Memory Spatial Span, Traveling Salesman Task, Breakfast Task	Within subjects (n = 165)	• EVET scores predicted by measures of retrospective memory, visuospatial planning, and spatial working memory • A limitation of the EVET is its lack of generalizability to other scenarios

(continued)

Table 2 (continued)

Study	Traditional tests	Design	Outcome
Pedroli et al. (2013) Virtual Multiple Errands Test (VMET)	MMSE, AVLT, DS, Corsi's Span, Supra-Span, Short Story, ToL, Verbal Fluency, Benton's JLO, WAIS-R, Naming Test, TMT, STAI, BDI	Within subjects PD (n = 3) Control (n = 21)	• The VMET showed good reliability • However, the System Usability Scale suggests that the VMET may need minor improvements to increase usability for patients
Rand et al. (2009) Virtual Multiple Errands Test (VMET)	Zoo Map Test, IADL, MET	Post-stroke (n = 9) Healthy adults (n = 20)	• VMET was able to distinguish between healthy and post-stroke • VMET was able to distinguish between older and younger cohorts
Raspelli et al. (2012) Virtual Multiple Errands Test (VMET)	MMSE, Star Cancellation Test, Token Test, Street's Completion Test, Test of Attentional Performance, Stroop Test, Iowa gambling task, DEX, ADL, IADL, State Trait Anxiety Index, BDI	Within subjects post-stroke (n = 9) Healthy adults (n = 10)	• Stroke patients showed the highest number of errors and slower reaction time on the VR-MET • Older adults showed higher number of errors and slower reaction time on the VR-MET compared to younger adults
Sauzeon et al. (2014) Virtual Human Object Memory for Everyday Scenes (virtual HOMES)	MMSE, MRT, Spatial Span, Stroop task, CVLT, SSQ, NTQ	Within subjects AD (n = 16) Young adults (n = 23) Older adults (n = 23)	• Alzheimer's patients demonstrated deficits in executive functioning • Older individuals showed signs of decline in free recall
Werner et al. (2009) Virtual Action Planning Supermarket (VAP-S)	BADS	Within-subjects MCI (n = 30) Control (n = 40)	• VAP-S was able to discriminate between MCI and the control group

Note RCT = Randomized Clinical Trial; PD = Parkinson's disease; AD = Alzheimer's disease; MMSE = Mini Mental State Examination; DS = Digit Span; TMT = Trail Making Test, FAB = Frontal Assessment Battery; ToL = Tower of London; BADS = Behavioural Assessment of the Dysexecutive Syndrome; AVLT = Auditory-Verbal Learning Test; JLO = Judgment of Line Orientation; MET = Multiple Errands Test; MRT; CVLT = California Verbal Learning Test; SSQ = Simulator Sickness Questionnaire; NTQ = New Technology Questionnaire; IADL = Instrumental Activities of Daily Living; ADL = Activities of Daily Living; DEX = Dysexecutive Questionnaire; OTDL-R = Revised Observed Tasks of Daily Living; BDI = Beck Depression Inventory; STAI = State and Trait Anxiety Index

Table 3 Assessment of executive functioning using function-led virtual reality

Study	Traditional tests	Design	Outcome
Avis et al. (2013) Virtual Reality Pedestrian Environment (VRPE)	N/A	1 within subjects EDS children (n = 33) Controls (n = 33)	• EDS children were much more likely to get hit in the virtual environment • Attention to traffic was not found to be significantly different between groups, but decision-making time did vary across groups, suggesting that children with EDS may take longer to determine whether it is safe to cross
Cao et al. (2010) Therapeutic Virtual Kitchen (TVK)	N/A	Within subjects Healthy (n = 13) TBI (n = 4) Stroke (N = 2) Meningoencephalitis (n = 1)	• Results revealed that a daily life task can be virtually simulated to assess executive functioning • Patients with TBI and normal participants could complete the task
Cook et al. (2013) Virtual Anticipating Consequences Task (VR-AC)	N/A	Within subjects TBI adolescents (n = 15) Healthy controls (n = 13)	• No significant differences were observed in the number of short-term consequences provided by the groups • However, the TBI group provided significantly more long-term consequences than the control group
Clancy et al. (2006) Road Crossing Virtual Apparatus	K-SADS-PL; Conners' Rating Scales—Revised; CBCL; New Zealand Socioeconomic Index of Occupational Status; word reading, spelling, pseudoword decoding (WIAT-II); Block Design, Vocabulary (WAIS-III)	Within subjects ADHD children (n = 24) Control (n = 24)	• ADHD adolescents had low margins of safety compared to controls • ADHD adolescents were hit twice as often as controls • ADHD adolescents walked slower and used less of the available space to cross the road

(continued)

Table 3 (continued)

Study	Traditional tests	Design	Outcome
Davis et al. (2013) Virtual Reality Pedestrian Environment (VRPE)	N/A	Within subjects Adolescents deprived of sleep (n = 55)	• Sleep restriction seems to be correlated with an increase in risky behaviors • Sleep-deprived participants did not pay as much attention to traffic, made poorer decisions when crossing, and took longer to make those decisions
Jovanovski et al. (2012a) Multitasking in the City Test (MCT)	WTAR, ToMM, COWAT, semantic fluency, WCST, MSET, TMT, WAIS-III, JOL, RCFT, CVLT-II, WMS-III, BDI, BAI, FSBS	Within-subjects Stroke or TBI (n = 13)	• Patients can be differentiated from normal samples • Significant correlations between the MCT and standardized neuropsychological assessments were also established
Jovanovski et al. (2012b) Multitasking in the City Test (MCT)	TMT, ToL, MSET, WTAR, JOL, Star Cancellation, RBMT—extended	Within subjects (n = 30)	• The MCT was found to have low associations with other tests of executive function, aside from the MSET • The MSE was correlated with the MCT plan score
Lamberts et al. (2009) Virtual Executive Secretarial Task (VEST)	DEX, TMT, 15 Words Test, BADS	Within subjects TBI (n = 35) Control (n = 57)	• The VEST successfully discriminated between the two groups • The VEST was able to give valuable information on real-life functioning in individuals with brain injury
Montgomery et al. (2011) Jansari-Agnew-Akesson-Murphy (JAAM) Task	N/A	Between-subjects—Alcohol versus placebo (n = 40)	• Alcohol group has significant impairments in both executive functioning and prospective memory • People who have had even a modest amount of alcohol may not realize the extent of their planning abilities and performance impairment

(continued)

Table 3 (continued)

Study	Traditional tests	Design	Outcome
Renison et al. (2012) Virtual Library Task (VLT)	Real Library Task, WTAR, LM-II, DS, WCST, Brixton Spatial Anticipation Test; Zoo Map Test; MSET	Within subjects TBI (n = 30) Control (n = 30)	• VLT was highly positively correlated with the real library task • VLT was able to discriminate between executive functions in TBI
Sweeney et al. (2010) Virtual Removals Task (VRT; versions 1 and 2)	N/A	Within subjects TBI (n = 17) Control (n = 17)	• VRT revealed differences between individuals with TBI and controls in executive functioning • VRT revealed differences in planning and prospective memory between TBI and control groups, with the TBI group showing greater deficits
Toet and van Schaik (2013) Virtual Town	N/A	Between-subjects Pleasant versus unpleasant versus neutral olfactory groups) (n = 69)	• Participants navigated a town while smelling either pleasant, unpleasant, or neutral odors. Odors did not seem to impact visual attention

Note EDS = Excessive Daytime Sleepiness; K-SADS-PL = Kiddie-SADS-Present and Lifetime Version; CBCL = Child Behavior Checklist; WIAT-II = Wechsler Individual Achievement Test; WAIS-III = Wechsler Adult Intelligence Scale; WMS-III = Wechsler Memory Scale; WTAR = Wechsler Test of Adult Reading; TOMM = Test of Memory Malingering; COWAT = Controlled Oral Word Association Test; WCST = Wisconsin Card Sorting Test; MSET = Modified Six Elements Test; TMT = Trail Making Test; JLO = Judgement of Line Orientation; RCFT = Rey Complex Figure Test; CVLT = California Verbal Learning Test; BDI = Beck Depression Inventory; BAI = Beck Anxiety Inventory; FSBS = Frontal Systems Behavioral Scale; ToL = Tower of London; RBMT = Rivermead Behavioral Memory Test; DEX = Dysexecutive Questionnaire; BADS = Behavioural Assessment of the Dysexecutive Syndrome; LM-II = Logical Memory II, DS = Digit Span that have reported no significant differences between control and brain-injured performances on the WCST (Alderman et al. 2003; Dawson et al. 2009; Ord et al. 2009). The authors contend that the disparity between the demands of functional assessments and traditional testing environments most likely accounts for the differences (Manchester et al. 2004).

3.2 *Driving Simulator Paradigm for Function-Led Assessments*

Another area of function-led assessments can be found in VE-based neuropsychological assessments that use driving simulators (see Table 4 for review of driving simulators over the past 10 years). The successful operation of a motor vehicle requires coordination of multiple functional behaviors. Given its complexity, driving is often an ability that becomes difficult for clinical populations. It is important to note that the literature on cognitive assessment using driving simulation is vast and beyond the scope of this review. Perhaps the most comprehensive review of executive function assessments in relation to fitness to drive is Asimakopulos et al. (2012). For additional articles about driving simulation, see Calhoun and Pearlson (2012) or Schultheis et al. (2007). Unfortunately, these reviews do not look at the construct-driven versus function-led approach that is discussed herein. As a result, this chapter would be remiss if it did not attempt to give a general summary of the efforts of researchers in this area.

VR driving simulators have been used to investigate driving performance in individuals with ADHD (Barkley et al. 2007; Barkley et al. 2005; Cox et al. 2008; Knouse et al. 2005); alcohol or drug impairment (Allen et al. 2009; Barkley et al. 2007); and brain injury (Liu et al. 1999; Milleville-Pennel et al. 2010; Schultheis and Mourant 2001; Schultheis et al. 2007; Wald and Liu 2001; Wald et al. 2000). While driving simulators may not assess driving capabilities in a manner exactly the same as an on-road driving test, both tests have their limitations as indicators of actual driving performance owing to different methods and demand characteristics. Further, past research has shown that virtual reality simulators have evidence of validity for predicting actual driving performance and risks (Bedard et al. 2010; Lee et al. 2003a, b).

While there is currently limited empirical evidence to determine the efficacy of driving simulation for function-led assessment of executive functioning, Bedard and colleagues (2010) found preliminary support for assessing driving performance in relation to cognitive functioning using driving simulations. Further, it may be best to view driving simulator results as complementary assessment data to traditional neuropsychological assessment data (Lew et al. 2005; Milleville-Pennel et al. 2010; Patomella et al. 2006).

Table 4 Function-led assessment of attention and executive functioning using driving simulators

Study	Traditional tests	Design	Outcome
Allen et al. (2009)	N/A	3 between subjects (placebo versus moderate alcohol versus high alcohol (n = 40))	• fMRI results indicated blood oxygen level decreased in the hippocampus, anterior cingulated, and dorsolateral prefrontal areas during the VR driving task • Since these brain areas affect attention and decision making, this may have implications for driving while under the influence of alcohol
Barkley et al. (2007)	Adult ADHD Rating Scale, Safe Driving Behavior Survey	3 × 3 (atomoxetine dose titration) within-subjects ADHD (n = 18)	• Although self-report results revealed perceived improvement in ADHD symptoms while performing simulated driving, behavioral observations did not reveal a significant improvement
Barkley et al. (2007)	N/A	2 (placebo versus alcohol) × 2 (0.04 BA between-subjects ADHD (n = 50) versus control (n = 40)	• Although alcohol produced greater inattention in persons with ADHD than control subjects, overall driving performance declined similarly for both groups
Barkley et al. (2005)	CPT	2 × 3 (dose titration) within subjects ADHD (n = 52)	• A high dose of methylphenidate reduced impulsiveness errors on the CPT and led to improved driving performance (less variability in steering and lowered driving speed)
Cox et al. (2008)	N/A	3 between-subjects (OROS MPH versus se-AMPH ER versus placebo) Adolescents with ADHD (n = 19)	• Results showed ORS MPH and se-AMPH ER were linked with significantly poorer performance of the VR driving simulator in comparison with the placebo
Knouse et al. (2005)	Driver History Survey, DBS, estimates of driving ability, estimated percentile score, examiner rating of safe driving behavior	6 within subjects ADHD (n = 44) versus control (n = 44	• Adults with ADHD overestimated driving performance and performed worse on the virtual reality driving task

(continued)

Table 4 (continued)

Study	Traditional tests	Design	Outcome
Mckeever et al. (2013)	N/A	2 within subjects (baseline loop versus task engaged loop) (n = 28)	• Texting appeared to have a detrimental effect on lane management, as participants paid less attention to the road while texting
Milleville-Pennel et al. (2010)	Alertness, Go/No-Go, divided attention, Visual Scanning (TAP); DS (WAIS-III); D2 Test, Stroop Color–Word Test, Zoo Map Test, TMT	10 within subjects TBI (n = 5) versus control (n = 6)	• Differences in planning and attention were found between participants with TBI and controls • Persons with TBI showed limited visual exploration compared to controls
Schultheis et al. (2007)	Digit Symbol (WAIS-III), PASAT, TMT, VR-DR User Feedback Questionnaire	5 within subjects acquired brain injury (n = 33) versus controls (n = 21)	• Persons with acquired brain injury had lower ratings of the VR-DR system than healthy controls

Note ADHD = Attention deficit/hyperactivity disorder, CPT = Continuous Performance Test, DBS = Driving Behavior Survey, ACT = Auditory Consonant Trigrams, PASAT = Paced Auditory Serial Addition Test, UFOV = Useful Field of View, WAIS-III = Wechsler Adult Intelligence Scale—Third Edition, TMT = Trail Making Test, TAP = Test for Attentional Performance, UFOV = Useful Field of View, WMS = Wechsler Memory Scale

4 Virtual Environments for Assessment of Memory

Virtual environments are increasingly being used for assessment of memory in experimentally controlled simulations of everyday activities with various levels of immersion and fidelity (Benoit et al. 2015; Mueller et al. 2012). Of particular interest to memory researchers is the balance of experimental control and simulation of everyday memory found in virtual environments (Plancher et al. 2010, 2012). By "everyday memory," these researchers mean the memory functioning embedded within daily activities and includes a multiplicity of autonomous or associated neurocognitive domains that function in a global and homogenous manner (Magnussen and Heilstrup 2007). An example of everyday memory would be maintaining the intention to purchase groceries while driving to one's apartment after work and concurrently seeing a certain café on the boulevard that calls to memory a conversation one had with a friend at the café. For neuropsychologists, the understanding of memory functioning in everyday life settings is critical for differential diagnoses, particularly when the patient is aging and/or has a brain injury.

Often neuropsychologists make use of laboratory tests designed to maintain experimental control while targeting specific memory constructs (e.g., episodic memory, working memory). While findings from these laboratory-administered and construct-driven tests reveal impaired memory, they often lack ecological validity because the same patients are often able to function well in everyday life. These conflicting results may reflect differences in demand levels between controlled laboratory tasks and everyday life. To extend ecological validity and gain a better understanding of their patients' everyday memory functioning, neuropsychologists often elicit subjective memory complaints via self-rating scales (Ossher et al. 2013; Trop et al. 2015). This veridical approach to ecological validity considers subjective ratings of everyday memory (Calabria et al. 2011) to be ecologically valid when the subjective ratings are significantly correlated with objective performances on construct-driven neuropsychological tests. Unfortunately, the self-report of memory performance used in the veridicality approach often shows only modest or non-significant correlations with performance on construct-driven neuropsychological assessments (Beaudoin and Desrichard 2011; Mascherak and Zimprich 2011). In fact, subjective ratings of overall memory performance show stronger correlations with affective factors such as depression and stress (Benito-León et al. 2010).

An alternative to veridicality is the verisimilitude approach, in which neuropsychologists seek to ensure that the characteristics of a test are similar to the environments, functions, and activities that their patients experience daily. Increasingly, new measures are being developed that more closely approximate everyday activities and behaviors. For example, the Rivermead Behavioral Memory Test (RBMT; Wilson et al. 1999) was developed by Barbara Wilson and colleagues to provide information on memory in everyday situations. The RBMT consists of eleven subtests designed to assess memory difficulties frequently encountered by patients with acquired brain damage. Review of the ecological validity of neuropsychological tests has provided support for the superiority of verisimilitude tests as the results from these measures tended to be more consistently related to the outcome measures than the traditional paper-and-pencil tests.

An unfortunate limitation for this approach is that although these neuropsychologists have developed instruments that more closely approximate skills required for everyday functioning, have not made use of advances in computer technology. As a result, they are in danger of continuing the negative trend that de-emphasizes psychology's role as a science. As Sternberg has contended, neurocognitive testing needs progress in ideas, not just new measures, for delivering old technologies. Given that virtual environments allow for participants to carry out neurocognitive and sensorimotor tasks while immersed in simulation of real-world activities, memory researchers may find it to be an important tool to add to their battery of memory tests. Virtual environment-based research has been used to study spatial learning and memory in young (e.g., Barra et al. 2012; Gras et al. 2013) and older adults (see Moffat 2009 for review). Interestingly, Gras et al. (2013) used a virtual environment to assess spatial memory and found that working memory components are involved in the construction of spatial memory. Further, individual differences modulate the involvement of working memory in that participants with higher visuospatial abilities used more spatial working memory than participants with lower spatial capacities.

4.1 *Virtual Environments for Episodic Memory in Complex Conditions*

Growing support is apparent for using virtual environments to investigate episodic memory in complex conditions (Sauzéon et al. 2011; Plancher et al. 2012). For example, memory researchers have used virtual environments for neuropsychological assessment of object memory (Matheis et al. 2007; Parsons and Rizzo 2008; Sauzéon et al. 2012; Widman et al. 2012). Matheis and colleagues (2007) used a virtual office to compare memory performance in participants with traumatic brain injury and healthy controls. During the assessment, participants were immersed in the virtual office and instructed to perform a list-learning memory test that was followed by recall and recognition trials after a short (30 min) and long (24 h) delay. The results indicated that virtual environment-based learning and memory testing has potential for distinguishing between participants from brain injury and control groups. A significant relation was found between the virtual office and a standard auditorily mediated (i.e., California Verbal Learning Test) neuropsychological measure of learning and memory.

In a similar study aimed at using virtual reality to assess object learning and memory, Parsons and Rizzo (2008) developed a virtual city task that reflected tasks found in the Hopkins Verbal Learning Test—Revised (HVLT-R) and the Brief Visuospatial Memory Test—Revised (BVMT-R). Before being immersed in the virtual city, participants took part in a learning task in which they were exposed to language- and graphic-based information without any context across three free learning trials. Next, they were immersed into the virtual environment and they followed a virtual human guide to five different zones of a virtual city. In each zone, participants searched the area for two target items (i.e., items from the learning phase). Following immersion in each of the five zones, participants performed short and long delay free and cued recall tasks. Parsons and Rizzo compared results from the virtual city to traditional paper-and-pencil tasks and found the virtual city was significantly related to paper-and-pencil measures (both individual and composites) of both visually and auditorily mediated learning and memory (convergent validity).

Other researchers have extended object memory to include contextual information such as the location, character, and moment associated with each object (Burgess et al. 2001, 2002; Rauchs et al. 2008; Plancher et al. 2010, 2012, 2013). For example, Arvind-Pala et al. (2014) assessed everyday-like memory using a virtual environment-based Human Object Memory for Everyday Scenes (HOMES) test. In this virtual paradigm that included a virtual apartment to simulate the California Verbal Learning Test, older adults and brain-injured patients displayed comparably poor recall and a recognition benefit.

4.2 Active Versus Passive Navigation

In a study investigating age-related episodic memory using a virtual town, Plancher et al. (2010) found that older adults had deficits in episodic recall compared to younger adults. It is important to note that some virtual environment studies have examined the role of active versus passive navigation in episodic memory performances. An example can be found in Brooks et al. (1999) comparison of participants assigned to a free active navigation (using a joystick) with participants assigned to a passive condition. Findings revealed that the active condition enhanced recall of spatial layout, but not the recall of objects observed during navigation. In a similar study, Sauzéon et al. (2011) found that episodic memory for objects placed in the rooms of two virtual apartments was increased by active compared to passive navigation. Likewise, active navigation was found by Plancher et al. (2012) to offer an advantage in an aging cohort. Although active navigation has been shown to increase feature binding (what–where–when), it has also been shown to have a negative impact on recall of perceptual details associated to elements (e.g., a car accident). The active navigation advantage has been argued to result from the enhancement of item-specific processing (Sauzéon et al. 2011; Plancher et al. 2012, 2013). Further, the loss might be contingent on the level of involvedness of active navigation (Wolbers and Hegarty 2010; Plancher et al. 2012). For some memory researchers, these inconsistencies may be due to inconsistencies in the experimental designs (Bakdash et al. 2008; Chrastil and Warren 2012). Bakdash et al. (2008) found that decision making with or without motor control is an essential cognitive process in active navigation that impacts spatial memory. In a related study, Plancher et al. (2013) found that motor interaction (unlike decision making) resulted in inferior memory for items. In another recent study, Jebara and colleagues (2014) examined the impact of action relative to passive navigation and the locus of decisional control (self or externally imposed) on episodic memory. Findings revealed an age-related decline for immediate and delayed feature binding. Further, active navigation was shown to enhance episodic memory when it is not too demanding for participant' cognitive resources.

4.3 Prospective Memory

Although the majority of neuropsychological assessments of memory focus on retrospective memory recall of a previously experienced episode, there is growing interest in prospective memory of a future intention after some period of delay or memory for intentions. A range of tasks exemplify prospective memory and remembering to remember that one needs to mail a letter, complete an errand at the grocery store, or take medication. Virtual environments have the potential to balance the demands of ecological validity with the sensitivity and specificity of traditional measures of prospective memory (Knight and Titov 2009). Three approaches to assessing prospective memory have been proposed: (1) Time-based prospective memory tasks include measures where the cue for action is a moment in time (e.g., calling someone at 2 p.m.); (2) event-based prospective memory tasks includes measures where the cue is some signal in the environment (e.g., oven alarm signals to remove cake); and (3) action-based prospective memory tasks that are less demanding (when compared to time- and event-based) tasks includes external cues that coincide with the end of an ongoing activity and thus do not require the interruption of the activity (e.g., turning off the lights when leaving a room). A number of virtual environments have been used to assess prospective memory based on time, events, and action (Jansari et al. 2013, 2014; Sweeney et al. 2010). Example virtual environments for prospective memory include virtual office (Jansari et al. 2004; Logie et al. 2011); virtual bungalow (Sweeney et al. 2012); virtual library task (Renison et al. 2012); virtual shopping (Canty et al. 2014; Kinsella et al. 2009), virtual breakfast task (Craik and Bialystok 2006); and virtual street (Knight and Titov 2009).

In a recent study of participants with TBI, Canty et al. (2014) developed and implemented a virtual reality shopping task to measure time- and event-based prospective memory. They aimed to assess the validity of this virtual measure via comparisons between groups (TBI and healthy controls) and traditional neuropsychological measures. In the virtual environment, the participant controls an avatar to achieve certain tasks, while also completing time-based (e.g., send a text message at a certain time) and event-based (e.g., press a key when participant hears the word "sale") prospective memory tasks. Results revealed sensitivity, convergent validity, and ecological validity of the virtual environment. Participants in the TBI group performed significantly worse than controls on event- and time-based prospective memory tasks in the virtual environment. Prospective memory performance in the virtual environment by the TBI group significantly correlated with performance on measures of mental flexibility (Trail Making Test: Parts A and B), verbal fluency, and verbal memory (Hopkins Verbal Learning Test—Revised). Findings such as these provide preliminary evidence of the promise of virtual environments for ecologically valid assessment of everyday prospective memory.

Recently, a virtual library task has been developed and validated to measure executive functioning and prospective memory (time- and event-based). In addition to virtual library task, participants (TBI group and healthy control group) were administered a real-life analogous task and neuropsychological measures (WCST; verbal fluency; Brixton Spatial Anticipation Test; Zoo Map; and Modified Six Elements Test) of executive functioning. Results revealed significant positive correlations between the virtual library task and the real-life analogous. Further, the participants in the TBI group performed significantly worse than controls on the virtual library task and the Modified Six Elements Test. Participants in the TBI group obtained significantly lower scores than participants in the control group on the VLT prospective working memory, time-based prospective memory, and event-based prospective memory. Interestingly, the other neuropsychological measures of executive functioning failed to differentiate participants from TBI and control groups. Authors suggest that since the virtual library task and the Modified Six Elements Test significantly predicted everyday executive functioning and prospective memory, they are both ecologically valid tools. These findings offer support for the use of virtual environments. While other neuropsychological measures failed to differentiate TBI participants from healthy controls, the virtual environment was able to differentiate between TBI and healthy control groups.

An interesting result for both spatial memory and episodic memory is that findings from studies using virtual environments at times reflect a reliance on executive functions and working memory. For spatial memory, Gras et al. (2013) found that working memory components are involved in the construction of spatial memory and individual differences modulate the involvement of working memory. It has also been shown that age-related memory differences after active navigation are mediated by executive functions (Gyselinck et al. 2013; Jebara et al. 2014; Taillade et al. 2013). Taillade and colleagues (2013) found that even when participants from an older cohort have equivalent spatial knowledge to younger adults, they had greater difficulties with the wayfinding task. They argued that this supports an executive decline view in age-related wayfinding difficulties. Likewise, Jebara and colleagues (2014) found that controlling both the pedals and a steering wheel in a complex virtual environment resulted in differing degrees of executive/attentional load. Given the results of these studies and those mentioned above for functional assessment of executive functioning, there appears to be growing need for research into the use of virtual environments for the fractionating of component neurocognitive processes.

5 Enhanced Ecological Validity via Virtual Environments for Affective Assessments

In addition to the cognitive processing assessments mentioned above, virtual environments are also being used to assess affective processes. Virtual reality has recently become an increasingly popular medium for assessment of various aspects of affective arousal and emotional dysregulation (Parsons and Rizzo 2008). It has been found to be an especially useful modality for intervening with a participant when real-world exposure would be too costly, time-consuming, or hazardous. In the following, a number of application areas for affective arousal using virtual environments are discussed: general fear conditioning; affective responses in everyday contexts; affective responses in threatening contexts; and affective processing of moral dilemmas. These areas were chosen because they cover the range of contexts for affective responding from simple fear conditioning to real-world moral dilemmas.

5.1 Virtual Environments for Studies of Fear Conditioning

One application of interest for affective neuroscience is the use of virtual environments for studies of fear conditioning (Alvarez et al. 2007; Baas et al. 2008). Virtual environments offer an ecologically valid platform for examinations of context-dependent fear reactions in simulations of real-life activities (Glotzbach 2012; Mühlberger et al. 2007). Neuroimaging studies utilizing virtual environments have been used to delineate brain circuits involved in sustained anxiety to unpredictable stressors in humans. In a study of contextual fear conditioning, Alvarez et al. (2008) used a virtual office and fMRI to investigate whether the same brain mechanisms that underlie contextual fear conditioning in animals are also found in humans. Results suggested that contextual fear conditioning in humans was consistent with preclinical findings in rodents. Specifically, findings support hot affective processing in that the medial aspect of the amygdala had afferent and efferent connections that included input from the orbitofrontal cortex. In another study using a virtual office, Glotzbach-Schoon et al. (2013) assessed the modulation of contextual fear conditioning and extinction by 5HTTLPR (serotonin transporter-linked polymorphic region) and NPSR1 (neuropeptide S receptor 1) polymorphisms. Results revealed that both the 5HTTLPR and the NPSR1 polymorphisms were related to hot affective (implicit) processing via a fear-potentiated startle. There was no effect of the 5HTTLPR polymorphism on cold cognitive (explicit) ratings of anxiety. Given the ability of virtual environments to place participants in experimentally controlled yet contextually relevant situations, there appears to be promise in applying this platform to future translational studies into contextual fear conditioning.

5.2 *Virtual Environments to Elicit Affective Responses in Threatening Contexts*

Recently, virtual environments have been applied to the assessment of both "cold" and "hot" processes using combat-related scenarios (Armstrong et al. 2013; Parsons et al. 2013). The addition of virtual environments allows affective neuroscience researchers to move beyond the ethical concerns related to placing participants into real-world situations with hazardous contexts. The goal of these platforms is to assess the impact of hot affective arousal upon cold cognitive processes (see Table 5). For example, Parsons et al. (2013) have developed a Virtual Reality Stroop Task (VRST) in which the participant is immersed in a simulated High Mobility Multipurpose Wheeled Vehicle (HMMWV) and passes through zones with alternating low threat (driving down a deserted desert road) and high threat (gunfire, explosions, and shouting among other stressors) while dual-task stimuli (e.g., Stroop stimuli) were presented on the windshield. They found that the high-threat zones created a greater level of psychophysiological arousal (heart rate, skin conductance, respiration) than did low-threat zones. Findings from these studies also provided data regarding the potential of military-relevant virtual environments for measurement of supervisory attentional processing (Parsons et al. 2013). Analyses of the effect of threat level on the color–word and interference scores resulted in a main effect of threat level and condition. Findings from the virtual environment paradigm support the perspective that (1) high information load tasks used for cold cognitive processing may be relatively automatic in controlled circumstances—for example, in low-threat zones with little activity, and (2) the total available processing capacities may be decreased by other hot affective factors such as arousal (e.g., threat zones with a great deal of activity). In a replication study, Armstrong et al. (2013) established the preliminary convergent and discriminant validity of the VRST with an active-duty military sample.

In addition to virtual environment-based neuropsychological assessments using driving simulators, a number of other military-relevant virtual environments have emerged for neurocognitive assessment of cold and hot processes. For example, Parsons et al. (2012, 2014) immersed participants into a Middle Eastern city and exposed participants to a cold cognitive processing task (e.g., paced auditory serial addition test) as they followed a fire team on foot through safe and ambush (e.g., hot affective—bombs, gunfire, screams, and other visual and auditory forms of threat) zones in a Middle Eastern city. In one measure of the battery, a route-learning task, each zone is preceded by a zone marker, which serves as a landmark to assist in remembering the route. The route-learning task is followed immediately by the navigation task in which the participants were asked to return to the starting point of their tour through the city. Courtney et al. (2013) found that the inclusion of hot affective stimuli (e.g., high-threat zones) resulted in a greater level of psychophysiological arousal (heart rate, skin conductance, respiration) and decreased performance on cold cognitive processes than did low-threat zones. Results from active-duty military (Parsons et al. 2012) and civilian (Parsons and

Table 5 Virtual environments to elicit affective responses in threatening contexts

Study	Traditional tests	Sample	Outcome
Armstrong et al. (2013) Virtual HMMWV VRST	BDI, DKEFS Color–Word Interference, PASAT ANAM (Stroop, Reaction Time, Code Substitution, Matching to Sample, Math Processing, Tower Test)	N = 49 active-duty soldiers	• Convergent validity of the VRST with the DKEFS Color-Word Interference Task and the ANAM Stroop Task • Discriminant validity with the VRST was established
Parsons and Courtney (2014) VR-PASAT	PASAT; DKEFS Color–Word Inference Test; ANAM (Code Substitution, Procedural Reaction Time, Mathematical Processing, Matching to Sample, Stroop)	N = 50 college-aged students	• Convergent validity of VR-PASAT was found via correlations with measures of attentional processing and executive functioning • Divergent validity of VR-PASAT was found via lack of correlations with measures of learning, memory, and visuospatial processing, showing discriminant validity • Likability of VR-PASAT was consistently rated higher than the traditional PASAT
Parsons et al. (2013) Virtual HMMWV VRST	ANAM Stroop Task, DKEFS Color–Word Interference	N = 50 college-aged students	• HUMVEE VRST showed the same Stroop pattern as the traditional DKEFS and ANAM Stroop measures • VRST offers the advantage of being able to assess exogenous and endogenous processing • HUMVEE VRST high-threat zones produced more psychophysiological arousal than the low-threat zones
Parsons et al. (2012) VR-PASAT	BDI, DKEFS Color–Word Interference, PASAT ANAM (Stroop, Reaction Time, Code Substitution, Matching To Sample, Math Processing, Tower Test)	N = 49 (94 % were male) military service members	• When compared to the paper-and-pencil version of the test, as well as the ANAM, the VR-PASAT appears to have enhanced capacity for providing an indication of a participant's performance while immersed in a military-relevant simulation
Parsons et al. (2011) Virtual HMMWV VRST	ANAM Stroop Task, DKEFS Color–Word Interference	N = 20 college-aged students	• Skin conductance level predicted threat level (higher skin conductance levels were observed in high-threat zones) • Cognitive workload was predicted by heart rate and behavioral data, and both heart rate and response time increased in the interference condition with the highest difficulty

(continued)

Table 5 (continued)

Study	Traditional tests	Sample	Outcome
Parsons et al. (2009) Virtual Attention Task and Memory Module	HVLT-R, BVMT, Digit Span, Digit Symbol Coding, TMT-B, semantic and phonemic Fluency, Stroop Color and Word Test	N = 67 healthy adults	• Results supported both convergent and discriminant validity • Stimulus complexity was found to impair attentional functioning • Immersive presentations were found to evoke more pronounced physiological responses than less immersive environments
Parsons et al. (2009) Virtual HMMWV Attention Task	TAS; ITQ; electromyography; electrodermal activity; electrocardiographic activity; and respiration	N = 6 West Point cadets and N = 9 civilians	• Cadets were found to have diminished startle eyeblink amplitude compared with civilians, which may reflect that cadets experienced less negative affect during the scenario in general • Heart rate data revealed that cadets had significantly lower heart rates than civilians in the "low" but not "high" immersion condition. This suggests that "low" immersion conditions may not have the ecological validity necessary to evoke consistent affect across cohorts
Parsons and Rizzo (2008) Virtual Iraq Memory Module	HVLT-R; BVMT-R; semantic and phonemic fluency; Digit Symbol Coding; Digit Span; WAIS-III; TMT; Stroop Color and Word Test; WTAR	N = 30 healthy adults	• Results supported both convergent validity and discriminant validity

Note ANAM = Automated Neuropsychological Assessment Metrics; BDI = Beck Depression Inventory; BVMT-R = Brief Visuospatial Memory Test—Revised; DKEFS = Delis–Kaplan Executive Function System; HMMWV = High Mobility Multipurpose Wheeled Vehicle; HVLT-R = Hopkins Verbal Learning Test—Revised; ITQ = Immersive Tendencies Questionnaire; PASAT = Paced Auditory Serial Addition Test; TAS = Tellegen Absorption Scale; TMT = Trail Making Test; VR-PASAT = Virtual Reality Paced Auditory Serial Addition Test; VRST = Virtual Reality Stroop Task; WAIS-III = Wechsler Adult Intelligence Scale—Third Edition; WTAR = Wechsler Test of Adult Reading

Courtney 2014) populations offer preliminary support for the construct validity of the VR-PASAT as a measure of attentional processing. Further, results suggest that the VR-PASAT may provide some unique information related to hot affective processing not tapped by traditional cold attentional processing tasks.

6 Conclusions

Virtual environment-based neuropsychological assessments afford several important advantages for clinical application in the assessment of deficits. Some positive attributes of these VE-based neuropsychological assessments include enhanced ecological validity, simulation customizability, affordability, safety and efficiency, applicability to a wide range of impairments, user-friendly interfaces, data capture, and real-time analyses of performance (Parsons 2011). While there is a great deal of optimism surrounding the potential of virtual environments for ecologically valid assessments of cognitive functioning, this chapter argues that this optimism may be decreased by the reality that many of these virtual environments are in fact simply placing traditional construct-driven stimuli into various simulations of real-life environments. Hence, the difficult issue facing neuropsychologists interested in adding virtual environments to their assessments of real-world functioning is the question of what constitutes an ecologically valid assessment of executive functioning. As Burgess and colleagues (2006) have pointed out, the majority of neuropsychological assessments currently in use today were developed to assess cognitive "constructs" without regard for their ability to predict "functional" behavior. Virtual environments that simply recycle these construct-driven paradigms run the risk of perpetuating a declining emphasis in the world of neuropsychological assessment. That said, there are a number of virtual environments reviewed that meet the standards laid out by Burgess et al. (2006) and emphasize a function-led approach to assessing executive functions using simulated environments.

Function-led virtual environment-based neuropsychological assessment is an emerging area of application. However, this area requires substantial research and development to establish acceptable psychometric properties and clinical utility. Regardless of the purported advantages of virtual environments, there are several critical areas that require further development. One area of note is the compatibility of current VE hardware and software components. Further, it is important to note that researchers of VE-based neuropsychological assessments have often sought to establish construct validity by demonstrating significant associations between construct-driven virtual environments with other traditional construct-driven measures (e.g., Armstrong et al. 2013; Matheis et al. 2007; Parsons and Rizzo 2008). In the area of function-led assessment, multiple cognitive domains may be involved in the simulation of real-world tasks, and associations with traditional construct-driven tests may be necessarily lower than is typically desired to establish construct validity. In this context, the degree to which a VE-based neuropsychological assessment modeled using a function-led approach accurately predicts relevant real-world behavior may be more important than large-magnitude associations with traditional construct-driven paper-and-pencil tests. Future research should consider this issue in the design of function-led VE-based neuropsychological assessment studies. In addition to these technical issues, clinicians, researchers, and policy-makers will need to scrutinize emerging VE-based neuropsychological assessments to ensure adherence to legal, ethical, and human safety guidelines. Finally, the matching of specific technologies to the needs and capacities of the patient will also require careful consideration be neuropsychologists.

A pressing need among neuropsychologists is the identification of VE-based neuropsychological assessments that reflect relevant underlying cognitive and behavioral capacities for assessments of varying degrees of cognitive deficits. VE-based neuropsychological assessments must demonstrate relevance beyond that available through simpler means of assessment. As such, there is specific need for VE-based neuropsychological assessments to be sufficiently standardized within the range and nature of responses available to participants within the virtual environment to allow for reliable measurement. Through the amassing of multiple studies of various clinical populations, VE-based neuropsychological assessments may reveal relevant responses that can be cataloged and defined as measurable factors in a virtual environment. This will require large-scale research trials for validation of measures and development of norms. For neurocognitive assessment of clinical populations, increased research is needed. This research will require large participant pools consisting of patients and normal controls from various samples.

Given the above, it is possible that VE-based neuropsychological assessments developed as function-led assessments can meaningfully inform a neuropsychologist's predictive statements about a patient's real-world functioning. Considering these aspects may lead to the missing of decrements in many aspects of cognition that are critical to competence in everyday life. Some progress has been made in various areas of VE-based neuropsychological assessment. Herein, a general scientific approach to the neuropsychology of executive function is proffered that stresses the importance of analyzing the demands made by real-world situations and then trying to mimic them in the laboratory. To the extent that this approach is correct, it is hoped that neuropsychologists interested in virtual environment-based will go from construct-driven to function-led assessments as a starting point both for the development of new and better clinical tests of executive function and also for basic neuropsychological investigations.

Part III
Next Generation Neuropsychological Applications

Chapter 6
Telemedicine, Mobile, and Internet-Based Neurocognitive Assessment

Another possibility for increasing throughput is to adopt less labor-intensive procedures for example, it is possible to collect information of certain behavioral features through assessment tools that can be self-administered over the Internet by individuals throughout the world.

—Freimer and Sabatti (2003)

A new medium for delivering neuropsychological assessments has emerged as a result of the Internet. Recent surveys have revealed that over 3.1 billion people now have access to the Internet. The distribution of this number by country reveals the following: China = 642 million; USA = 280 million; India = 243 million; Japan = 109 million; Brazil = 108 million; Russia = 84 million, among others (Internet Live Stats 2015). In the USA, 86.75 % of the residents have access to the Internet. Telemedicine is an area that has developed for the use and exchange of medical information from one site to another via electronic communications, information technology, and telecommunications. When researchers are discussing "telemedicine," they typically mean synchronous (interactive) technologies such as videoconferencing or telephony to deliver patient care. When the clinical services involve mental health or psychiatric services, the terms "telemental health" and "telepsychiatry" are generally used (Yellowlees et al. 2009).

Recently, the term "teleneuropsychology" has emerged for cognitive assessments that act as natural extensions of the movement in health care to expand the availability of specialty services (Cullum and Grosch 2012). Within the teleneuropsychology framework, neuropsychologists use video teleconferencing, smartphones, and Web-based assessment for remote assessment of patients in rural areas (Hilty et al. 2006). As a specialty service, teleneuropsychology allows for the assessment of patients potentially impacted by neurocognitive impairments that are geographically isolated. Evaluation of the patient is performed via a personal computer, digital tablet, smartphone, or other digital interface to administer, score, and aide interpretation of neuropsychological assessments (Cullum et al. 2014). Preliminary evaluation of patient acceptance of this methodology has revealed that teleneuropsychology appears to be well accepted by consumers. Parikh et al.

T.D. Parsons, *Clinical Neuropsychology and Technology*,
DOI 10.1007/978-3-319-31075-6_6

(2013) found 98 percent satisfaction and approximately two-thirds of participants reported no preference between assessment via video teleconferencing and traditional in-person assessment.

While teleneuropsychology offers a great deal of promise for in general, there are strengths in weaknesses for various modalities and approaches that need to be discussed. For example, the most widely studied medium in teleneuropsychology is video teleconferencing, which represents an excellent advance in the incorporation of advanced technology for connecting neuropsychologists with patients in underserved areas. However, video teleconferencing falls far short of the stimulus presentation and logging found in Neuropsychological Assessment 2.0 and 3.0. Instead, it uses video teleconferencing to administer the sorts of paper-and-pencil measures found in Neuropsychological Assessment 1.0. Further, it fails to add to the ecological validity of assessments and simply continues a construct-driven approach that falls short in the assessment of affect. A much more promising teleneuropsychology will also embrace smartphones (including ecological momentary assessment) and Web-based neuropsychological assessment. These approaches offer much of the promise found in Neuropsychological Assessment 2.0, and some of the enhanced ecological validity found in Neuropsychological Assessment 3.0.

The plan of this chapter is as follows: First, there will be a discussion of video teleconferencing and the studies comparing it to in-person assessments. Next, there will be a discussion of construct-driven and affective possibilities found in smartphones and Web-based approaches. The chapter will conclude with a discussion of the possibilities of enhanced data collection and database building for personalized medicine.

1 Video Teleconferencing for Teleneuropsychological Assessment

The use of video teleconferencing for teleneuropsychological assessment involves a set of videoconferencing platforms. One set of equipment is situated at the neuropsychologist's location, and another set is located remotely at the client location. There are now a number of studies comparing the administration of neuropsychological measures via video teleconferencing to in-person administrations, and research in this area is being further developed and validated. In addition to video teleconferencing with healthy participants (Hildebrand et al. 2004; Jacobsen et al. 2003), a number of clinical studies have been performed: medical disorders (Ciemins et al. 2009; Menon et al. 2001), intellectual disability (Temple et al. 2010), alcohol abuse (Kirkwood et al. 2000), and dementia (Barton et al. 2011; Cullum et al. 2006; Grosch et al. 2015; Hanzevacki et al. 2011; Harrell et al. 2014; Loh et al. 2004, 2007; McEachern et al. 2008; Vestal et al. 2006).

1.1 Mini Mental State Examination via Remote Administration

Teleneuropsychology investigations have varied in their assessment measures and populations. Many have focused on cognitive screens such as the Mini Mental State Examination (MMSE; Ciemins et al. 2009; Loh et al. 2004, 2007; McEachern et al. 2008). For example, Ciemins et al. (2009) examined the reliability of MMSE administrations via remote administration. Their primary focus was to evaluate the auditory and visual components of the administration. The MMSE was administered only once to 72 participants with Type II diabetes. Responses from patients were recorded by both a remote administrator and an in-person examiner. Findings revealed that 80 % of individual items demonstrated remote to in-person agreement. In a related study administering the MMSE via video teleconferencing, McEachern et al. (2008) assessed elderly individuals referred to a memory clinic. Following an initial assessment, patients were seen at 6- and 12-week follow-ups. Findings revealed that MMSE scores did not differ significantly between remote and in-person assessments. In a similarly designed study, Loh et al. (2004) aimed to determine the interrater reliability of the Mini Mental State Examination through video teleconferencing as compared to in-person administration. Results revealed that the correlation between in-person and remote MMSE scores was 0.90. Findings suggest that remote assessments with the MMSE using video teleconferencing methods yielded similar results to direct assessments (see Table 1).

Table 1 Comparison of MMSE in video teleconference and face-to-face modalities

Authors	Demographics	Participant groups	Results
Ciemens et al. (2009)	63 s (45 % F), mean age: 61 yrs	Type 2 diabetes; 17 % with associated depression	80 % of individual items demonstrated VTC to in-person agreement of ≥95 % and all items were ≥85.5 % in agreement
Loh et al. (2007)	20 subjects (9 M, average age was 79 years over 65 years	20 cognitive impairments	The average of the standard MMSE total score was 23.3 (SD 3.6), and average MMSE by VTC was 24.2 (SD 3.7)
McEachern et al. (2008)	71 s (34 M), age 72 yrs ± 11	37 AD, 11 MCI, 4 VD, 10 other pathology, 9 normal	No difference between VTC MMSE score vs. in-person ($p = 0.223$)
Timpano et al. (2013)	342 sbj (134 M) 50 > age < 94; 0 > yrs l < 18	Cognitively impaired and healthy subjects	There were high levels of sensitivity and specificity for the optimal VMMSE cutoff identification and an accuracy of 0.96

1.2 *Neuropsychological Batteries via Video Teleconferencing*

While the cognitive screening studies are helpful, many neuropsychologists are interested in the results of comparing larger neuropsychological batteries via video teleconferencing to in-person administrations (see Table 2). Jacobsen and colleagues (2003) evaluated the reliability of administering a broader neuropsychological assessment remotely using healthy volunteers. The battery was made up of twelve measures that covered eight cognitive domains: attention, information processing, visuomotor speed, nonverbal memory, visual perception, auditory

Table 2 Neuropsychological battery and video teleconference and face-to-face modalities

Authors	Demographics	Participant groups	Results
Cullum et al. (2006)	33 subjects (mean age 73.3)	MCI, mild-to-moderate AD	Robust agreement between VTC and in-person testing Digit Span (p = 0.81), category fluency (p = 0.58), letter fluency (p = 0.83), and BNT (p = 0.88)
Cullum et al. (2014)	N = 200 (mean age = 68.5)	Cognitive impairment; healthy controls	Similar findings across VTC and in-person conditions; with significant intraclass correlations (mean = 0.74; range: 0.55–0.91) between test scores
Khan et al. (2012)	N = 205 (mean age 75.6)	MCI, dementia, and healthy subject	Agreement for the VTC group (P < 0.0001) and agreement for the in-person group (P < 0.0001) were both statistically significant (P < 0.05). VTC was not inferior to in-person assessment
Loh et al. (2007)	N = 20 (mean age = 79 years)	Cognitive impairment	The medium and standard deviation of VTC and in-person did not show significant differences in GDS (remote: 2.6 ± 2.1; direct: 2.8 ± 2.1), in IQCODE (remote: 3.8 ± 0.7; direct: 4.2 ± 0.6), and in ADL (remote: 3.0 ± 2.4; direct: 3.0 ± 2.3)
Sano et al. (2010)	N = 48 (mean age = 82.1)	Nondemented	The time for overall direct evaluation was lowest for IVR (Mn = 44.4; SD = 21.5), followed by MIP (Mn = 74.9; SD = 29.9), and followed by KIO Mn = 129.4; SD = 117.0). The test–retest reliability of all experimental measures was moderate
Vestal et al. 2006)	N = 10 (mean age 73.9)	Mild AD	Wilcoxon signed-rank test indicated no significant difference on performance between VTC and in-person assessment for Picture Description Test, BNT, Token Test, ACWP and Controlled Oral Word Association Test

Note VTC = Video teleconferencing

attention, verbal memory, and verbal ability. Results revealed that for most of the measures, the in-person and remote scores were highly correlated (reliability coefficients ranging from 0.37 to 0.86; median value of 0.74).

In addition to some important reviews of the teleneuropsychology literature, Cullum, Grosch, and colleagues have completed a set of studies comparing video teleconference-based diagnostic interviewing with conventional in-person assessment (Cullum et al. 2006, 2012, 2014; Grosch et al. 2011, 2015). In an early study, Cullum et al. (2006) made this comparison with a sample of 33 participants, with 14 older persons having mild cognitive impairment and 19 participants with mild-to-moderate Alzheimer's disease. The neuropsychology battery included the MMSE, Hopkins Verbal Learning Test-Revised, Boston Naming Test (short form), Digit Span, letter fluency, and category fluency. Robust correlations were found between video teleconference and in-person testing: MMSE ($r = 0.89$), Boston Naming ($r = 0.88$), digit span ($r = 0.81$), category fluency ($r = 0.58$), and letter fluency ($r = 0.83$), and showed excellent agreement. It is important to note that while there was a significant correlation between two conditions for the HVLT-R, verbal percentage retention score exhibited considerable variability in each test session. This suggests that this score may not be as reliable as the other memory indices. These results offer further support for the validity of video teleconferencing for conducting neuropsychological evaluations of older adults with cognitive impairment. Cullum and colleagues (2014) performed a follow-up study with a larger sample size. They examined the reliability of video teleconference-based neuropsychological assessment using the following: MMSE, Hopkins Verbal Learning Test-Revised, Boston Naming Test (short form), letter and category fluency, digit Span forward and backward, and clock drawing. The sample consisted of two hundred and two (cognitive impairment $N = 83$; healthy controls $N = 119$) adult participants. Highly similar results were found across video teleconferencing and in-person conditions regardless of whether participants had cognitive impairment. These findings suggest that video teleconferencing-based neuropsychological testing is a valid and reliable alternative to traditional in-person assessment. In a more recent study, this team aimed to validate remote video teleconferencing for geropsychiatry applications. Findings suggest that brief telecognitive screening is feasible in an outpatient geropsychiatry clinic and produces similar results for attention and visuospatial ability in older patients. The patients of neuropsychologists may benefit from a remote assessment and diagnosis because teleneuropsychology allows the neuropsychologist to overcome the barriers of displacing patients (and their caregivers) living in rural areas that are far from health institutions.

1.3 Gerontology Applications of Videoconference-Based Assessment

The role of teleneuropsychology is expected to expand, providing increased access to clinical care for geographically isolated geriatric patients in rural settings

(Ramos-Ríos et al. 2012). Teleneuropsychology-based programs using video teleconferencing for gerontological care have been positively received by persons living in nursing homes, community dwelling patients, caregivers, and physicians. Video teleconferencing has also been shown to have adequate reliability with in-person assessment (Azad et al. 2012). To replicate best practices from traditional approaches found in memory clinic settings, interdisciplinary models for the care of elders with cognitive impairment have also been applied via video teleconferencing (Barton et al. 2011). Of specific interest to neuropsychologists are studies showing the feasibility and reliability of using video teleconferencing for administering objective cognitive testing with screening instruments (Cullum et al. 2006; Grosch et al. 2015; Hanzevacki et al. 2011; Loh et al. 2004, 2007; McEachern et al. 2008; Parikh et al. 2013; Turner et al. 2012; Vestal et al. 2006).

1.4 Language Assessments

In a study that emphasized the effectiveness of language assessment in mild Alzheimer's patients, Vestal and colleagues (2006) compared video teleconferencing with in-person language assessments: Boston Naming Test, Picture Description (auditory response), Token Test, Aural Comprehension of Words and Phrases, and the Controlled Oral Word Association Test. Results from the Wilcoxon signed-rank test indicated no significant difference for performance on each of the five language tasks between the video teleconference and in-person conditions. It is important to note that the overall acceptance of the video teleconferencing evaluation in an elderly population was rated at a high level. Given these results, video teleconferencing appears to have promise for speech and language evaluation services in dementia.

1.5 Acceptability of Neuropsychological Screening Delivered via Telehealth

Although the above studies provide support for the feasibility, validity, and acceptability of neuropsychological screening delivered via telehealth, there have only been a couple studies that discuss the feasibility of neuropsychological assessment for a comprehensive dementia care program that services patients with limited accessibility (Barton et al. 2011; Harrell et al. 2014; Martin-Khan et al. 2012; Vestal et al. 2006). For example, Barton et al. (2011) employed a platform to administer multidisciplinary, state-of-the-art assessment of neurocognitive impairment by video teleconferencing. The participants were patients at a rural veteran's community clinic that were referred by their local provider for evaluation of memory complaints. The neuropsychological evaluation was integrated into the typical clinical configuration and involved a neurological evaluation and neuropsychological testing via video teleconferencing. Results revealed that for each patient, the video teleconferencing format permitted the clinical team to arrive at a working diagnosis and relevant treatment recommendations were made. The evaluation results were discussed with providers who joined the post-clinic conference via video teleconferencing. These findings suggest that video teleconferencing may offer an effective way to provide consultation and care to rural residents.

Similar results were found in a study designed to determine the validity of the diagnosis of dementia via video teleconferencing. Martin-Khan and colleagues (2012) evaluated 205 patients using video teleconferencing and in-person administrations of neuropsychological tests: MMSE, Rowland Universal Dementia Assessment Scale (RUDAS), verbal fluency, animal naming, and the clock face test. Results revealed significant agreement between the video teleconference group and the in-person group. The summary kappa statistic indicated that video teleconferencing was similar to the in-person assessment. Findings suggested that incorporating video teleconferencing and in-person assessments has promise as a reliable process for differential diagnosis of dementia.

In summary, teleneuropsychology has emerged as a natural extension of the movement in health care to expand the availability of specialty services via telecommunication. Within the teleneuropsychology framework, neuropsychologists use video teleconferencing for remote assessment of patients in rural areas. A limitation of video teleconferencing is that it falls far short of the sorts of progress discussed in this manuscript. It continues a construct-driven approach and falls short in assessment of affect. Further, in terms of progress, video teleconferencing appears to be little more than Neuropsychological Assessment 1.0 using advanced technology. This is apparent in the low ecological validity of the tests that simply administer traditional construct-driven paper-and-pencil tests using video teleconferencing. Finally, video teleconferencing also fails to bring in any affective assessments beyond paper-and-pencil measures.

2 Smartphones for Telephone-Based Neuropsychological Assessment

Contemporary technological advances such as telemedicine and teleneuropsychology paradigms have been shown to have promise a multiplicity of settings (Cullum et al. 2006, 2011, 2014; Cullum and Grosch 2012; Rajan 2012; Clifford and Clifton 2012; Rogante et al. 2012). One approach to teleneuropsychology is the use of smartphones which include computing capabilities. Given their mobility and ubiquity in the general population, smartphones are increasingly part of medicine-related applications that have the potential for use in clinical settings. A number of papers have described the promise of smartphone-based applications for assisting in a broad range of clinical research areas and patient point-of-care services (Boulos et al. 2011; Doherty and oh 2012; Doherty et al. 2011; Fortney et al. 2011). Of particular interest for neuropsychologists is the potential of smartphones for research in cognitive science (Dufau et al. 2011). A handful of smartphone applications have emerged for cognitive assessment (Brouillette et al. 2013; Gentry et al. 2008; Kwan and Lai 2013; Lee et al. 2012; Svoboda et al. 2012; Thompson et al. 2012).

In one of these smartphone applications, Brouillette et al. (2013) developed a new application that utilizes touch screen technology to assess attention and processing speed. Initial validation was completed using an elderly nondemented population. Findings revealed that their color shape test was a reliable and valid tool for the assessment processing speed and attention in the elderly. These findings support the potential of smartphone-based assessment batteries for attentional processing in geriatric cohorts.

Smartphones move beyond the Neuropsychological Assessment 1.0 (paper and pencil) found in video teleconferencing. Given their use of advanced technologies (i.e., smartphones instead of paper-and-pencil), smartphone-based cognitive assessment represents Neuropsychological Assessment 2.0. That said, smartphone-based cognitive assessment does not extend ecological validity because it incorporates construct-driven and veridical assessments that lack assessment of affective processing.

3 Ecological Momentary Assessments

Neuropsychologists are interested in the everyday real-world behavior of their patients because brain injury and its functional impairments are expressed in real-world contexts. An unfortunate limitation is that many neuropsychological assessments are construct-driven (e.g., working memory) assessments that do little to tap into the affective aspects of their patient's functioning. Instead, evaluation of activities of daily living, quality of life, affective processing, and life stressors is surveyed using global, summary, or retrospective self-reports. For example, a neuropsychologist may ask a patient how often they experience frustration, how many times they forgot their intentions during the past week or month, or how depressed their mood has been. The prominence of global questionnaires can keep neuropsychologists from observing and studying the dynamic fluctuations in behavior over time and across situations. Further, these questionnaires may obfuscate the ways in which a patient's behavior varies and is governed by context. In reaction to the frequent reliance of neuropsychologists on global, retrospective reports (and the serious limits they place on accurately characterizing, understanding, and changing behavior in real-world settings), some neuropsychologists are turning to Ecological Momentary Assessment (EMA; Cain et al. 2009; Schuster et al. 2015; Waters and Li 2008; Waters et al. 2014). EMA is characterized by a series of (often computer-based) repeated assessments of then current cognitive, affective (including physiological), and contextual experiences of participants as they take part in everyday activities (Jones and Johnston 2011; Shiffman et al. 2008).

EMA moves beyond the Neuropsychological Assessment 1.0 (paper-and-pencil) found in video teleconferencing and to some extent the Neuropsychological Assessment 2.0 found in smartphone-based cognitive assessments. The EMA approach also moves beyond the frequent reliance of neuropsychologists on retrospective reports offers a series of computer-based repeated assessments of cognitive, affective (including physiological), and contextual experiences of participants as they take part in everyday activities. While this is a new application in neuropsychological assessment, it does offer promise (once adequately validated) for enhancing the ecological validity of neuropsychological assessments.

4 Web-Based Computerized Assessments

Web-based computerized assessments have the capacity for adaptive testing strategies that are likely to multiply efficiency in construct measurement (Bilder 2011). In one study, Gibbons and colleagues (2008) found that use of a computerized adaptive test resulted in a 95 % average reduction in the number of items administered. The potential of adaptive Web-based neurocognitive assessment protocols can be seen in the capacity to large sample of participants in relatively short periods of time. While there may be concerns that the neuropsychologist cannot be sure of the identity of the test-takers or that they are performing tasks as instructed, validity indicators, online video surveillance, and anthropometric identifiers can be included to remove these concerns. For example, algorithms can be implemented that allow for item-level response monitoring and automated consistency checks. Further, neuroinformatics algorithms are available that will allow for detection of outlying response patterns of uncertain validity.

While some Web-based neuropsychological assessments are limited to a single domain (e.g., attention and processing speed; Bart et al. 2014; Erlanger et al. 2003; Raz et al. 2014), there is an emerging suite of online batteries. Some of these Web-based assessments consist primarily of informant reports of cognitive decline (Brandt et al. 2013), but there are an increasing number of cognitive screens (Medalia et al. 2005; Scharre et al. 2014) and some larger batteries (Elbin et al. 2011; Gur et al. 2001; Schatz and Sandel 2013; Silverstein et al. 2007; Troyer et al. 2014). A recent battery called BRAINScreen was developed by Zakzanis and Azarbehi (2014) to offer a Web-based and real-time examination of cognitive functioning. The Web-based screening battery includes a number of cognitive measures: visual attention and information-processing speed; list learning and recall; spatial orientation-type task; and forward and backward Digit Span. Initial psychometric validation revealed (when combined into a composite score) a correlation with age, ability to distinguish normal from clinical groups, and robust overall reliability. BRAINScreen offers a straightforward and manageable

Web-based automated screen for neurocognitive impairment with real-time interpretive results.

In another project, Troyer and colleagues (2014) developed a Web-based cognitive assessment for use with middle-aged and older adults. The Web-based battery emphasizes measures of memory and executive attention processes: spatial working memory task; stroop interference task; face–name association task; and number–letter alternation task. Results from a normative study revealed adequate internal consistency, construct validity, test–retest reliability, and alternate version reliability. Each of the neurocognitive tasks loaded on the same principle component. Demographically corrected z-scores from the individual tasks were combined to create an overall score, which showed good reliability and classification consistency. Scores were correlated with age. These findings suggest that the Web-based neuropsychological screening measure may be useful for identifying middle-aged and older adults with lower than expected scores who may benefit from further evaluation by a clinical neuropsychologist.

One of the most widely used and validated of the new Web-based neuropsychology batteries is WebNeuro. The battery includes assessments of the following domains of neurocognitive function: sensorimotor, memory, executive planning, attention, and emotion perception (social cognition; see Table 3; Mathersul et al. 2009; Silverstein et al. 2007; Williams et al. 2009). In addition to cognitive assessments, the WebNeuro battery also includes affective assessments of emotion recognition and identification: immediate explicit identification followed by implicit recognition (within a priming protocol). The WebNeuro protocol was developed as a Web-based version of the IntegNeuro computerized battery. The IntegNeuro battery was developed by a consortium of scientists interested in establishing a standardized international called Brain Resource International Database (BRID; Gordon 2003; Gordon et al. 2005; Paul et al. 2005). IntegNeuro and WebNeuro are part of the BRID project's aim to move beyond outdated approaches to aggregating neuropsychological knowledgebases and develop standardized testing approaches that facilitate the integration of normally independent sources of data (genetic, neuroimaging, psychophysiological, neuropsychological, and clinical). The WebNeuro platform allows for data to be acquired internationally with a centralized database infrastructure for storage and manipulation of these data.

Psychometric evaluation of the WebNeuro platform has revealed robust correlations with IntegNeuro, indicating high convergent validation. The correlation between the WebNeuro and IntegNeuro factor scores exceeded 0.56 in all cases, reflecting a statistically significant degree of overlap between the two variables (Silverstein et al. 2007). In further validation studies with a large sample ($n = 1000$; 6–91 years, 53.5 % female), the WebNeuro tests of emotion identification and recognition and tests of general cognitive function revealed seven domains of general cognition: information-processing speed, executive function, sustained attention/vigilance, verbal memory, working memory capacity, inhibition/impulsivity, and sensorimotor function (Mathersul et al. 2009; Silverstein et al. 2007; Williams et al. 2009).

Table 3 WebNeuro Cognitive and Affective Assessments

Test name	Construct assessed	Test output	Traditional test equivalent
Cognitive assessments			
Finger tapping	Motor coordination: capacity to quickly execute finger tapping	Number of taps. Variability of pauses between taps	Finger tapping
Choice reaction time	Decision speed: capacity to recognize changes and choose the correct response under time demands	Reaction time	Corsi blocks
Memory recognition	Verbal memory: capacity to remember and retrieve factual information (e.g., lists)	Immediate recall accuracy; delayed recall accuracy	RAVLT, CVLT
Digit Span	Working memory: capacity to hold information for multitasking	Total number of digits recalled	WAIS—III; digit Span
Verbal interference	Cognitive control: capacity to inhibit a prepotent response	Reaction time (color) Reaction time (word) Reaction time interference (color–word)	Stroop test
Switching of attention	Processing speed: capacity to link information logically and flexibly under time demands	Accuracy; completion time	Trail Making Test
Go/No-Go	Response inhibition: capacity to switch from automatic reactions to withholding	False alarm errors; false miss errors; % accuracy; reaction time	Go/No-Go
CPT	Attention: capacity to focus on the assigned task	False alarm errors; false miss errors; reaction time	CPT
Maze	Planning: capacity to plan ahead and learn from mistakes	Completion time; % accuracy	Austin Maze
Affective assessments			
Explicit emotion identification	Emotion bias: identification of facial expressions of emotion (e.g., fear and happiness). Tendency to read neutral and positive emotion as negative	% of misidentification as another emotion	Penn Emotion Test
Implicit emotion recognition	Influence of emotion: preoccupied by specific emotions that influence decision making	Reaction time for recognizing a previously seen face	Repetition priming tasks

Note RAVLT = Rey Auditory Verbal Learning Test; CVLT = California Verbal Learning Test; CPT = Continuous Performance Task

While the normative findings for a Web-based neuropsychological assessment are promising, the greatest potential appears to be WebNeuro's relation to Brain Resource International Database. The data from WebNeuro are linked to insights and correlations in a standardized and integrative international database (see www.BrainResource.com; www.BRAINnet.com). The WebNeuro data is incorporated as additional (in addition to other markers: genetic, neuroimaging, psychophysiological, neuropsychological, and clinical) clinical markers that can be incorporated into databases as new marker discoveries emerge from personalized medicine.

5 Summary and Conclusions

Despite breakthroughs in the human neurosciences (cognitive, social, and affective), neuroimaging, psychometrics, human–machine interfaces, and neuroinformatics, the neuropsychological assessments in use today have barely changed over the past century. In addition to failing to advance with technological innovations, traditional print publishing like the WAIS-IV/WMS-IV revisions has fallen short in terms of back-compatibility that may invalidate clinical interpretations (Loring and Bauer 2010). This lack of back-compatibility is especially disappointing given the fact that even modest updates to paper-and-pencil batteries take years. Neuropsychologists are increasingly interested in the potential for advanced psychometrics, online computer-automated assessment methods, and neuroinformatics for large-sample implementation and the development of collaborative neuropsychological knowledge bases (Bilder 2011; Jagaroo 2009). The use of modern psychometric theory and neuroinformatics enables preservation of robust back-compatibility with prior test versions and enables the introduction of new content and new constructs. This will become increasingly important as evidence-based medicine is systematically adopted within the context of clinical neuropsychology (e.g., Chelune 2010). There is increasing interest among neuropsychologists in adopting consolidated standards for the reporting of clinical trials that include neuropsychological endpoints that will ultimately serve to strengthen the empirical evidence and scientific base of neuropsychology (Loring and Bowden 2014; Miller et al. 2014).

Some neuropsychologists are also calling for greater inclusion of computer-automated assessments (Bilder 2011; Jagaroo 2009). It is important to note that some neuropsychologists have concerns that computerized neuropsychological assessment devices will somehow replace human neuropsychologists and/or overlook significant clinical information. However, computerized neuropsychological assessments are just tools for enhanced presentation and logging of stimuli. When properly used, computer-automated assessments can greatly enhance the assessment in terms of precision and rapid implementation of adaptive algorithms. Further, as Bilder (2011) points out, a distinct improvement of computer timing precision is that it allows for enactment of procedures from the human neurosciences that rely on more refined task operations and trial-by-trial analyses that may be more sensitive and specific to individual differences in neural system function. The exponential increase in access to computers and the Internet across the life span allows for interactive Web-based cognitive assessments (Bart et al. 2014; Raz et al. 2014; Wagner et al. 2010). Access to and use of computers are becoming increasingly more common among older adults. Currently, 59 % of those persons that are 64 years or older go online, and this number is increasing at a rapid pace (Smith 2014). Online neurocognitive assessment may enhance dissemination of testing because tests could be administered in a variety of settings (e.g., office, home, school), at different times of the day, and by multiple persons at the same time.

Chapter 7
Neuropsychological Rehabilitation 3.0: State of the Science

It seems highly likely that virtual reality assessments and treatment approaches will become the norm in neuropsychology and rehabilitation within the next decade.
—Wilson (2013)

1 Introduction

Neuropsychological rehabilitation represents a multidisciplinary approach to address the range of cognitive, emotional, psychosocial, and behavioral factors that impact care. Persons with neurocognitive impairments may experience decreased functioning in multiple domains including attention, self-awareness, memory, reasoning, and judgment. Such impairments represent significant obstacles to the patient's activities of daily living. Within neurocognitive rehabilitation, the patient may perform systematically presented and functionally oriented therapeutic activities that are based upon an assessment and understanding of brain–behavior deficits. From a clinical perspective, neurocognitive rehabilitation typically connotes methodical intervention intended to aid the patient impacted by cognitive and/or behavioral deficits. In general, the goal is to enable patients to increase their ability to perform activities of daily living.

Therapeutic interventions occurring within neurocognitive rehabilitation often aim at the achievement of functional changes through reestablishing previously learned behavior patterns or establishing new patterns of cognitive activity or compensatory mechanisms. Other approaches focus upon increasing activities of daily living by systematically evaluating current performance and reducing impairment by equipping the patient with success strategies from a range of settings. Traditionally, these approaches to treatment and rehabilitation of the cognitive, psychological, and motor sequelae of central nervous system dysfunction have relied upon assessment devices to inform diagnosis and to track changes in clinical status. Although typical assessments employ standard paper-and-pencil psychometrics and training methodologies for impairment assessment and rehabilitation, these approaches have been criticized as limited in the area of ecological validity, that is,

T.D. Parsons, *Clinical Neuropsychology and Technology*,
DOI 10.1007/978-3-319-31075-6_7

the degree of relevance or similarity that a test or training system has relative to the real world and in its value for predicting or improving daily functioning.

A further common method applied in the rehabilitation sciences employs behavioral observation and ratings of human performance in the real world or via physical mock-ups of functional environments. Activities of daily living within mock-up environments (i.e., kitchens and bathrooms) and workspaces (i.e., offices and factory settings) are typically built, within which persons with motor and/or neurocognitive impairments are observed, while their performance is evaluated. Aside from the economic costs to physically build these environments and to provide human resources to conduct such evaluations, this approach is limited in the systematic control of real-world stimulus challenges and in its capacity to provide detailed performance data capture.

2 History of Rehabilitation in Neuropsychology

The earliest rehabilitation interventions may be traced back to ancient trepanation practices on persons with brain damage and behavioral deficits. Although the Greeks and Romans endeavored to understand the brain and restoration of function, much of their theorizing was limited by the religious and cultural beliefs of their time. The first neuroanatomical documentation that can be considered scientific did not occur until Vesalius in the sixteenth century. In the seventeenth century, Thomas Willis published two medical texts. The first, *Cerebri anatome,* included anatomical drawings of the brain and cranial nerves. The second was a complementary text on brain pathology and physiology. Also in the seventeenth century, Rene Descartes proffered a theory of mind–body dualism in his *Passions of the Soul* and *The Description of the Human Body.* For Descartes, the body functioned as a machine with material properties and the mind was nonmaterial and beyond the laws of nature. Although today Cartesian dualism is no longer a tenable philosophy of mind, in the seventeenth century, Descartes set the agenda for a philosophical discussion of the mind–body problem for many years (Damasio 2008). In the eighteenth century, another influential but flawed theory was postulated by Franz Gall. According to Gall's theory of phrenology, measurements of the human skull reveal specific mental functions. Although Gall's theory was pseudoscience, it remained very popular in the nineteenth century and is viewed by many as a precursor for work on localization of brain functions. The localizationist Paul Broca developed a program of rehabilitation for an adult patient that lost the ability to read aloud (Berker et al. 1986; as cited in Boake 2003). Another localizationist, Carl Wernicke, built on Broca's ideas and postulated that brain function is best understood as a series of interconnected neural regions. Shepherd Franz also built on Broca's ideas to develop techniques that focus on learning compensatory strategies for cognitive rehabilitation (Prigatano 2005; Witsken et al. 2008).

In the twentieth century, a number of developments occurred in neuropsychological rehabilitation during and after the First and Second World Wars.

Throughout this time, rehabilitation centers were established in Europe to treat brain-injured soldiers. Kurt Goldstein worked at one of these centers where he documented his treatment recommendations for deficits in speech, reading, and writing. Goldstein's work provided a template for rehabilitation efforts focusing upon preserved areas to compensate for lost skills and behavioral methods for shaping desired behaviors (Boake 2003; Witsken et al. 2008). Goldstein's work is especially notable for including long-term follow-up of patients, emphasis upon limitations of psychometric techniques, observation of each patient's preferred compensatory strategies, the impact of fatigue during treatment, individual differences, personality deficits, and the connection between cognitive rehabilitation and functional activities (Newcombe 2002; Witsken et al. 2008). During this time, another early rehabilitation neuropsychologist named Alexander Luria was working with brain-injured veterans. Although Luria's primary work in rehabilitation occurred later in his career, it was during this time that Luria extended rehabilitation beyond aphasia to include rehabilitation of motor planning, visuospatial perception, and executive functioning (Christensen and Castano 1906; Prigatano 2005; Witsken et al. 2008). In 1947, the Zangwill (1947) made a significant contribution to neuropsychological rehabilitation by establishing three aspects of rehabilitation: (1) substitution of alternate strategies in place of those affected by impaired functions; (2) compensation by using alternative strategies to solve problems caused by impaired functioning; and (3) restoration using direct retraining of impaired areas (Johnstone and Stonnington 2009).

Throughout the twentieth century, cognitive rehabilitation strategies and techniques continued to develop. Emphasis was increasingly placed upon psychosocial difficulties and the potential for anxiety and behavioral problems to reduce the effectiveness of intervention programs. The interaction among all these aspects of human functioning was recognized by pioneers who argued for the holistic approach to brain injury rehabilitation: Diller (1976), Ben-Yishay (1978), and Prigatano (1986). Emphasis upon the emotional needs and responses of brain-injured patients and their families is also apparent in Muriel Lezak's (1986) work. Building on this work, Cicerone (2002) explored the relationship between emotional and cognitive dysfunction (see also Cicerone et al. 1983; Cicerone and Kalmar 1997; Cicerone and Fraser 2000). Prigatano (1999, 2005) and Sohlberg and Mateer (1989, 2001) aided our understanding, treatment, and management of attentional deficits. Wilson et al. (2000) offered a British version of the holistic program that is based on the principles of Ben-Yishay (1978) and Prigatano (1986). Finally, the work of Williams (2003) and colleagues has aided work in neuropsychological rehabilitation via emphasis upon the rehabilitation of emotional disorders following brain injury.

While the work of these pioneers offers hope for a fully realized field of neuropsychological rehabilitation, research supporting the utility and efficacy of cognitive rehabilitation techniques varies widely in terms of designs, measures, and outcomes. As a result, many neuropsychologists are skeptical of the utility of cognitive rehabilitation procedures (Bowen and Lincoln 2007) and Cochrane Reviews have offered only "limited evidence" for the effectiveness of neuropsychological rehabilitation for deficits in attention, memory, and language following stroke (Turner-Stokes et al. 2005). Further, an array of challenging methodological confounds and limitations (heterogeneity of disorders, duration/level of recovery, level of cognitive disability; heterogeneity of measurement and intervention techniques) have been found to exist in most of the studies involving neuropsychological rehabilitation (Cicerone 2008). Nevertheless, there are neuropsychologists who have alluded to the unique contribution neuropsychologists have to make in the process of neuropsychological rehabilitation. For example, Wilson (2008) described neuropsychological rehabilitation as a broader field than pure cognitive rehabilitation because it encompasses attempts to ameliorate the affective, psychosocial, and behavioral deficits caused by brain injury. In the following, there will be an attempt to describe the evolution of neuropsychological rehabilitation technologies.

3 Neuropsychological Rehabilitation 2.0

There has been a recent proliferation of computer-assisted and other multimedia methods in neuropsychological rehabilitation, which reflects a general trend toward leveraging technology to improve the accuracy and efficiency of data capture procedures. Rehabilitation neuropsychologists are increasingly moving beyond the limited technologies found in Neuropsychological Rehabilitation 1.0 to more sophisticated technologies in Neuropsychological Rehabilitation 2.0. For example, the "memory notebooks" used for training memory-impaired patients within a Neuropsychological Rehabilitation 1.0 framework would typically be small three-ring binders used for remembering appointments and other important information. In Neuropsychological Rehabilitation 2.0, these "memory notebooks" are handheld electronic devices such as smart phones, iPads, personal computers, and many other types of computerized devices. It is important to note that recent research suggests that up to 90 % of paper diary respondents enter multiple backlogged entries instead of completing the diary in real time and electronic diaries contain significantly fewer completion errors (Stone et al. 2003). The technology in Neuropsychological Rehabilitation 2.0 also supports the use of innovative time-dependent data collection methods such as momentary time sampling, a method in which responses are recorded at predetermined intervals (Cain et al. 2009). Momentary time sampling procedures move beyond retrospective methods in that they do not depend on the capacity to summarize events that occurred in the distant past. During Neuropsychological Rehabilitation 1.0, momentary time sampling data were collected using paper diaries. In Neuropsychological Rehabilitation 2.0, the feasibility and accuracy of these methods have been improved with the availability of personal digital assistants, text messaging, and cell phones (Dale and Hagen 2006). An important application of technology to rehabilitation is the adaptation of technology to the individual needs of a given patient with neurocognitive deficits. For example, computers and other electronic devices may be used to for neuropsychological assessment, implementation of compensatory strategies, training, and neurocognitive prosthetics. Further, the use of these technologies provides a method and system for reminding patients to record data and a device through which data can be recorded, stored, and electronically transmitted to a secure database.

4 Electronic Devices for Cognitive Aids

Early incorporation of technology into neuropsychological rehabilitation can be seen in work with left visual neglect due to stroke. Boake (2003) includes discussion of some of the early computer-based cognitive rehabilitation programs. In particular, he describes a scanner that consisted of a stimulus board and two rows of colored light bulbs. The apparatus was controlled from a console operated by the neuropsychologist. Patients visually scanned the stimulus board from left to right and tried to detect which lights were illuminated. In addition to large-scale visual scanners that take up a wall of the clinician's office, early work by neuropsychologists also included electronic aids in tackling real-life problems such as using a digital alarm chronograph as a memory aid in early dementia (Kurlychek 1983); an interactive task guidance system to assist brain-injured people in performing functional tasks (Kirsch et al. 1987); telephone calls to a voicemail service and general reminders to "stop, think, organize, and plan" for prospective memory (Fish et al. 2007); and a paging system for reducing the everyday problems of neurologically impaired people with memory and/or planning difficulties (Fish et al. 2008; Wilson et al. 2001).

5 Computerized Skills Training Software

In addition to use of electronic devices for cognitive aids, computerized skills training software programs have emerged for a variety of populations. For example, in pediatric cohorts, beneficial effects of adaptive working memory training have used in cohorts of children with attention deficit hyperactivity disorder (ADHD). A number of studies with pediatric cohorts have made use of the Captain's Log Computerized Cognitive Training System (Sanford 2007). The "Captain's Log" consists of 35 multilevel brain-training exercises that were designed to help develop and remediate a wide range of cognitive skills. Studies using "Captain's Log" reveal improvements in attention and maze learning abilities of children with ADHD (Slate et al. 1998), cancer (Hardy 2011), cerebral malaria (Bangirana et al. 2009, 2011), and HIV-related cognitive impairment (Boivin et al. 2010). In a study using an online cognitive rehabilitation program, Kesler et al. (2011) found improvements in processing speed, flexibility, and declarative memory in pediatric cancer survivors.

6 Computerized Attention Training Programs

A number of computerized attention training programs have been developed that are organized into a hierarchy of tasks to sequentially and systematically increase the difficulty of treatment (Stierwalt and Murray 2002; Fasotti et al. 2000). Examples of attentional rehabilitation programs are now computerized that include Attention Process Training-3, Attentional Training System, Orientation Remedial Module, and Bracy Cognitive Rehabilitation Program. In a randomized controlled study, computerized mass practice of spatial working memory improved performance in a span board task in a small sample of children with ADHD (Klingberg et al. 2002). In a follow-up study with a larger sample of children with ADHD, Klingberg et al. (2005) replicated their results and found improved spatial working memory with computerized practice, as well as improvements on a task measuring response inhibition. Further, the exposure of children with ADHD to computerized massed practice was associated with improved executive functioning (i.e., reduction of inattentive, hyperactive, and impulsive symptoms). These improvements in span board performance remained evident 3 months after the training. While there have been some positive results, findings have been mixed. Findings from MacDonald and Wiseman-Hakes (2010) suggest that computer training for attention is not well supported by evidence unless it includes functional goals and clinician input (Sohlberg and Mateer 2010; Riccio and French 2004).

7 Computer-Based Cognitive Rehabilitation for Brain Injury

Computer-based cognitive rehabilitation has been shown to be an effective intervention since the early 1980s in treating the neurocognitive impairments of patients with brain injury, dementia, or schizophrenia (Gontkovsky 2002; Lynch 2002; McGurk 2007; Stern 1999). During computer-based cognitive rehabilitation, a computer is used as an intervention tool to provide feedback to patient responses and reaction speed via input devices like a keyboard or joystick, and the results of tasks are viewed on a monitor (Gray et al. 1992; Thornton et al. 2008). A number of computer-based cognitive rehabilitation studies have shown improvements in patients' response time, attention, and verbal memory and decrease in psychiatric negative symptoms immediately after training (Benedict 1994; Burda et al. 1991; Giles et al. 1989). Further, computerized neuropsychological rehabilitation approaches have shown efficacy for enhancing attentional processing in persons with attentional deficits (Larose et al. 1989), schizophrenia (Eack et al. 2009), multiple sclerosis (Flavia et al. 2010), and stroke patients (Westerberg et al. 2007). In another study that focused on errorless learning of computer-generated words in a patient with semantic dementia, the patient was able to relearn words (Jokel et al. 2010). Beneficial effects of adaptive working memory training have been found in adults after stroke (Westerberg et al. 2007) and traumatic brain injury (Serino et al. 2007).

While computerized training of attention has been of questionable import, summative findings from systematic reviews have revealed moderate support for direct attention training for patients who have experienced a moderate to severe TBI (Snell et al. 2009; Comper et al. 2005; Gordon et al. 2006). The Cogmed program has been widely used in various populations. Cogmed is a rehabilitation program that uses videogame-based programs for children and adults that are practiced 30 min a day, 5 days/week for 5 weeks. The Cogmed consists of coaching, education, and peer support with the goal of training and improving working memory capacity. Brehmer and colleagues (2012) used Cogmed QM to investigate the benefits of computerized working memory exercises in 55 younger adults and 45 cognitively intact older adults. Results indicated that participants (both younger and older adults) showed significant improvements on the following neuropsychological measure: verbal and nonverbal working memory (Spatial Span and Digit Span), sustained attention and working memory (PASAT), and self-report of cognitive functioning. Improvements were not seen in the areas of memory, nonverbal reasoning, or response inhibition (Brehmer et al. 2012). In a study with a clinical population of 18 adults with moderate to severe acquired brain injuries, Johansson and Tournmalm (2012) had participants use the Cogmed QM training software for 8 weeks for a total of 12 h. Findings revealed improvements on trained working memory tasks and self-reports of functioning. An unfortunate limitation of the study is that it had no control group. In another study that included a control group Westerberg et al. (2007) had participants use Cogmed QM for 40 min daily, 5 days a week for 5 weeks. The treatment group performed significantly better than the control group on Spatial and Digit Span, PASAT, and Ruff 2&7, but no differences emerged between groups on the Stroop, Ravens progressive matrices, or the word list test (see Table 1).

8 Neuropsychological Rehabilitation 3.0

A perceived weakness for both Neuropsychological Rehabilitation 1.0 and Neuropsychological Rehabilitation 2.0 is the limited ability to replicate the challenges that may occur outside a sterile office or hospital setting. With advances in technology, the possibility of simulating real-world situations while being able to control stimulus delivery and measurement is closer to fruition (Wilson 2011, 2013). The virtual environments found in Neuropsychological Rehabilitation 3.0 permit individuals to control dynamic three-dimensional environments, which are becoming rapidly more complex, refined, and interactive (Riva 2009). These immersive environments include depictions of home settings, libraries, grocery stores, classrooms, and even combat environments. With advances in technology, the head-mounted displays are decreasing in size, weight, and cost. Motion tracking allows the individual to interact with the virtual environment. Further, computer

Table 1 Recent studies using the Cogmed program

Authors citation	Groups	Time to onset	Design	Intervention duration	Outcome measures	Main findings
Cogmed QM Westerberg et al. (2007)	9 stroke patients 9 controls	12–36 months	Randomized pilot design	40 min, 5 per week for 5 weeks	Span board, Digit Span, Stroop, Raven's PM, word list repetitions, PASAT, RUFF, CFQ	Significant decrease in cognitive problems as measured by CFQ. Systematic WM training can significantly improve WM and attention more than one year post-stroke
Parrot software Li et al. (2013)	12 ABI patients	21.27 months	Quasi-experimental prepost test design	60 min., 10 per session, 1 session per week for 8 sessions	Cognistat Attention, memory	Significant improvement in memory and attention
Cogmed QM Lundqvist et al. (2010)	10 stroke and ABI patients 11 controls	37 months	Controlled crossover experimental design	45–60 min., 5 per week for 5 weeks	PASAT; CWIT; Block Span; LST; Picture Span	Significant improvement in trained WM tasks; WM test; and rated occupational performance
Cogmed QM Johansson and Tommalm (2012)	18 TBI and tumor patients	7 years	Prospective cohort design	30–45 min., 3 per week for 7–8 weeks	Built-in parameter; CFQ	Significant improvement on trained WM tasks
Cogmed QM Bjorkdahl et al. (2013)	20 stroke and TBI patients 18 controls	27 weeks	Randomized controlled design	30–45 min., 5 days per week for 5 weeks	Digits Backward; RBMT II; WM Q	Significant improvement on Digit Span and the WM questionnaire

(continued)

Table 1 (continued)

Authors citation	Groups	Time to onset	Design	Intervention duration	Outcome measures	Main findings
Cognitive PC-training De Luca et al. (2014)	15 stroke and TBI patients 20 control	Not spec	Control design	24 sessions, 3 per week for 8 weeks	RML; Attentive Matrices; MMSE; CVF; LVF; RAVLT Recall; Constructional Apraxia; ADLs; Barthel Index; HADS	Significant cognitive improvement on nearly all the neuropsychological tests
Cogmed QM Akerlund (2013)	8 patients 10 controls	Not spec	Randomized controlled design	Baseline and at follow-ups at 6 and 18 weeks	Digit Span, Arithmetic, Letter-NumberSequences, Spatial Span, BNIS; DEX and HADS	Significant improvement in WM, BNIS, and in Digit Span
Cogmed QM Hellgren et al. (2015)	48 ABI patients	29 month	Randomized controlled design (crossover)	Patients tested at baseline and 20 weeks	PASAT; Forward and backward block repetition; LST	Significantly improved WM,neuropsychological test scores, and self-estimated health scores

Note ADAS = Alzheimer's Disease Assessment Scale; BCPM = Behavioral Checklist of prospective Memory Task; BNIS = Barrow Neurological Institute Screen; CAMPROMT = Cambridge Prospective Memory Test; CBTT = Corsi Block-Tapping Test; CFQ = Cognitive Failures Questionnaire; CIQ = Community Integration Questionnaire; CST = Corsi Supraspan Test; CTT,Color Trail Test; CVF = Category Verbal Fluency; CWIT = Color Word Interference Test; FAB = Frontal Assessment Battery; HAD = Hamilton Anxiety and Depression; LST = Listening Span Task; LVF = letter verbal fluency; RAVLT = Rey Auditory Verbal, Learning Test; Lawton IADL = Instrumental Activities of Daily Living Scale; Min-minutes; MMSE = Mini–mental state examination; NCSE = Neurobehavioral Cognitive Status; PASAT = Paced Auditory Serial Addition Test; Raven's PM = Progressive Matrices; RBMT = Rivermead Behavioral Memory Test; SADI = Self-Awareness of Deficit Interview; TMT = Trial Making Test; TONI-3 = Test of Nonverbal Intelligence–3rd Edition; WFT = Word Fluency Test; WM = Working Memory graphics have advanced to the point of presenting high-fidelity three-dimensional images through stereo vision. This technology allows precise presentation and control of stimuli across different sensory modalities, such as haptic, visual, auditory, olfactory, and even ambulatory conditions (Bohil et al. 2011). Recording, measurement, and computational modeling of these behavioral responses may help clinicians better understand and treat patient problems in their daily and complex routines (Wilson 2011, 2013) (Table 2).

Advances in virtual reality technology and improved access (via cost reductions; and ease of use interfaces) permit a wide range of physical, affective, and neurocognitive deficits to be clinically targeted. More importantly, these ecologically valid virtual environments can be used for assessment (Parsey and Schmitter-Edgecombe 2013) and rehabilitation (Koenig et al. 2009; Marusan et al. 2006; Parsons et al. 2009; Probosz et al. 2009). Virtual environments make use of symbols, stimuli, and concepts frequently experienced by the clinical population being assessed and therefore consider the sociocultural milieu and not only injury or illness-related information (Imam and Jarus 2014). As a result, virtual environments have been utilized in the treatment of psychological disorders. Anxiety disorders including social anxiety, specific phobias, and post-traumatic stress disorder have garnered the most attention and shown promising preliminary results (McCann et al. 2014; Motraghi et al. 2012, 2014). Virtual environments have the potential for the presentation of fear invoking stimuli across multiple sensory modalities which lends itself to traditional principles of graded exposure therapy (Parsons and Rizzo 2008). A virtual reality graded exposure therapy paradigm can update with contextually relevant information, based on an individual response or treating professional's preference. This form of in vivo exposure therapy would be predicted to be more efficacious than reliance upon imagination or other more passive approaches in selected patients, but well-controlled comparison studies have not been conducted. As vulnerable populations have greater rates of repeat traumas, this skill-based approach to preventative care holds extensive promise (Fortier et al. 2009; Neigh et al. 2009; Pineles et al. 2011).

The ability to create a visual representation of an emotion or pain experience in a virtual environment could potentially translate into improved awareness and understanding of such concepts (Keefe et al. 2012; Hoffman et al. 2011). In a similar fashion, virtual environments could serve as an adjunct treatment in non-pharmacological pain management treatment (Wender et al. 2010). For example, in using various imagery techniques and relaxation strategies, traditional psychological interventions can be enhanced with the visual feedback. Furthermore, visual feedback could help patients internalize a sense of control over and even modify the pain experience (Parsons and Trost 2014; Trost and Parsons 2014). This potential is exemplified by exploratory virtual reality techniques to address phantom pain after amputation. For example, a few groups have modified the classic mirror-box treatment, which creates the visual illusion of moving the missing limb, with less cognitively taxing VR that allows for a broader range of movement (Aphonso et al. 2002; Murray 2009).

Table 2 Virtual reality rehabilitation studies

Authors citation	Groups	Design and analyses	Experimental control intervention	Intervention duration	Outcome measures	Main findings
Castiello et al. (2004)	6 stroke patients (age 67–75) and 6 neurologically healthy controls (age unknown)	2 (group: stroke vs control) × 2 (task: sensory versus motor) × 2 (location: left versus right) between-subjects ANOVA	*Experimental*: Virtual objects were presented in different locations and subjects reported location of, or reached toward, objects; *Control*: None	3 sessions in one day	Task performance measured by percent successful detection of objects in sensory task and percent successful reaching trials in motor task	Neglect patients improved in ability to reach toward objects in affected hemisphere
Rand et al. (2009)	4 patients with remote history of stroke (age = 53–70)	Within-subjects; descriptive statistics (Mean, SD) pretest and post-test	*Experimental*: 10 sessions of VR intervention; *Control*: None	10 sessions, 60 min each, over 3 week period	MET test performance and clinician ratings of instrumental activities of daily living	Mean number of errors on MET-HV decreased from pre- to post-test and mean clinician ratings improved
Gamito et al. (2011)	TBI case study (age = 20)	Case study; nonparametric pairwise comparisons at pretest, intermediate, and post-test	*Experimental*: 10 sessions of VR consisting of finding one's way to and from a supermarket and finding figures embedded in scenery; *Control*: None	10 sessions	PASAT test performance	Subject's PASAT scores improved from pretest to post-test
Fong et al. (2010)	24 stroke, TBI, or other neurological injury patients (age = 18–63)	S; Mann–Whitney U-test (pre-test vs. post-test)	*Experimental*: 1 instruction session + 6 training sessions; *Control*: VR training in basic ATM skills	6 training sessions: 60 min each, 2/week for 3 weeks	Cognistat test performance and in vivo task completion (withdraw money from an ATM)	Improvement in reaction time and accuracy of cash withdrawals; no difference in money transfers

(continued)

Table 2 (continued)

Authors citation	Groups	Design and analyses	Experimental control intervention	Intervention duration	Outcome measures	Main findings
Optale et al. (2010)	15 older adults with memory deficits (mean age = 78.5) and 16 older adults in a randomized controlled trial (mean age = 81.6)	2 (group) × time mixed model ANOVA	*Experimental*: 36 initial sessions and 24 booster sessions; VR pathfinding exercise; *Control*: music therapy	36 initial sessions for 30 min each over 3 months and 24 booster sessions for 30 min each over 3 months	Test performance on MMSE, Digit Span, VSR test, phonemic verbal fluency, dual test performance, cognitive estimation test, clock drawing test, Geriatric Depression Scale clinician ADL ratings	There were improvements on all outcome measure tests, but no gains on clinician ratings
Jacoby et al. (2011)	6 TBI patients (age = 19–55) and 6 randomized controls (age = 19–55)	Within-subjects; Mann–Whitney U-test (pre-test vs. post-test)	*Experimental*: 10 sessions; *Control*: 10 standard occupational therapy sessions	10 sessions for 45 min each	MET-SV and executive function performance test	There was improvement on virtual task performance (shopping, cooking), improvement on real-world activities, and improvement on outcome tests (MET-SV and EFPT subtests)
Kim et al. (2011)	16 stroke patients (mean age = 66.5) and 13 randomized controls (mean age = 62)	Wilcoxon signed-rank test and within-subjects Mann–Whitney U-test (pre-test vs. post-test)	*Experimental*: 20 sessions alternating between ComCog exercises and IREX VR exercises; *Control*: 20 sessions including ComCog exercises	20 sessions for 30 min each over 4 weeks	CPT and visual span test performance; clinical rating on activities of daily living	Both groups improved on neuropsychological measures from pre- to post-test. VR group showed greater improvement than controls on CPT and backward VST

(continued)

Table 2 (continued)

Authors citation	Groups	Design and analyses	Experimental control intervention	Intervention duration	Outcome measures	Main findings
Man et al. (2012)	20 patients with questionable dementia (mean age = 80.3) and 14 randomized controls (mean age = 80.28)	Two-way repeated measures ANCOVA (groups x time)	*Experimental*: 10 sessions; *Control*: 10 sessions of paper-and-pencil memory exercises	10 sessions for 30 min each over 4 weeks	Test performance on clinical Dementia Rating Scale, MMSE, Fuld object memory evaluation, and clinician ratings of instrumental ADLs	The experimental (VR) group improved more on neuropsychological tests of memory and on self-report ratings of memory strategy implementation
Gerber et al. (2012)	19 patients with remote history of TBI (meanage = 50.4)	Within-subjects; descriptive statistics, correlations of standardized tests with improvement in time	*Experimental*: Single session of 4 VR tasks w/3 repetitions each. Tasks were to remove tools from a workbench, compose 3-letter words, make a sandwich, and hammer nails; *Control*: none	1 session with 4 tasks repeated 3 times	VR Task performance; Purdue Pegboard test performance; Clinician ratings of neurobehavioral symptom inventory and Boredom Propensity Scale	All subjects improved on task performance from pre-test to post-test
Dvorkin et al. (in press)	TBI case study (age = 20)	Case study; analysis of descriptive statistics	*Experimental*: 10 sessions of VR target acquisition exercise; *Control*: 10 sessions of standard OT and speech therapy	10 sessions, 40 min each	Task performance (duration of on-task behavior in each session)	Time on task improved earlier during VR sessions than on standard therapy

(continued)

Table 2 (continued)

Authors citation	Groups	Design and analyses	Experimental control intervention	Intervention duration	Outcome measures	Main findings
Larson et al. (2011)	18 patients with severe TBI (age = 23–56)	Within-subjects; descriptive statistics (mean, SD); repeated measures ANOVA of target acquisition time across trials	*Experimental*: 2 sessions of VR target acquisition exercise; *Control*: None	2 sessions for 40 min each over 2 days	Task performance (target acquisition time) and clinician rating on modified agitated behavior scale	There was improvement on target acquisition time task performance and improvement in clinician ratings (lower modified Agitated Behavior Scale scores)
Lloyd et al. (2009)	20 patients with brain injury or stroke (mean age = 42.5)	Within-subjects; paired sample t tests of errors by condition (errorless learning versus trial and error); ANOVA (time 1 versus time 2 versus time 3)	*Experimental*: One session of errorless learning route-finding exercise (demonstration trial and learning trials); *Control*: One session of trial-and-error learning route-finding exercise (demonstration trial and learning trials)	1 session	Task performance as measured by number of errors	Route recall was more accurate during experimental errorless learning condition than during control trial-and-error learning condition
Gagliardo et al. (2013)	10 patients with stroke (mean age = 54.8)	Within-subjects; descriptive statistics (mean, SD) and t tests (pre- and post-test)	*Experimental*: 40 sessions running Neuro@Home exercises (attention, categorization, and working memory); *Control*: None	40 sessions for 60 min each over 8 weeks	Task performance as measured by number of correct responses	There was improvement from pre- to post-test observed on all three exercises

(continued)

Table 2 (continued)

Authors citation	Groups	Design and analyses	Experimental control intervention	Intervention duration	Outcome measures	Main findings
Devos et al. (2009)	42 patients with stroke and 41 randomized controls (mean age = 54)	Nonparametric statistical comparison (baseline, post-test, follow-up)	*Experimental*: 15 sessions in VR simulator running 12 driving scenarios; *Control*: 15 sessions playing commercially available games involving cognitive skills required by driving	15 sessions for 60 min each	Test performance on Test Ride for Investigating Practical fitness to drive (TRIP)—Belgian version	Both groups improved on all aspects of on-road performance; VR group showed greater improvements in overall on-road performance
Sorita et al. (2012)	13 TBI patients (mean age = 31.1) and 14 randomized controls (mean age = 31.5)	Between-subjects; descriptive statistics (mean, SD); ANOVA and Mann–Whitney U–test for # of errors by task (real versus VR)	*Experimental*: 4 sessions of Barrash Route-learning task in virtual environment; *Control*: 4 sessions of Barrash route-learning task in urban environment	4 sessions for 15 min each over 2 days	Test performance on sketch map test, map recognition test, and scene arrangement test	The real environment group scored better than VR group only on scene arrangement; VR group performed as well as real environment group on sketch map test and map recognition test

(continued)

Table 2 (continued)

Authors citation	Groups	Design and analyses	Experimental control intervention	Intervention duration	Outcome measures	Main findings
Yip and Man (2013)	19 acquired brain injury patients (mean age = 37.8) and 18 randomized controls (mean age = 38.5)	Between-subjects; descriptive statistics (mean, SD); paired and independent t tests	*Experimental*: 12 sessions of VR; *Control*: Reading and table game activities	12 sessions for 30–45 min each, twice per week for 5–6 weeks	Test performance on Cambridge Prospective Memory Test–Chinese Version, Hong Kong List Learning Test, Frontal Assessment Battery, Word Fluency Test–Chinese Version, Color Trails Test and in vivo task completion (remembering events)	The VR group improved for both tests and on in vivo task completion
Man, Poon and Lam (2013)	20 TBI patients (age = 18–55) and 20 randomized controls (age = 18–55)	Between-subjects; descriptive statistics (mean, SD); repeated measures ANOVA	*Experimental*: 12 sessions of VR; *Control*: 12 sessions of psycho-educational vocational training system	12 sessions for 20–25 min each	Test performance on WCST and Tower of London Test; In vivo task completion	The VR group improved more on WCST; there were no differences between groups on employment conditions

Virtual environments are also increasingly being used for the management of behavioral problems and social skills training with developmental disorders and psychiatric populations (Kandalaft et al. 2013; Park et al. 2011; Parsons et al. 2009; Rus-Calafell et al. 2014). Such programs may use virtual humans and incorporate programming that allows the treating professional to track desired and undesired responses/interactions. Coaching can also be integrated to capitalize on real-time feedback. Again, the appeal of creating a more ecologically valid and modifiable therapy session speaks to the exciting potential of VR technologies with even the most challenging of populations.

Within the psychological specialties more focused upon the detection, diagnosis, and treatment of neurocognitive deficits, virtual reality has increasingly been seen as a potential aid to assist in detection and treatment of neurocognitive impairments (Koenig et al. 2009; Marusan et al. 2006; Probosz et al. 2009). Specifically, virtual environment-based assessments and rehabilitation programs have been explored in depth following brain injury. For example, virtual environments have been developed that assess way-finding skills and then provide training of spatial orientation skills via programming that allows increased complexity as participants progress though the program (Koenig et al. 2009). Virtual reality research has been transitioning more recently to a focus upon clinical treatment of cognitive disorders (Imam and Jarus 2014; Larson et al. 2014; Spreij 2014). This includes innovative rehabilitation of stroke patients to reduce paresis and dyspraxias that impact expressive speech via multisensorial brain stimulation (Probosz et al. 2009). Various researchers have promoted the use of mental rotation paradigms—felt to be an essential skill in multiple cognitive functions—in the neurorehabilitation setting to enhance memory, reasoning, and problem solving in everyday life (Marusan et al. 2006; Podzebenko et al. 2005). Some neuropsychological interventions have been translated into virtual formats, such as the VR version of the Multiple Errands Test (MET; Burgess et al. 2006). This virtual environment has been used to provide training the executive functions: strategic planning, cognitive flexibility, and inhibition. The MET has been validated on stroke and TBI patients (Jacoby et al. 2013). These attempts at clinical treatment represent the next stage of transitioning VR from research laboratories to mainstream interventions.

8.1 *Brain–Computer Interfaces for Rehabilitation*

In an attempt to widen the utility of computer-assisted devices in rehabilitation, brain–computer interface (BCI) technology has generated a great deal of interest (Collinger et al. 2013; Ikegami et al. 2011; Mak and Wolpaw 2009; Shih et al. 2012). From a rehabilitation psychology standpoint, BCI technology can be envisioned as a possible tool for cognitive assessment and intervention, pain management, stress management, and leisure activity exploration. BCI has been described as linking brain patterns to motor or mental intent in an effort to bypass the reliance upon peripheral nerves and muscles that may be compromised (Cincotti 2008;

Millian 2010). To date, a primary focus of BCIs has revolved around motor-based activity and communication. Case examples and a few small studies have highlighted how BCI can be applied to neurorehabilitation populations such as stroke, amyotrophic lateral sclerosis, locked-in syndrome, and SCI (Enzinger et al. 2008; Ikegami et al. 2011; Kaufmann et al. 2013; Kiper et al. 2011; Schreuder et al. 2013; Salisbury et al. 2015). Still, much of the technology is not ready for mainstream implementation, and the various challenges inherent with such interventions have been well detailed (see Danziger 2014; Hill et al. 2014; Millian et al. 2010; Mak and Wolpaw 2009; Shih et al. 2012).

The potential of BCI beyond motor and communication augmentation has received less attention, but is increasingly viewed as a fruitful area of application for assessment (Allanson and Fairclough 2004; Nacke et al. 2011; Wu et al. 2010; Wu et al. 2014) and training (Berka et al. 2007; Parsons and Courtney 2011; Parsons and Reinebold 2012). This avenue of BCI research would be consistent with increasing support that psychological, social, and nonmotor-based factors are key aspects in perceived quality of life following injury (Tate 2002). Studies have begun exploring the use of BCI in nonmedical populations to recognize emotions (Inventado et al. 2011; Jatupaiboon et al. 2013; McMahan et al. 2015a; Pham and Tran 2012), assess specific psychological symptoms (Dutta et al. 2013), mediate artistic expression (Fraga et al. 2013), and evaluate cognitive workload (Anderson et al. 2011; Allison et al. 2010; McMahan et al. 2015b, c; Treder and Blankertz 2010).

Interest in BCI among individuals with SCI, particularly for augmentation of motor functioning, has been detailed in the literature (Collinger et al. 2013; Rupp 2014; Tate 2011). In a recent review of the use of BCI in persons with SCI, Rupp (2014) concluded that while BCIs seem to be a promising assistive technology for individuals with high SCI, systematic investigations are needed to obtain a realistic understanding of the feasibility of using BCIs in a clinical setting. Rupp identified three potentially limiting factors related to feasibility that should be considered: (1) availability of technology for signal acquisition and processing; (2) individual differences in user characteristics, and (3) infrastructure and healthcare-related constraints.

8.2 Challenges in Technology Application

The clear enthusiasm for technology must be tempered by an acknowledgement of potential barriers. The key concerns involve issues surrounding the utility of virtual environments, management of technological problems, and financial feasibility. Many virtual environments used in clinical studies are not commercially available, and only a few research laboratories have access to them. Further, a number of virtual reality systems use arrays of screens to allow for full-body interactions, costing many thousands of dollars. From a utility standpoint, projects typically range from simple visual stimuli to more advanced depictions of real-world settings. Still, there may be a need for more realistic visual paradigms. Studies are needed to assess the impact of various levels of stimulus fidelity, immersion, and presence upon rehabilitation efficacy. Only with such studies will we know whether further advances in graphic feedback naturalism are important for the progression of virtual interventions within the realm of psychological care and assessment.

The studies discussed in this chapter involved collaboration among clinicians and experts in the area of technology and psychology who can provide any needed assistance in a timely manner. The presence of an information technology support staff is also typically available as part of the hospital system. Further, during most studies, there are times when technology does not work properly resulting in delayed intervention or the need to reschedule. Such complications speak to the challenges of implementing interventions dependent upon technology within inpatient and outpatient rehabilitation settings. Any delays in these fast paced settings, requiring the coordination of various disciplines, can be quite disruptive to the milieu. The need to train staff and have support service available is paramount when considering using advanced technology as a core component of a rehabilitation program.

Finally, the financial feasibility of virtual environments will largely be determined by future outcome research. Unless there is support for clinical gain in the form of improved outcomes, decreased complications, or secondary decline in medical costs (e.g., decreased length of stay or less use of future medical services), cost concerns may prohibit adoption of such technologies. Mainstream implementation in rehabilitation would be a financial challenge considering the trend of declining reimbursement for clinical services and emphasis on bundled services with recent healthcare changes. The initial cost must be coupled with the previously mentioned planning for technology maintenance, staff training, and statistician support by individuals trained to analyze the data formats associated with this technology. Additionally, virtual environments require a private space that limits distractions that are all too frequent in rehabilitation settings. Private rooms or dedicated areas for such interventions would be ideal yet allocation of such space is often a challenge.

8.3 Summary

As highlighted in the reviewed studies, the potential for advanced technology appears far reaching in the field of neuropsychological rehabilitation. Ultimately, more sophisticated programming may foster greater immersive experiences tailored to the patient's therapeutic goals. Thus, invaluable real-time clinician feedback could guide targeted therapeutic interventions that relate to daily situations. With repeat use, immersive training environments may capitalize on procedural memory that often remains relatively better preserved among patients with brain damage (Imam and Jarus 2014; Larson et al. 2014; Spreij 2014). Virtual environment paradigms could be systematically altered to meet changing patient care needs and goals based on the course of recovery. Furthermore, integration of patient-specific training prompts and cues may improve patient self-monitoring, guide problem solving, and promote less reliance on rehabilitation staff and caregivers (Christansen et al. 1998; Imam and Jarus 2014; Larson et al. 2014; Spreij 2014). The core challenges to bringing technology into a multidisciplinary rehabilitation milieu include the initial costs of collaboration with research laboratories developing (and validating) the technologies, staff training, and confirming that these interventions have superior outcomes to traditional care.

Part IV
Conclusions

Chapter 8
Future Prospects for a Computational Neuropsychology

Neuropsychology is poised for transformations of its concepts and methods, leveraging advances in neuroimaging, the human genome project, psychometric theory, and information technologies. It is argued that a paradigm shift toward evidence-based science and practice can be enabled by innovations.

—Robert Bilder (2011)

Throughout this book, there is an emphasis upon the importance of (1) enhancing ecological validity via a move from construct-driven assessments to tests that are representative of real-world functions—it is argued that this will proffer results that are generalizable for prediction of the functional performance across a range of situations; (2) the potential of computerized neuropsychological assessment devices (CNADs) to enhance: standardization of administration, accuracy of timing presentation and response latencies, ease of administration and data collection, and reliable and randomized presentation of stimuli for repeat administrations; and (3) novel technologies to allow for precise presentation and control of dynamic perceptual stimuli—provides ecologically valid assessments that combine the veridical control and rigor of laboratory measures with a verisimilitude that reflects real-life situations.

Neuropsychologists are increasingly interested in the potential for advanced psychometrics, online computer-automated assessment methods, and neuroinformatics for large-sample implementation and the development of collaborative neuropsychological knowledgebases (Bilder 2011; Jagaroo 2009). In this chapter, the focus will be upon using technology to develop repositories for linking neuropsychological assessment results with data from neuroimaging, psychophysiology, and genetics. It is argued that clinical neuropsychology is ready to embrace technological advances and experience a transformation of its concepts and methods. To develop this aspect of Neuropsychology 3.0, clinical neuropsychologists should incorporate findings from the human genome project, advances in psychometric theory, and information technologies. Enhanced evidence-based science and praxes is possible if neuropsychologists do the following: (1) develop formal definitions of neuropsychological concepts and tasks in cognitive ontologies;

T.D. Parsons, *Clinical Neuropsychology and Technology*,
DOI 10.1007/978-3-319-31075-6_8

(2) create collaborative neuropsychological knowledgebases; and (3) design novel assessment methods. These focus areas have been reinforced by a growing body of literature calling for increased emphasis upon neuroinformatics in the future of clinical neuropsychology (Bilder 2011; Jararoo 2009; Nichols and Pohl 2015).

1 Formal Definitions of Neuropsychological Concepts and Tasks in Cognitive Ontologies

1.1 Covariance Among Neuropsychology Measures of Differing Domains

An important growth area for neuropsychology is the capacity for sharing knowledge gained from neuropsychological assessments with related disciplines. Obstacle to this shared knowledge approach includes the covariance among measures and the lack of operational definitions for key concepts and their interrelations. The covariance that exists among neuropsychological measures designed to assess overlapping cognitive domains limits categorical specification into well-delineated domains. As such, neuropsychological assessment batteries may be composed of multiple tests that measure essentially the same performance attributes. According to Dodrill (1997), poor test specificity may be revealed in the median correlations for common neuropsychological tests. For example, Dodrill asserts that while the median correlation within domain groupings on a test was 0.52, the median correlation between groupings was 0.44. From this, Dodrill extrapolates that the tests are not unambiguously domain specific because the median correlations should be notably higher for the within groupings and lower for the between groupings. Consequently, the principal assessment measures used by practitioners may not be quantifying domains to a level of specificity that accounts for the covariance among the measures (Dickinson and Gold 2008; Parsons et al. 2005). Future studies should look at multivariate approaches found in neuroinformatics that will allow for elucidation of the covariance information latent in neuropsychological assessment data.

1.2 Lack of Back-Compatibility in Traditional Print Publishing

An additional concern is that revisions found in traditional print publishing like the Wechsler Adult Intelligence Scale (WAIS) and the Wechsler Memory Scale (WMS) have fallen short in terms of back-compatibility that may invalidate clinical interpretations. Loring and Bauer (2010) contend that the significant alterations in the structure and content of the WAIS-IV/WMS-IV may decrease the potential for accurate patient classification if algorithms developed using earlier versions (e.g., WAIS III) are employed. While the revisions to the Wechsler scales offer enhanced psychometric validity, there are presently insufficient clinical data in neurologic populations to assure that they are appropriate for use in neuropsychological evaluations. This lack of back-compatibility is especially disappointing given the fact that even modest updates to paper-and-pencil batteries take years. The use of modern psychometric theory and neuroinformatics enables preservation of robust back-compatibility with prior test versions and enables the introduction of new content and new constructs. This will become increasingly important as evidence-based medicine is systematically adopted within the context of clinical neuropsychology (e.g., Chelune 2010). There is increasing interest among neuropsychologists in adopting consolidated standards for the reporting of clinical trials that include neuropsychological endpoints that will ultimately serve to strengthen the empirical evidence and scientific base of neuropsychology (Loring and Bowden 2014; Miller et al. 2014).

1.3 Neuropsychology's Need for Cognitive Ontologies

In addition to novel stochastic approaches to limiting covariance among measures, there is need for formalizing neuropsychological concepts into ontologies that offer formal descriptions of content domains. While ontologies abound in other biomedical disciplines, neuropsychological assessment lags in its development of formal ontologies (Bilder et al. 2009; Jararoo 2009; Price and Friston 2005). The idea of "ontologies" in neuroinformatics reflects the formal specification of entities that exist in a domain and the relations among them (Lenartowicz et al. 2010). A given ontology contains designations of separate entities along with a specification of ontological relations among entities that can include hierarchical relations (e.g., "is-a" or "part-of") or spatiotemporal relations (e.g., "preceded-by" or "contained-within"). These knowledge structures allow for consistent representations across models, which can facilitate communication among domains by providing an objective, concise, common, and controlled vocabulary. This consistency also allows for enhanced interoperability and provision of links among levels of analysis. Such ontologies have become central within many areas of neuroscience. In the realm of neuropsychology, several projects have been initiated to cognitive ontologies at the Consortium for Neuropsychiatric Phenomics (www.phenomics.ucla.edu). This consortium aims to enable more effective collaboration and facilitation of knowledge sharing about cognitive phenotypes to other levels of biological knowledge (Bilder et al. 2009).

Although there is great need for neuropsychology to develop cognitive ontologies for data garnered from neuropsychological assessment data, there are some roadblocks. Neurocognitive functioning involves interrelated dimensional constructs that refer to a hypothetical cognitive resource whose existence is inferred from research findings (Burgess et al. 2006). Take for example "working memory."

Instead of being a unitary concept, working memory is a latent construct that is estimated in a given study by one or more neuropsychological measures (directly observable behavioral output). Sabb et al. (2008) developed a collaborative annotation database (www.Phenowiki.org) to facilitate representation and sharing of empirical information. As a proof of concept, they examined over 478 articles to evaluate the relationship among estimates of heritability, behavioral measures, and component constructs of executive function. After applying a phrase search algorithm to isolate key terms most commonly used in the neuropsychology literature, they isolated a set of five terms that summarized the literature on executive functions: "cognitive control," "response inhibition," "response selection," "task switching," and "working memory." The latter four terms were selected because of their frequency of co-occurrence with the term "cognitive control." Further, these terms revealed high internal consistency for their indicators and associated heritability measures. This suggests that they may effectively capture distinct components of executive functions. Conversely, Sabb et al. (2008) also found that the same indicators associated with the term "cognitive control" had also been associated with the other constructs. While some suggest that this may reflect shared neural systems that can be important in establishing distinct cognitive constructs (Lenartowicz et al. 2010), there is also the possibility that the neurocognitive assessments themselves may be to blame. Although for some measures there was good consistency across studies in the use of a specific indicator (e.g., Digit Span Backwards only used one indicator: correct recall of digits), other measures had considerable variation in the specific indicator used (e.g., each of three studies reporting Go/No-go performance used different indicators and versions of the test). The result is an inconsistency that greatly increases the difficulty of pooling data and interpreting results across studies. That said, the work of Sabb and colleagues (2008) to develop a collaborative annotation database offers an approach to collaborative knowledge building. Such work enables neuropsychologists in their selection and prioritization of endophenotypes for translational research.

2 Web 2.0 and Collaborative Neuropsychological Knowledgebases

In addition to shared definitions of neuropsychological constructs, the development of ontologies enables systematic aggregation of neuropsychological knowledge into shared databases. Technological developments in the use of the Internet for collective knowledge building are apparent in Web 2.0 practices that involve specialized Web tools (O'Reilly 2007). Web 2.0 represents a trend in open platform Internet use that incorporates user-driven online networks and knowledgebases. While there are no large Internet-based repositories for neuropsychological data, efforts have been made to allow users to input individual test scores via a Web portal (www.neuropsychnorms.com) and obtain immediate reports comparing a patient's neuropsychological data to published findings (Mitrushina et al. 2005). Another online application is the Cognitive Atlas (http://www.cognitiveatlas.org/) which was developed to address the need for a collaborative knowledgebase that captures the comprehensive collection of conceptual structures within neuropsychology (Miller et al. 2010). To do this, the Cognitive Atlas project describes the "parts" and processes of the cognitive functioning in a manner similar to descriptions of the cell's component parts and functions in gene ontology. While this project does offer promise, it is still in its infancy and requires development if it is to provide a solid basis for annotation of neuropsychological (e.g., neuroimaging of cognitive processes) data. Further, like other collaborative knowledgebases (e.g., Wikipedia), its realization will depend on the involvement of a large number of interested neuropsychologists (Poldrack 2010).

Some neuropsychologists are calling for greater inclusion of Web-based neurocognitive assessments (Bilder 2011; Jagaroo 2009). The exponential increase in access to computers and the Internet across the life span allows for interactive Web-based neuropsychological assessments (Bart et al. 2014; Raz et al. 2014; Wagner et al. 2010). It is important to note that some neuropsychologists have concerns that Web-based neuropsychological assessment devises will somehow replace human neuropsychologists and/or overlook significant clinical information. However, Web-based neuropsychological assessments are just tools for enhanced presentation and logging of stimuli. When properly used, Web-based assessments can greatly enhance the assessment in terms of precision and rapid implementation of adaptive algorithms. Online neurocognitive assessment may enhance dissemination of testing because tests could be administered in a variety of settings (e.g., office, home, school), at different times of the day, and by multiple persons at the same time.

A distinct improvement of computer timing precision is that it allows for enactment of procedures from the human neurosciences that rely on more refined task operations and trial-by-trial analyses that may be more sensitive and specific to individual differences in neural system function. Web-based computerized assessments have the capacity for adaptive testing strategies that are likely to multiply efficiency in construct measurement (Bilder 2011). In one study, Gibbons and colleagues (2008) found that the use of a computerized adaptive test resulted in a 95 % average reduction in the number of items administered. The potential of adaptive Web-based neurocognitive assessment protocols can be seen in the capacity to large sample of participants in relatively short periods of time. While there may be concerns that the neuropsychologist cannot be sure of the identity of the test-takers or that they are performing tasks as instructed, validity indicators, online video surveillance, and anthropometric identifiers can be included to remove these concerns. For example, algorithms can be implemented that allow for item-level response monitoring and automated consistency checks. Further, neuroinformatics algorithms are available that will allow for the detection of outlying response patterns of uncertain validity.

One of the most widely used and validated of the new Web-based neuropsychology batteries is WebNeuro. The battery includes assessments of the following domains of neurocognitive function: sensorimotor, memory, executive planning, attention, and emotion perception (social cognition; Mathersul et al. 2009; Silverstein et al. 2007; Williams et al. 2009). In addition to cognitive assessments, the WebNeuro battery also includes affective assessments of emotion recognition and identification: immediate explicit identification followed by implicit recognition (within a priming protocol). The WebNeuro protocol was developed as a Web-based version of the IntegNeuro computerized battery. The IntegNeuro battery was developed by a consortium of scientists interested in establishing a standardized international called Brain Resource International Database (BRID; Gordon 2003; Gordon et al. 2005; Paul et al. 2005). IntegNeuro and WebNeuro are part of the BRID project's aim to move beyond outdated approaches to aggregating neuropsychological knowledgebases and develop standardized testing approaches that facilitate the integration of normally independent sources of data (genetic, neuroimaging, psychophysiological, neuropsychological, and clinical). The WebNeuro platform allows for data to be acquired internationally with a centralized database infrastructure for storage and manipulation of these data.

While the normative findings for a Web-based neuropsychological assessment are promising (Mathersul et al. 2009; Silverstein et al. 2007; Williams et al. 2009), the greatest potential appears to be WebNeuro's relation to Brain Resource International Database. The data from WebNeuro are linked to insights and correlations in a standardized and integrative international database (see www.BrainResource.com; www.BRAINnet.com). The WebNeuro data are incorporated as additional (in addition to other markers: genetic, neuroimaging, psychophysiological, neuropsychological, and clinical) clinical markers that can be incorporated into databases as new marker discoveries emerge from personalized medicine.

3 Construct-Driven and Function-Led Redux

Earlier in this book, we discussed the limitations of construct-driven tasks and the need for function-led neuropsychological assessments. While the original goal of many neuropsychological assessments was lesion localization, there is increasing need for assessments of everyday functioning. This new role for neuropsychologists has resulted in increased emphasis upon the ecological validity of neuropsychological instruments (Chaytor et al. 2006). As a result, neuropsychologists have been compelled to move beyond the limited generalizability of results found in construct-driven measures to tests that more closely approximate real-world function. The function-led approach allows the neuropsychologist to move from construct-driven assessments to tests that are representative of real-world functions and proffer results that are generalizable for prediction of the functional performance across a range of situations.

A number of investigators have argued that performance on traditional neuropsychological construct-driven tests (e.g., Wisconsin Card Sorting Test, Stroop) has little correspondence to activities of daily living (Bottari et al. 2009; Manchester et al. 2004; Sbordone 2008). According to Chan et al. (2008), most of these traditional construct-driven measures assess at the veridicality level and do not capture the complexity of response required in the many multistep tasks found in everyday activities. The "function-led approach" to creating neuropsychological assessments will include neuropsychological models that proceed from directly observable everyday behaviors backward to examine the ways in which a sequence of actions leads to a given behavior in normal functioning and the ways in which that behavior might become disrupted. These neuropsychological assessments should meet the usual standards of reliability, but discussions of validity should include both sensitivity to brain dysfunction and generalizability to real-world function.

However, this raises a problem for the development of cognitive ontologies and collaborative knowledgebases. These approaches rely on construct-driven and computer-automated neuropsychological assessment devices. One approach would be to have two streams of research: (1) use traditional (paper-and-pencil and computerized neuropsychological assessment devices) construct-driven assessments to develop cognitive ontologies and collaborative knowledgebases and (2) use virtual environment-based function-led assessments for return-to-capacity decisions. While this approach seems to have promise in the short term, it seems to miss the rich data that could come from an approach that used simulation technologies as a special case of computerized neuropsychological assessment devise.

3.1 *Virtual Environments for Assessing Polymorphisms*

While little neuroinformatic work has included virtual reality immersion, neuroimaging studies utilizing virtual environments have been used to delineate brain circuits involved in sustained anxiety to unpredictable stressors in humans. In a study of contextual fear conditioning, Alvarez et al. (2008) used a Virtual Office and fMRI to investigate whether the same brain mechanisms that underlie contextual fear conditioning in animals are also found in humans. Results suggested that contextual fear conditioning in humans was consistent with preclinical findings in rodents. Specifically, findings support hot affective processing in that the medial aspect of the amygdala had afferent and efferent connections that included input from the orbitofrontal cortex. In another study using a Virtual Office, Glotzbach-Schoon et al. (2013) assessed the modulation of contextual fear conditioning and extinction by 5HTTLPR (serotonin-transporter-linked polymorphic region) and NPSR1 (neuropeptide S receptor 1) polymorphisms. Results revealed that both the 5HTTLPR and the NPSR1 polymorphisms were related to hot affective (implicit) processing via a fear potentiated startle. There was no effect of the 5HTTLPR polymorphism on cold cognitive (explicit) ratings of anxiety. Given the ability of virtual environments to place participants in experimentally controlled yet contextually relevant situations, there appears to be promise in applying this platform to future translational studies into contextual fear conditioning. The ability to differentiate cold cognitive from hot affective processing could be used to develop ontologies for future research.

3.2 *Neuropsychological Assessment Using the Internet and Metaverse Platforms*

A further development of the emerging Neuropsychological Assessment 3.0 paradigm for clinical neuropsychologists may be found in the expanding Metaverse of virtual worlds found on the Internet. Technological advances in computing and the World Wide Web in the last couple decades (Abbate 1999) have allowed for Internet-based virtual worlds testing with potentially more diverse samples in respect to socioeconomic status, sex, and age than traditional samples that are often drawn from undergraduate university students (Gosling et al. 2004). Virtual worlds are made up of online communities in which persons interrelate in simulated environments. The continued progress in the development of robust technologies such as more rapid and secure Internet connections has led to the ever-increasing interest in social networks (Boulos and Wheeler 2007). Parsons (2012) described a number of advantages of Internet-delivered online virtual worlds:

- Systematic presentation of cognitive tasks targeting both construct-driven and function-led neuropsychological performance beyond what is currently available using traditional computerized neuropsychological assessment devices.
- Reliability of function-led neuropsychological assessment and treatment of affective and cognitive disorders can be enhanced in online virtual worlds by better control of the perceptual environment, more consistent stimulus presentation, and more precise and accurate scoring.
- Online virtual worlds may also improve the validity of neurocognitive measurements via the increased quantification of discrete behavioral responses, allowing for the identification of more specific cognitive domains.
- Online virtual worlds could allow for cognition and affect to be assessed and treated in situations that are more ecologically valid. Participants can be evaluated in an online virtual world that simulates the real world, not a contrived testing environment.
- Online virtual worlds offer the option to produce and distribute identical "standard" simulation environments to large samples in which performance can be measured and treated.

Within such digital scenarios, normative data can be accumulated for performance comparisons needed for assessment/diagnosis and for treatment/rehabilitation purposes. In this manner, reusable archetypical online virtual worlds constructed for one purpose can also be applied for applications addressing other clinical targets.

One example is Second Life (SL; Linden Lab, San Francisco, Calif.), which proffers tools (i.e., scripting and graphics) and environments that facilitate the creation of virtual environments that can be made available to potentially thousands of research subjects in an economical manner (Bainbridge 2007). The population of users in Second Life has reached more than six million virtual citizens (Boulous 2007). Virtual worlds provide users to experience social interaction as they participate in individual and group activities. The virtual world Second Life proffers multiple medical and health educational projects (Boulos et al. 2007). Although these programs focus primarily on the dissemination of medical information and the training of clinicians, a handful of private islands in Second Life (e.g., Brigadoon for Asperger's syndrome; Live2give for cerebral palsy) have been created for therapeutic purposes. In a recent article by Gorini et al. (2008), the authors describe such sites and the development and implementation of a form of tailored immersive e-therapy in which current technologies (e.g., virtual worlds; bio and activity sensors; and personal digital assistants) facilitate the interaction between real and 3-D virtual worlds and may increase treatment efficacy. In a recent article in science, Bainbridge (2007) discussed the robust potential of virtual worlds for research in the social and behavioral sciences. For social and behavioral science researchers, virtual worlds reflect developing cultures, each with an emerging ethos and supervenient social institutions (for a discussion of supervenience see Hare 1984). In addition to the general social phenomena emerging from virtual world communities, virtual worlds provide novel opportunities for studying them. According to Bainbridge (2007), virtual worlds proffer environments that facilitate the creation of online laboratories that can recruit potentially thousands of research subjects in an automated and economically feasible fashion. Virtual worlds like Second Life offer scripting and graphics tools that allow even a novice computer user the means necessary for building a virtual laboratory. Perhaps even more important is the fact that social interactions in online virtual worlds (e.g., Second Life) appear to reflect social norms and interactions found in the physical world (Yee et al. 2007). Finally, there is the potential of virtual worlds to improve access to medical rehabilitation. Klinger and Weiss (2009) describe the evolution of virtual worlds along to two dimensions: (1) the number of users and (2) the distance between the users. According to Klinger and Weiss, single user and locally used virtual worlds have developed into three additional venues: (1) multiple users located in the same setting, (2) single users remotely located, and (3) multiple users remotely located. According to Klinger and Weiss, single user, locally operated virtual worlds will continue to be important for rehabilitation within a clinical or educational setting. However, the literature, to date, has been limited to descriptions of system development and reports of small pilot studies (Brennan et al. 2009). It is anticipated that this trend is changing and future years will see evidence of the effectiveness of such virtual worlds for therapy.

4 Computational Neuropsychology

4.1 Virtual Environments as a Special Case of Computerized Neuropsychological Assessment Devices

In this book, we have looked at the development of technologies for neuropsychological assessment. An argument has been made that ecologically valid assessments should include both cognitive constructs and functions in affect sensitive simulations that represent real-world functions. One approach suggested in Neuropsychological Assessment 3.0 was to extend computerized neuropsychological assessment devices to virtual environments. Virtual environments represent a special case of computerized neuropsychological assessment devices because they have enhanced computational capacities for administration efficiency, stimulus presentation, automated logging of responses, and data analytic processing. Since VEs allow for precise presentation and control of dynamic perceptual stimuli, they can provide ecologically valid assessments that combine the veridical control and rigor of laboratory measures with a verisimilitude that reflects real-life situations. Additionally, the enhanced computation power allows for increased accuracy in the recording of neurobehavioral responses in a perceptual environment that systematically presents complex stimuli. Such simulation technology appears to be distinctively suited for the development of ecologically valid environments, in which three-dimensional objects are presented in a consistent and precise manner (Schultheis et al. 2002). VE-based neuropsychological assessments can provide a balance between naturalistic observation and the need for exacting control over key variables (Campbell et al. 2009; Parsons 2011). In summary, VE-based neuropsychological assessments allow for real-time measurement of multiple neurocognitive abilities in order to assess complex sets of skills and behaviors that may more closely resemble real-world functional abilities (Matheis et al. 2007).

4.2 Extending Computer-Automated Construct-Driven Ontologies to Virtual Environments

A possible place to start for extending cognitive ontologies from computer-automated neuropsychological assessment devices is to extend the annotations to construct-driven virtual environments like the virtual apartment Stroop task. The virtual apartment superimposes construct-driven stimuli (e.g., Stroop and CPT) onto a large television set in a virtual living room (Henry et al. 2012). A series of construct-driven stimuli appear on the flatscreen television with in the environment, while a female voice states the names of colors (red, blue, and green). Participants are instructed to click a mouse button as quickly as possible when the spoken color matches the color of the rectangle on the virtual flatscreen television and to withhold a response if the colors do not match. A total of 144 stimuli are presented, with 72 targets and 72 nontargets. During the task, distracters appear in different field of view locations in the environment. Some distracters are audio–visual: School bus passing on the street and a sports utility vehicle viewed through window on the right; iPhone ringing and vibrating on the table (in front of participant); and toy robot moving and making noise on the floor (center). Auditory distractors include the following: crumple paper (left); drop pencil (left); doorbell (left); clock (left) vacuum cleaner (right); jack hammer (right); sneeze (left); and jet noise (center). Visual distractors include the following: paper airplane (flying from left to right in front of the participant) and woman walking in the kitchen (center). The conditions were designed to assess reaction times (simple and complex), selective attention (matching the auditory and visual stimuli), and external interference control (environmental distracters). Computational neuropsychologists could compare construct-driven virtual environment performance with and without distractors to computer-automated neuropsychological assessment devices.

4.3 Construct-Driven and Function-Led Virtual Environments for Hot and Cold Processing

Recently, virtual environments have been applied to the assessment of both "Cold" and "Hot" processes using combat-related scenarios (Armstrong et al. 2013; Parsons et al. 2013). The addition of virtual environments allows neuropsychologists to move beyond the ethical concerns related to placing participants into real-world situations with hazardous contexts. The goal of these platforms is to assess the impact of hot affective arousal upon cold cognitive processes. For example, Parsons et al. (2013) have developed a Virtual Reality Stroop Task (VRST) in which the participant is immersed in a simulated High Mobility Multipurpose Wheeled Vehicle (HMMWV) and passes through zones with alternating low threat (driving down a deserted desert road) and high threat (gunfire, explosions, and shouting among other stressors), while construct-driven stimuli (e.g., Stroop stimuli) were presented on the windshield. They found that the high-threat zones created a greater level of psychophysiological arousal (heart rate, skin conductance, respiration) than did low-threat zones. Findings from these studies also provided data regarding the potential of military relevant virtual environments for the measurement of supervisory attentional processing (Parsons et al. 2013). Analyses of the effect of threat level on the color–word and interference scores resulted in a main effect of threat level and condition. Findings from the virtual environment paradigm support the perspective that (1) high information load tasks used for cold cognitive processing may be relatively automatic in controlled circumstances—for example, in low-threat zones with little activity; and (2) the total available processing capacities may be decreased by other hot affective factors such as arousal (e.g., threat zones with a great deal of activity). In a replication study, Armstrong et al. (2013) established the preliminary convergent and discriminant validity of the VRST with an active duty military sample.

In addition to virtual environment-based neuropsychological assessments using driving simulators, a number of other military relevant virtual environments have emerged for neurocognitive assessment of Cold and Hot processes. For example, Parsons et al. (2012, 2014) immersed participants into a Middle Eastern city and exposed participants to a cold cognitive processing task (e.g., paced auditory serial addition test) as they followed a fire team on foot through safe and ambush (e.g., hot affective—bombs, gunfire, screams, and other visual and auditory forms of threat) zones in a Middle Eastern city. In one measure of the battery, a route-learning task, each zone is preceded by a zone marker, which serves as a landmark to assist in remembering the route. The route-learning task is followed immediately by the navigation task in which the participants were asked to return to the starting point of their tour through the city. Courtney et al. (2013) found that the inclusion of hot affective stimuli (e.g., high-threat zones) resulted in a greater level of psychophysiological arousal (heart rate, skin conductance, respiration) and decreased performance on cold cognitive processes than did low-threat zones. Results from active duty military (Parsons et al. 2012) and civilian (Parsons and Courtney 2014) populations offer preliminary support for the construct validity of the VR-PASAT as a measure of attentional processing. Further, results suggest that the VR-PASAT may provide some unique information related to hot affective processing not tapped by traditional Cold attentional processing tasks.

While the above virtual environments fall short of a truly function-led environment in that they include construct-driven stimuli, they go beyond other construct-driven virtual environments because they include affective stimuli. It may be possible to take this paradigm and extend it to the ontological annotation of other executive control tasks. This would involve new neuroinformatic approaches to deal with the massively enhanced dataset. That said, neuroinformatics for neuropsychologists is in its earliest stages and it will not be long before collaborative knowledgebases will be developed for construct-driven assessments. A computational neuropsychological approach that uses artificial neural networks and machine learning could allow for enhanced assessment of construct-driven stimuli embedded in virtual environments. The end result would be a collaborative knowledgebase of function-led virtual environments to describe both the functions and the operational constructs involved in everyday activities.

References

Acker, M. B. (1990). Review of the ecological validity of neuropsychological tests. In D. E. Tupper & K. D. Cicerone (Eds.), *The neuropsychology of everyday life: Assessment and basic competencies* (pp. 19–55). Boston: Kluwer Academic Publishers. (Chapter 2).

Adams, K. M. (1986). Concepts and methods in the design of automata for neuropsychological test interpretation. In S. B. Filskov & T. J. Boll (Eds.), *Handbook of clinical neuropsychology* (vol. 2, pp. 561–576). New York: Wiley.

Adams, K. M., & Brown, G. C. (1986). The role of the computer in neuropsychological assessment. In I. Grant & K. M. Adams (Eds.), *Neuropsychological assessment of neuropsychiatric disorders* (pp. 87–89). New York: Oxford.

Adams, K. M., & Heaton, R. K. (1985). Automated interpretation of the neuropsychological test data. *Journal of Consulting and Clinical Psychology, 53*, 790–802.

Adams, K. M., & Heaton, R. K. (1987). Computerized neuropsychological assessment: Issues and applications. In J. N. Butcher (Ed.), *Computerized psychological assessment* (pp. 355–365). New York: Basic Books.

Adams, K. M., Kvale, V. I., & Keegan, J. F. (1984). Relative accuracy of three automated systems for neuropsychological interpretation. *Journal of Clinical Neuropsychology, 6*, 413–431.

Adams, R., Finn, P., Moes, E., Flannery, K., & Rizzo, A. (2009). Distractibility in attention deficit/hyperactivity disorder (ADHD): The virtual reality classroom. *Child Neuropsychology, 15*, 120–135.

Adolphs, R., Baron-Cohen, S., & Tranel, D. (2002). Impaired recognition of social emotions following amygdale damage. *Journal of Cognitive Neuroscience, 14*(8), 1264–1274.

Åkerlund, E., Esbjörnsson, E., Sunnerhagen, K. S., & Björkdahl, A. (2013). Can computerized working memory training improve impaired working memory, cognition, and psychological health? *Brain Injury, 27*, 13–14.

Akhutina, T. V., Vygotsky, L. S., & Luria, A. R. (2003). Foundations of neuropsychology. *Journal of Russian and East European Psychology, 41*(3), 159–190.

Allanson, J., & Fairclough, S. H. (2004). A research agenda for physiological computing. *Interacting with Computers, 16*, 857–878.

Alderman, N., Burgess, P. W., Knight, C., & Henman, C. (2003). Ecological validity of a simplified version of the multiple errands shopping test. *Journal of the International Neuropsychological Society, 9*, 31–44.

Allen, L. M, I. I. I., Iverson, G. L., & Green, P. (2003). Computerized assessment of response bias in forensic neuropsychology. *Journal of forensic neuropsychology, 3*(1-2), 205–225.

Allen, A. J., Shashwath, A. M., Skudlarski, P., Calhoun, V., Astur, R., Ruopp, K. C., & Pearlson, G. D. (2009). Effects of alcohol on performance of distraction task during simulated driving. *Alcohol Clinical Experimental Research, 33*, 617–625.

Allen, B. J., & Gfeller, J. D. (2011). The immediate post-concussion assessment and cognitive testing battery and traditional neuropsychological measures: A construct and concurrent validity study. *Brain Injury, 25*(2), 179–191.

T.D. Parsons, *Clinical Neuropsychology and Technology*,
DOI 10.1007/978-3-319-31075-6

Allison, B. Z., Brunner, C., Kaiser, V., Müller-Putz, G. R., Neuper, C., & Pfurtscheller, G. (2010). Toward a hybrid brain-computer interface based on imagined movement and visual attention. *Journal of Neural Engineering*, *7*(2).

Alphonso, A. L., Monson, B. T., Zeher, M. J., Armiger, R. S., Weeks, S. R., Burck, J. M., & Tsao, J. W. (2012). Use of a virtual integrated environment in prosthetic limb development and phantom limb pain. *Studies in Health Technology and Informatics, 181*, 305–309.

Alvarez, R. P., Johnson, L., & Grillon, C. (2007). Contextual-specificity of short-delay extinction in humans: Renewal of fear-potentiated startle in a virtual environment. *Learning and Memory, 14*(4), 247–253.

Anastasi, A., & Urbina, S. (1997). *Psychological testing* (7th ed.). New York: McMillian.

Anderson, E. W., Potter, K. C., Matzen, L. E., Shepherd, J. F., Preston, G. A., & Silva, C. T. (2011). A user study of visualization effectiveness using EEG and cognitive load. *Computer Graphics Forum, 30*, 791–800.

Anthony, W. Z., Heaton, R. K., & Lehman, R. A. W. (1980). An attempt to cross-validate two actuarial systems for neuropsychological test interpretation. *Journal of Consulting and Clinical Psychology, 48*, 317–326.

Ardila, A. (2008). On the evolutionary origins of executive functions. *Brain and Cognition, 68*, 92–99.

Armstrong, C., Reger, G., Edwards, J., Rizzo, A., Courtney, C., & Parsons, T. (2013). Validity of the virtual reality stroop task (VRST) in active duty military. *Journal of Clinical and Experimental Neuropsychology, 35*, 113–123.

Asimakopulos, J., Boychuck, Z., Sondergaard, D., Poulin, V., Ménard, I., & Korner-Bitensky, N. (2012). Assessing executive function in relation to fitness to drive: A review of tools and their ability to predict safe driving. *Australian Occupational Therapy Journal, 59*, 402–427.

Avis, K., Gamble, K., & Schwebel, D. (2014). Does excessive daytime sleepiness affect children's pedestrian safety? *SLEEP, 37*, 283–287.

Azad, N., Amos, S., Milne, K., & Power, B. (2012). Telemedicine in a rural memory disorder clinic-remote management of patients with dementia. *Canadian Geriatrics Journal, 15*, 96e100.

Baas, J. M. P., van Ooijen, L., Goudriaan, A., & Kenemans, J. L. (2008). Failure to condition to a cue is associated with sustained contextual fear. *Acta Psychologica, 127*(3), 581–592.

Backs, R. W., & Seljos, K. A. (1994). Metabolic and cardiorespiratory measures of mental effort: The effects of level of difficulty in a working memory task. *International Journal of Psychophysiology, 16*, 57–68.

Baddeley, A. (1981). The cognitive psychology of everyday life. *British Journal of Psychology, 72* (2), 257–269.

Baddeley, A. (2011). How does emotion influence working memory? Attention, representation, and human performance: Integration of cognition, emotion, and motivation, 3–18.

Baddeley, A. (2012). How does emotion influence working memory? In S. Masmoudi, D. Y. Dai, & A. Naceur (Eds.), *Attention, representation, and human performance: Integration of cognition, emotion, and motivation* (pp. 3–18). Psychology Press.

Bakdash, J. Z., Linkenauger, S. A., & Profitt, D. (2008). Comparing decision-making and control for learning a virtual environment: backseat drivers learn where they are going. *Proceedings of the Human Factors and Ergonomics Society Annual Meeting, 52*, 2117–2121.

Banaji, M. R., & Crowder, R. G. (1989). The bankruptcy of everyday memory. *American Psychologist, 44*(9), 1185.

Bangirana, P., Giordani, B., John, C. C., Page, C., Opoka, R. O., & Boivin, M. J. (2009). Immediate neuropsychological and behavioral benefits of computerized cognitive rehabilitation in Ugandan pediatric cerebral malaria survivors. *Journal of Developmental and Behavioral Pediatrics: JDBP, 30*(4), 310–318.

Bangirana, P., Allebeck, P., Boivin, M. J., John, C. C., Page, C., Ehnvall, A., & Musisi, S. (2011). Cognition, behaviour and academic skills after cognitive rehabilitation in Ugandan children surviving severe malaria: A randomised trial. *BMC Neurology, 11*(1), 96.

Barkley, R. A., Anderson, D. L., & Kruesi, M. (2007). A pilot study of the effects of atomoxetine on driving performance in adults with ADHD. *Journal of Attention Disorders, 10*, 306–316.

Barkley, R. A., & Murphy, K. R. (2011). The nature of executive function (EF) deficits in daily life activities in adults with ADHD and their relationship to performance on EF tests. *Journal of Psychopathology and Behavioral Assessment, 33*(2), 137–158.

Barkley, R., Murphy, K., O'connell, T., Anderson, D., & Connor, D. (2006). Effects of two doses of alcohol on simulator driving performance in adults with attention-deficit/hyperactivity disorder. *Neuropsychology, 20*, 77-87.

Barkley, R. A., Murphy, K. R., O'Connell, T., & Connor, D. F. (2005). Effects of two doses of methylphenidate on simulator driving performance in adults with attention deficit hyperactivity disorder. *Journal of Safety Research, 36*, 121–131.

Barr, W. B. (2008). Historical development of the neuropsychological test battery. In J. E. Morgan & J. H. Ricker (Eds.), *Textbook of clinical neuropsychology* (pp. 3–17). New York: Taylor & Francis.

Barra, J., Laou, L., Poline, J. B., Lebihan, D., & Berthoz, A. (2012). Does an oblique/slanted perspective during virtual navigation engage both egocentric and allocentric brain strategies? *PLoS ONE, 7*, e49537.

Barrett, A. M., Buxbaum, L. J., Coslett, H. B., Edwards, E., Heilman, K. M., Hillis, A. E., & Robertson, I. H. (2006). Cognitive rehabilitation interventions for neglect and related disorders: moving from bench to bedside in stroke patients. *Journal of Cognitive Neuroscience, 18*(7), 1223-1236.

Barton, C., Morris, R., Rothlind, J., & Yaffe, K. (2011). Video-telemedicine in a memory disorders clinic: evaluation and management of rural elders with cognitive impairment. *Telemedicine and e-Health, 17*(10), 789–793.

Bartram, D., & Bayliss, R. (1984). Automated testing: Past, present and future. *Journal of Occupational Psychology, 57*(3), 221–237.

Bauer, R. M., Iverson, G. L., Cernich, A. N., Binder, L. M., Ruff, R. M., & Naugle, R. I. (2012). Computerized neuropsychological assessment devices: Joint position paper of the American Academy of Clinical Neuropsychology and the National Academy of Neuropsychology. *The Clinical Neuropsychologist, 26*(2), 177–196.

Baxendale, S., & Thompson, P. (2010). Beyond localization: the role of traditional neuropsychological tests in an age of imaging. *Epilepsia, 51*(11), 2225–2230.

Bayless, J. D., Varney, N. R., & Roberts, R. J. (1989). Tinker Toy Test performance and vocational outcome in patients with closed-head injuries. *Journal of Clinical and Experimental Neuropsychology, 11*, 913–917.

Beaudoin, M., & Desrichard, O. (2011). Are memory self-efficacy and memory performance related? A meta-analysis. *Psychological Bulletin, 137*, 211–241.

Beaumont, J. G. (1975). The validity of the Category Test administered by on-line computer. *Journal of Clinical Psychology, 31*, 458–462.

Bechara, A., Damasio, A. R., Damasio, H., & Anderson, S. W. (1994). Insensitivity to future consequences following damage to human prefrontal cortex. *Cognition, 50*, 7–15.

Bechara, A., Tranel, D., Damasio, H., & Damasio, A. R. (1996). Failure to respond autonomically to anticipated future outcomes following damage to prefrontal cortex. *Cerebral Cortex, 6*, 215–225.

Bechara, A., Damasio, H., Tranel, D., & Damasio, A. R. (1997). Deciding advantageously before knowing the advantageous strategy. *Science, 275*, 1293–1295.

Bechara, A., Damasio, H., Tranel, D., & Anderson, S. W. (1998). Dissociation of working memory from decision making within human prefrontal cortex. *Journal of Neuroscience, 18*, 428–437.

Bechara, A., Damasio, H., & Damasio, A. R. (2000). Emotion, decision making, and the orbitofrontal cortex. *Cerebral Cortex, 10*, 295–307.

Bechara, A. (2004). The role of emotion in decision-making: evidence from neurological patients with orbitofrontal damage. *Brain and Cognition, 55*(1), 30–40.

Bechara, A. (2007). Iowa gambling task professional manual. Psychological Assessment Resources, Inc.

Bechara, A., & Damasio, A. R. (2005). The somatic marker hypothesis: A neural theory of economic decision. *Games and Economic Behavior, 52*, 336–372.

Bechtel, W., & Abrahamsen, A. (1990). *Connectionism and the mind.* Cambridge: Blackwell.

Bedard, A. C., Ickowicz, A., & Tannock, R. (2002). Methylphenidate improves Stroop naming speed, but not response interference, in children with attention deficit hyperactivity disorder. *Journal of Child and Adolescent Psychopharmacology, 12*, 301–309.

Bedard, A. C., Martinussen, R., Ickowicz, A., & Tannock, R. (2004). Methylphenidate improves visual-spatial memory in children with attention-deficit/hyperactivity disorder. *Journal of the American Academy of Child & Adolescent Psychiatry, 43*, 260–268.

Bedard, M., Parkkari, M., Weaver, B., Riendeau, J., & Dahlquist, M. (2010). Assessment of driving performance using a simulator protocol: Validity and reproducibility. *American Journal of Occupational Therapy, 64*, 336–340.

Benedict, R. H. B., Harris, A. E., Markow, T., McCormick, J. A., Nuechterlein, K. H., & Asarnow, R. F. (1994). Effects of attention training on information processing in schizophrenia. *Schizophrenia Bulletin, 20*(3), 537–546.

Benito-León, J., Mitchell, A. J., Vega, S., & Bermejo-Pareja, F. (2010). A population-based study of cognitive function in older people with subjective memory complaints. *Journal of Alzheimer's Disease, 22*, 159–170.

Benoit, M., Guerchouche, R., Petit, P. D., Chapoulie, E., Manera, V., Chaurasia, G., & Robert, P. (2015). Is it possible to use highly realistic virtual reality in the elderly? A feasibility study with image-based rendering. *Neuropsychiatric Disease and Treatment, 11*, 557.

Benton, A. L. (1985). Some problems associated with neuropsychological assessment. *Bulletin of Clinical Neuroscience, 50*, 11–15.

Benton, A. L., & Howell, I. L. (1941). The use of psychological tests in the evaluation of intellec-tual function following head injury. *Psychosomatic Medicine, 3*, 138–51.

Benton, A. L. (1967). Problems of test construction in the field of aphasia. *Cortex, 3*, 32–58.

Ben-Yishay, Y. (Ed.). (1978). *Working Approaches to Remediation of Cognitive Deficits in Brain Damaged Persons. Rehabilitation Monograph 59.* New York: New York University Medical Center.

Berka, C., Levendowski, D. J., Lumicao, M. N., Yau, A., Davis, G., & Zivkovic, V. T. (2007). EEG correlates of task engagement and mental workload in vigilance, learning, and memory tasks. *Aviation, Space, and Environmental Medicine, 78*, B231–B244.

Berker, E. A., Berker, A. H., & Smith, A. (1986). Translation of Broca's 1865 report. Localization of speech in the third left frontal convolution. *Archives of Neurology, 43*(10), 1065–1072.

Berlucchi, G., Aglioti, S., & Tassinari, G. (1997). Rightward attentional bias and left hemi-sphere dominance in a cue-target light detection task in a callosotomy patient. *Neuropsy-chologia, 35* (7), 941–952.

Bezeau, S., & Graves, R. (2001). Statistical power and effect sizes of clinical neuropsycholo-gy research. *Journal of Clinical and Experimental Neuropsychology, 23*(3), 399–406.

Bigler, E. D. (2007). A motion to exclude and the 'fixed' versus 'flexible' battery in 'foren-sic' neuropsychology: Challenges to the practice of clinical neuropsychology. *Archives of Clinical Neuropsychology, 22*(1), 45–51.

Bigler, E. D. (2013). Neuroimaging biomarkers in mild traumatic brain injury (mTBI). *Neuropsychology Review, 23*(3), 169–209.

Bilder, R. M. (2011). Neuropsychology 3.0: evidence-based science and practice. *Journal of the International Neuropsychological Society, 17*(01), 7–13.

Binet, A., & Henri, V. (1896). La psychologie individuelle (Individual psychology). *L'Annee Psychologique, 2*, 411–465.

Binet, A., & Henri, V. (1898). *La fatigue intellectuelle (Intellectual tiredness).* Paris: Schlei-cher.

Binet, A., & Simon, T. (1905). Methodes nouvelles pour le diagnostic du niveau intellectuel des anormaux (New methods to diagnose the intellectual level of abnormals). *L'Annee Psychologique, 11*, 245–366.

Binet, A., & Simon, T. (1908). Le developpement de l'intelligence chez les enfants (The de-velopment of intelligence in children). *L'Annee Psychologique, 14*, 1–94.

Bioulac, S., Lallemand, S., Rizzo, A., Philip, P., Fabrigoule, C., & Bouvard, M. P. (2012). Impact of time on task on ADHD patients' performances in a virtual classroom. *European Journal of Paediatric Neurology, 16*, 514–521.

Boake, C. (2003). Stages in the history of neuropsychological rehabilitation. Neuropsychological rehabilitation: Theory and practice, 11–21.

Bohil, C. J., Alicea, B., & Biocca, F. A. (2011). Virtual reality in neuroscience research and therapy. *Nature Reviews Neuroscience, 12*, 752–762.

Boivin, M. J., Busman, R. A., Parikh, S. M., Bangirana, P., Page, C. F., Opoka, R. O., & Giordani, B. (2010). A pilot study of the neuropsychological benefi ts of computerized cognitive rehabilitation in Ugandan children with HIV. *Neuropsychology, 24*(5), 667–673.

Boller, F. (1998). History of the International Neuropsychological Symposium: a reflection of the evolution of a discipline. *Neuropsychologia, 37*(1), 17–26.

Bolles, M., & Goldstein, K. (1938). A study of the impairment of "abstract behavior" in schizophrenic patients. *Psychiatric Quarterly, 12*, 42–65.

Boller, F., & Forbes, M. M. (1998). History of dementia and dementia in history: an over-view. *Journal of the Neurological Sciences, 158*(2), 125–133.

Bonelli, R. M., & Cummings, J. L. (2007). Frontal-subcortical circuitry and behavior. *Dialogues in Clinical Neuroscience, 9*(2), 141.

Bottari, C., Dassa, C., Rainville, C., & Dutil, E. (2009). The criterion-related validity of the IADL Profile with measures of executive functions, indices of trauma severity and sociodemographic characteristics. *Brain Injury, 23*, 322–335.

Boulos, M. N., Wheeler, S., Tavares, C., & Jones, R. (2011). How smartphones are changing the face of mobile and participatory healthcare: an overview, with example from eCAALYX. *BioMedical Engineering OnLine, 10*, 24.

Boutcher, Y. N., & Boutcher, S. H. (2006). Cardiovascular response to Stroop: Effect of verbal response and task difficulty. *Biological Psychology, 73*, 235–241.

Bowen, A., & Lincoln, N. B. (2007). Cognitive rehabilitation for spatial neglect following stroke. *Cochrane Database of Systematic Reviews, 2*, CD003586.

Bowman, H. C., Evans, Y. E. C., & Turnbull, H. O. (2005). Artificial time constraints on the Iowa Gambling Task: The effects on behavioral performance and subjective experience. *Brain and Cognition, 57*(1), 21–25.

Brehmer, Y., Westerberg, H., & Backman, L. (2012). Working-memory training in younger and older adults: training gains, transfer, and maintenance. *Frontiers in Human Neuroscience, 6*, 63.

Brinton, G., & Rouleau, R. A. (1969). Automating the Hidden and Embedded Figure Tests. *Perceptual and Motor Skills, 29*, 401–402.

Broca, P. (1865). Sur le siège de la faculté du langage articulé. *Bulletine de Société Anthro-Pologique, 6*, 337–339.

Brock, L. L., Rimm-Kaufman, S. E., Nathanson, L., & Grimm, K. J. (2009). The contributions of "hot" and "cool" executive function to children's academic achievement, learning-related behaviors, and engagement in kindergarten. *Early Childhood Research Quarterly, 24*, 337–349.

Broglio, S. P., Ferrara, M. S., Macciocchi, S. N., Baumgartner, T. A., & Elliott, R. (2007). Test-retest reliability of computerized concussion assessment programs. *Journal of Athletic Training, 42*(4), 509.

Brookings, J. B., Wilson, G. F., & Swain, C. R. (1996). Psychophysiological responses to changes in workload during simulated air traffic control. *Biological Psychology, 42*, 361–377.

Brouillette, R. M., Foil, H., Fontenot, S., Correro, A., Allen, R., Martin, C. K., & Keller, J. N. (2013). Feasibility, reliability, and validity of a smartphone based application for the assessment of cognitive function in the elderly. *PloS one, 8*(6), e65925.

Bruce, D. (1985). On the origin of the term "Neuropsychology". *Neuropsychologia, 23*, 813–814.

Brunswick, E. (1955). Symposium of the probability approach in psychology: Representative design and probabilistic theory in a functional psychology. *Psychological Review, 62*, 193–217.

Buelow, M. T., & Suhr, J. A. (2009). Construct validity of the Iowa gambling task. *Neuropsychology Review, 19*(1), 102–114.

Burda, P. C., Starkey, T. W., & Dominguez, F. (1991). Computer administered treatment of psychiatric inpatients. *Computers in Human Behavior, 7*(1), 1–5.

Burgess, N., Maguire, E. A., Spiers, H. J., & O'Keefe, J. (2001). A temporoparietal and prefrontal network for retrieving the spatial context of lifelike events. *Neuroimage, 14*(2), 439–453.

Burgess, N., Maguire, E. A., & O'Keefe, J. (2002). The human hippocampus and spatial and episodic memory. *Neuron, 35*(4), 625–641.

Burgess, P. W. (2000). *Real-world multitasking from a cognitive neuroscience perspective* (pp. 465–472). Control of Cognitive Processes: Attention and performance XVIII.

Burgess, P. W., Alderman, N., Forbes, C., Costello, A., Coates, L., Dawson, D. R., et al. (2006). The case for the development and use of "ecologically valid" measures of executive function in experimental and clinical neuropsychology. *Journal of the International Neuropsychological Society, 12*(02), 194–209.

Burgess, P. W., Veitch, E., Costello, A., & Shallice, T. (2000). The cognitive and neuroanatomical correlates of multitasking. *Neuropsychologia, 38*, 848–863.

Buxbaum, L., Dawson, A., & Linsley, D. (2012). Reliability and validity of the virtual reality lateralized attention test in assessing hemispatial neglect in right-hemisphere stroke. *Neuropsychology, 26*, 430–441.

Cain, A. E., Depp, C. A., & Jeste, D. V. (2009). Ecological momentary assessment in aging research: A critical review. *Journal of Psychiatric Research, 43*, 987–996.

Calabria, M., Manenti, R., Rosini, S., Zanetti, O., Miniussi, C., & Cotelli, M. (2011). Objective and subjective memory impairment in elderly adults: a revised version of the everyday memory questionnaire. *Aging Clinical and Experimental Research, 23*(1), 67–73.

Calhoun, V. D., & Pearlson, G. D. (2012). A selective review of simulated driving studies: Combining naturalistic and hybrid paradigms, analysis approaches, and future directions. *NeuroImage, 59*, 25–35.

Calvert, E. J., & Waterfall, R. C. (1982). A comparison of conventional and automated administration of Raven's Standard Progressive Matrices. *International Journal of Man-Machine Studies, 17*, 305–310.

Camara, W. J., Nathan, J. S., & Puente, A. E. (2000). Psychological test usage: Implications in professional psychology. *Professional Psychology: Research and Practice, 31*, 141–154.

Campbell, Z., Zakzanis, K. K., Jovanovski, D., Joordens, S., Mraz, R., & Graham, S. J. (2009). Utilizing virtual reality to improve the ecological validity of clinical neuropsychology: An fMRI case study elucidating the neural basis of planning by comparing the Tower of London with a three-dimensional navigation task. *Applied Neuropsychology, 16*, 295–306.

Canini, M., Battista, P., Della Rosa, P. A., Catricalà, E., Salvatore, C., Gilardi, M. C., & Castiglioni, I. (2014). Computerized neuropsychological assessment in aging: Testing efficacy and clinical ecology of different interfaces. *Computational and Mathematical Methods in Medicine*.

Canty, A. L., Fleming, J., Patterson, F., Green, H. J., Man, D., & Shum, D. H. (2014). Evaluation of a virtual reality prospective memory task for use with individuals with severe traumatic brain injury. *Neuropsychological Rehabilitation, 24*, 238–265.

Cao, X., Douguet, A. S., Fuchs, P., & Klinger, E. (2010). Designing an ecological virtual task in the context of executive functions: a preliminary study. *Proceedings of the 8th International Conference on Disability, Virtual Reality and Associated Technologies* (vol. 31, pp. 71–78).

Capuana, L. J., Dywan, J., Tays, W. J., Elmers, J. L., Witherspoon, R., & Segalowitz, S. J. (2014). Factors influencing the role of cardiac autonomic regulation in the service of cognitive control. *Biological Psychology, 102*, 88–97.

Carelli, L., Morganti, F., Weiss, P. L., Kizony, R., & Riva, G. (2008). A virtual reality paradigm for the assessment and rehabilitation of executive function deficits post stroke: feasibility study. *Virtual Rehabilitation* (pp. 99–104). IEEE.

Carlsson, A. (2001). A paradigm shift in brain research. *Science, 294*, 1021–1024.

Carroll, D., Turner, J. R., & Hellawell, J. C. (1986). Heart rate and oxygen consumption during active psychological challenge: The effects of level of difficulty. *Psychophysiology, 23*, 174–181.

Carter, S., & Pasqualini, M. C. S. (2004). Stronger autonomic response accompanies better learning: a test of Damasio's somatic marker hypothesis. *Cognition and Emotion, 18*, 901–911.

Cernich, A. N., Brennana, D. M., Barker, L. M., & Bleiberg, J. (2007). Sources of error in computerized neuropsychological assessment. *Archives of Clinical Neuropsychology, 22*, 39–48.

Chan, R. C. K., Shum, D., Toulopoulou, T., & Chen, E. Y. H. (2008). Assessment of executive functions: Review of instruments and identification of critical issues. *Archives of Clinical Neuropsychology*, *23*(2), 201–216.

Chaytor, N., & Schmitter-Edgecombe, M. (2003). The ecological validity of neuropsychological tests: A review of the literature on everyday cognitive skills. *Neuropsychology Review, 13*, 181–197.

Chaytor, N., Schmitter-Edgecombe, M., & Burr, R. (2006). Improving the ecological validity of executive functioning assessment. *Archives of Clinical Neuropsychology, 21*(3), 217–227.

Chelune, G. J., & Moehle, K. A. (1986). Neuropsychological assessment and everyday functioning. In D. Wedding, A. M. Horton, & J. Webster (Eds.), *The neuropsychology handbook* (pp. 489–525). New York: Springer.

Choca, J. P., & Morris, J. (1992). Administering the category test by computer: Equivalence of results. *Clinical Neuropsychologist, 6*, 9–15.

Chrastil, E. R., & Warren, W. H. (2012). Active and passive contributions to spatial learning. *Psychonomic Bulletin and Review, 19*, 1–23.

Christensen, A. L. (1975). *Luria's neuropsychological investigation* (2nd ed.). Copenhagen, Denmark: Munksgaard.

Christensen, A. L. (1996). Alexandr Romanovich Luria (1902-1977): Contributions to neuropsychological rehabilitation. *Neuropsychological Rehabilitation, 6*(4), 279–304.

Cicerone, K. D. (2008). Principles in evaluating cognitive rehabilitation research. In D. T. Stuss, G. Winocur, & I. H. Robertson (Eds.), *Cognitive neurorehabilitation* (pp. 106–118). New York: Cambridge University Press.

Ciemins, E. L., Holloway, B., Jay Coon, P., McClosky-Armstrong, T., & Min, S. J. (2009). Telemedicine and the Mini-Mental State Examination: assessment from a distance. *Tele-medicine and e-Health, 15*(5), 476–478.

Cincotti, F., Mattia, D., Aloise, F., Bufalari, S., Schalk, G., Oriolo, Babiloni, F. (2008). Non-invasive brain-computer interface system: Towards its application as assistive technology. *Brain Research Bulletin, 75*(6), 796-803.

Cipresso, P., La Paglia, F., La Cascia, C., Riva, G., Albani, G., & La Barbera, D. (2013). Break in volition: A virtual reality study in patients with obsessive-compulsive disorder. *Experimental Brain Research, 229*, 443–449.

Clancy, T. A., Rucklidge, J. J., & Owen, D. (2010). Road-crossing safety in virtual reality: A comparison of adolescents with and without ADHD. *Journal of Clinical Child and Adolescent Psychology, 35*, 203–215.

Clark, L., Manes, F., Nagui, A., Sahakian, B. J., & Robbins, T. W. (2003). The contributions of lesion laterality and lesion volume to decision-making impairment following frontal lobe damage. *Neuropsychologia, 41*, 1474–1483.

Clark, L., & Manes, F. (2004). Social and emotional decision-making following frontal lobe injury. *Neurocase, 10*(5), 398–403.

Clifford, G. D., & Clifton, D. (2012). Wireless technology in disease management and medicine. *The Annual Review of Medicine, 63*, 479–492.

CogState (2011). CogState research manual (Version 6.0). New Haven: CogState Ltd.

Cohen, S., & Pressman, S. D. (2006). Positive affect and health. *Current Directions in Psychological Science, 15*(3), 122–125.

Coley, N., Andrieu, S., Jaros, M., Weiner, M., Cedarbaum, J., & Vellas, B. (2011). Suitability of the clinical dementia rating-sum of boxes as a single primary endpoint for Alzheimer's disease trials. *Alzheimer's Dementia, 7*, 602–610.

Collie, A., Maruff, P., Falleti, M., Silbert, B., & Darby, D. G. (2002). Determining the extent of cognitive change following coronary artery bypass grafting: A review of available statistical procedures. *Annals of Thoracic Surgery, 73*, 2005–2011.

Collie, A., & Maruff, P. (2003). Computerised neuropsychological testing. *British Journal of Sports Medicine, 37*(1), 2–2.

Collie, A., Maruff, P., Makdissi, M., McCrory, P., McStephen, M., & Darby, D. (2003). CogSport: reliability and correlation with conventional cognitive tests used in postconcussion medical evaluations. *Clinical Journal of Sport Medicine, 13*(1), 28–32.

Collinger, J. L., Boninger, M. L., Bruns, T. M., Curley, K., Wang, W., & Weber, D. J. (2013). Functional priorities, assistive technology, and brain-computer interfaces after spinal cord injury. *Journal of Rehabilitation Research and Development, 50*(2), 145–159.

Comper, P., Bisschop, S. M., Carnide, N., & Triccio, A. (2005). A systematic review of treatments for mild traumatic brain injury. *Brain Injury, 19*(11), 863–880.

Conkey, R. (1938). Psychological changes associated with head injuries. *Archives of Psychology, 33*, 5–22.

Conway, M. A. (1991). In defense of everyday memory. *American Psychologist, 46*, 19–26.

Cook, L., Hanten, G., Orsten, K., Chapman, S., Li, X., Wilde, E., et al. (2013). Effects of moderate to severe Traumatic Brain Injury on anticipating consequences of actions in adults: a preliminary study. *Journal of the International Neuropsychological Society, 19*, 508–517.

Costa, L. (1983). Clinical neuropsychology: A discipline in evolution. *Journal of Clinical Neuropsychology, 5*, 1–11.

Costa, L., & Spreen, O. (Eds.). (1985). Studies in neuropsychology: Selected papers of Arthur Benton. New York: Oxford University Press.

Courtney, C., Dawson, M., Rizzo, A., Arizmendi, B., & Parsons, T. D. (2013). Predicting navigation performance with psychophysiological responses to threat in a virtual environment. *Lecture Notes in Computer Science, 8021*, 129–138.

Cox, D., Moore, M., Burket, R., Merkel, R., Mikami, A., & Kovatchev, B. (2008). Rebound effects with long-acting amphetamine or methylphenidate stimulant medication preparations among adolescent male drivers with Attention-Deficit/Hyperactivity Disorder. *Journal of Child and Adolescent Psychopharmacology, 18*, 1–10.

Critchley, H. D. (2005). Neural mechansims of autonomic, affective, and cognitive integration. *The Journal of Comparative Neurology, 493*, 154–166.

Cromwell, H. C., & Panksepp, J. (2011). Rethinking the cognitive revolution from a neural perspective: how overuse/misuse of the term 'cognition' and the neglect of affective controls in behavioral neuroscience could be delaying progress in understanding the BrainMind. *Neuroscience and Biobehavioral Reviews, 35*, 2026–2035.

Crone, E. A., Somsen, R. J. M., van Beek, B., & van der Molen, M. W. (2004). Heart rate and skin conductance analysis of antecedents and consequences of decision making. *Psychophysiology, 41*, 531–540.

Crook, T. H., Ferris, S., & McCarthy, M. (1979). The Misplaced-Objects Task: A brief test for memory dysfunction in the aged. *Journal of the American Geriatrics Society, 27*, 284–287.

Crook, T. H., Ferris, S. H., McCarthy, M., & Rae, D. (1980). Utility of digit recall tasks for assessing memory in the aged. *Journal of Consulting and Clinical Psychology, 48*, 228–233.

Crook, T. H., Kay, G. G., & Larrabee, G. J. (2009). Computer-based cognitive testing. In I. Grant & K. M. Adams (Eds.), *Neuropsychological assessment of neuropsychiatric and neuromedical disorders* (3rd ed., pp. 84–100). New York: Oxford University Press.

Cubelli, R. (2005). The history of neuropsychology according to Norman Geschwind: Conti-nuity and discontinuity in the development of science. *Cortex, 41*(2), 271–274.

Cuberos-Urbano, G., Caracuel, A., Vilar-López, R., Valls-Serrano, C., Bateman, A., & Verdejo-García, A. (2013). Ecological validity of the Multiple Errands Test using predictive models of dysexecutive problems in everyday life. *Journal of Clinical and Experimental Neuropsychology, 35*, 329–336.

Cullum, C. M., Weiner, M. F., Gehrmann, H. R., & Hynan, L. S. (2006). Feasibility of tele-cognitive assessment in dementia. *Assessment, 13*(4), 385–390.

Cullum, C. M., & Grosch, M. G. (2012). Teleneuropsychology. In K. Myers & C. Turvey (Eds.), *Telemental health: Clinical, technical and administrative foundations for evidence-based practice* (pp. 275–294). Amsterdam: Elsevier.

Cullum, M., Hynan, C., Grosch, L., Parikh, M., & Weiner, M. F. (2014). Teleneuropsychology: Evidence for video teleconference-based neuropsychological assessment. *Journal of the International Neuropsychological Society, 20*(10), 1028–1033.

Cummings, J., Gould, H., & Zhong, K. (2012). Advances in designs for Alzheimer's disease clinical trials. *American Journal of Neurodegenerative Disease, 1*(3), 205–216.

Cyr, A., Stinchcombe, A., Gagnon, S., Marshall, S., Hing, M. M., & Finestone, H. (2009). Driving difficulties of brain-injured drivers in reaction to high-crash-risk simulated road events: A question of impaired divided attention? *Journal of Clinical and Experimental Neuropsychology, 31*, 472–482.

Dale, O., & Hagen, K. B. (2006). Despite technical problems personal digital assistants outperform pen and paper when collecting patient diary data. *Journal of Clinical Epidemiology, 60*(1), 8–17.

Damasio, A. R. (1994). *Descartes' error: Emotion, rationality and the human brain*. New York: GP Putnam.

Damasio, A. R. (1996). The somatic marker hypothesis and the possible functions of the prefrontal cortex. *Philosophical Transactions of the Royal Society of London—Series B: Biological Sciences, 351*, 1413–1420.

Damasio, A. (2008). Descartes' error: Emotion, reason and the human brain. Random House.

Daniel, M. H. (2012). Equivalence of Q-interactiveTM administered cognitive tasks: CVLT-II and selected D-KEFS subtests, Q-Interactive Tech. Rep. No. 3. Bloomington, MN: NCS Pearson, Inc.

Daniel, M. H. (2013). Equivalence of Q-interactive™ and paper administration of WMS®-IV cognitive tasks, Q-Interactive Tech. Rep. No. 6. Bloomington, MN: NCS Pearson, Inc.

Davis, A., Avis, K., & Schwebel, D. (2013). The effects of acute sleep restriction on adolescents' pedestrian safety in a virtual environment. *Journal of Adolescent Health, 53*, 785–790.

Davidson, R. J., & Sutton, S. K. (1995). Affective neuroscience: The emergence of a discipline. *Current Opinion in Neurobiology, 5*, 217–224.

Dawson, D. R., Anderson, N. D., Burgess, P., Cooper, E., Krpan, K. M., & Stuss, D. T. (2009). Further development of the Multiple Errands Test: Standardized scoring, reliability, and ecological validity for the Baycrest version. *Archives of Physical Medicine and Rehabilitation, 90*, S41–S51.

Danziger, Z. (2014). A reductionist approach to the analysis of learning in brain-computer interfaces. *Biological Cybernetics, 108*(2), 183–201.

Delaney, J. P. A., & Brodie, D. A. (2000). Effects of short-termpsychological stress on the time and frequency domains of heart rate variability. *Perceptual and Motor Skills, 91*, 515–524.

Delis, D. C., Kaplan, E., & Kramer, J. H. (2001). Delis-Kaplan executive function system (D-KEFS). Psychological Corporation.

Delis, D. C., Kramer, J. H., Kaplan, E., & Ober, B. A. (2000). *CVLT-II*. New York: The psychological corporation.

De Luca, R., Calabrò, R. S., Gervasi, G., DeSalvo, S., Bonanno, L., Corallo, F., et al. (2014). Is computer-assisted training effective in improving rehabilitative outcomes after brain injury? A case-control hospital-based study. *Disability and Health Journal, 7*, 356–360.

de Freitas, S., & Liarokapis, F. (2011). Serious Games: A new paradigm for education? In *Serious games and edutainment applications* (pp. 9–23). Springer London.

De Jager, C. A., Milwain, E., & Budge, M. (2002). Early detection of isolated memory deficits in the elderly: the need for more sensitive neuropsychological tests. *Psychological Medicine, 32*, 483–491.

De Marco, A. P., & Broshek, D. K. (2014). Computerized cognitive testing in the management of youth sports-related concussion. *Journal of Child Neurology*, 0883073814559645.

de Oliveira, M. O., & Brucki, S. M. D. (2014). Computerized neurocognitive test (CNT) in mild cognitive impairment and Alzheimer's disease. *Dementia and Neuropsychologia, 8*(2), 112–116.

deWall, C., Wilson, B. A., & Baddeley, A. D. (1994). The extended rivermead behavioral memory test: A measure of everyday memory performance in normal adults. *Memory, 2*, 149–166.

Diaz-Orueta, U., Garcia-Lopez, C., Crespo-Eguilaz, N., Sanchez-Carpintero, R., Climent, G., & Narbona, J. (2014). AULA virtual reality test as an attention measure: Convergent validity with Conners' continuous performance test. *Child Neuropsychology, 20*, 328–342.

Diller, L. (1976). A model for cognitive retraining in rehabilitation. *Clinical Psychology, 29*, 13–15.

Dimeff, L. A., Paves, A. P., Skutch, J. M., & Woodcock, E. A. (2011). Shifting paradigms in clinical psychology: How innovative technologies are shaping treatment delivery. In D. H. Barlow (Ed.), *The Oxford handbook of clinical psychology* (pp. 618–648). New York: Oxford University Press.

Di Sclafani, V., Tolou-Shams, M., Price, L. J., & Fein, G. (2002). Neuropsychological performance of individuals dependent on crack-cocaine, or crack-cocaine and alcohol, at 6 weeks and 6 months of abstinence. *Drug and Alcohol Dependence, 66*, 161–171.

Dodrill, C. B. (1997). Myths of neuropsychology. *The Clinical Neuropsychologist, 11*, 1–17.

Dodrill, C. B. (1999). Myths of neuropsychology: Further considerations. *The Clinical Neuropsychologist, 13*(4), 562–572.

Doherty, S. T., & Oh, P. (2012). A multi-sensor monitoring system of human physiology and daily activities. *Telemedicine Journal and e-Health, 18*, 185–192.

Dolcos, F., & McCarthy, G. (2006). Brain systems mediating cognitive interference by emotional distraction. *The Journal of Neuroscience, 26*(7), 2072–2079.

Dufau, S., Dunabeitia, J. A., Moret-Tatay, C., McGonigal, A., Peeters, D., et al. (2011). Smart phone, smart science: how the use of smartphones can revolutionize research in cognitive science. *PLoS One, 6*, e24974.

Dunn, E. J., Searight, H. R., Grisso, T., Margolis, R. B., & Gibbons, J. L. (1990). The relation of the Halstead-Reitan neuropsychological battery to functional daily living skills in geriatric patients. *Archives of Clinical Neuropsychology, 5*, 103–117.

Dutta, A., Kumar, R., Malhotra, S., Chugh, S., Banerjee, A., & Dutta, A. (2013). A low-cost point-of-care testing system for psychomotor symptoms of depression affecting standing balance: A preliminary study in India. Depression Research and Treatment.

Eack, S. M., Greenwald, D. P., Hogarty, S. S., Cooley, S. J., DiBarry, A. L., Montrose, D. M., & Keshavan, M. S. (2009). Cognitive enhancement therapy for early-course schizophrenia: Effects of a two-year randomized controlled trial. *Psychiatric Services, 60*(11), 1468–1476.

Eckerman, D. A., Carroll, J. B., Forre, C. D., Guillen, M., & Lansman, M. (1985). An approach to brief field testing for neurotoxicity. *Neurobehavioral Toxicology and Teratology, 7*, 387–393.

Égerházi, A., Berecz, R., Bartók, E., & Degrell, I. (2007). Automated neuropsychological test battery (CANTAB) in mild cognitive impairment and in Alzheimer's disease. *Progress in Neuro-Psychopharmacology and Biological Psychiatry, 31*(3), 746–751.

Elbin, R. J., Schatz, P., & Covassin, T. (2011). One-year test-retest reliability of the online version of ImPACT in high school athletes. *The American Journal of Sports Medicine, 39*(11), 2319–2324.

Eling, P., Derckx, K., & Maes, R. (2008). On the historical and conceptual background of the Wisconsin Card sorting test. *Brain and Cognition, 67*, 247–253.

Elkind, J. S., Rubin, E., Rosenthal, S., Skoff, B., & Prather, P. (2001). A simulated reality scenario compared with the computerized Wisconsin Card sorting test: An analysis of preliminary results. *Cyber Psychology and Behavior, 4*, 489–496.

Ellis, H. C., & Ashbrook, P. W. (1988). Resource allocation model of the effects of depressed mood states on memory. In K. Fiedler & J. Forgas (Eds.), *Affect, cognition, and social behavior: New evidence and integrative attempts* (pp. 25–43). Toronto: Hogrefe.

Elwood, D. J. (1969). Automation of psychological testing. *American Psychologist, 24*, 287–289.

Elwood, D. J. (1972). Validity of an automated measure of intelligence in borderline retarded subjects. *American Journal of Mental Deficiency, 7*(1), 90–94.

Elwood, D. L., & Griffin, R. (1972). Individual intelligence testing without the examiner. *Journal of Consulting and Clinical Psychology, 38*, 9–14.

Elwood, R. W. (2001). MicroCog: Assessment of cognitive functioning. *Neuropsychology Review, 11*(2), 89–100.

Embretson, S. E., & Reise, S. P. (2013). Item response theory. Psychology Press.

Erlanger, D. M., Feldman, D. J., Kutner, K. (1999). Concussion resolution index. New York: HeadMinder, Inc.

Enzinger, C., Ropele, S., Fazekas, F., Loitfelder, M., Gorani, F., Seifert, T., & Müller-Putz, G. (2008). Brain motor system function in a patient with complete spinal cord injury following extensive brain-computer interface training. *Experimental Brain Research, 190*(2), 215–223.

Erlanger, D. M., Feldman, D., Kutner, K., Kaushik, T., Kroger, H., Festa, J., et al. (2003). Development and validation of a web-based neuropsychological test protocol for sports-related return-to-play decision making. *Archives of Clinical Neuropsychology, 18*, 293–316.

Ernst, M., Bolla, K., Mouratidis, M., Contoreggi, C., Matochik, J. A., Kurian, V., et al. (2002). Decision-making in a risk-taking task: A PET study. *Neuropsychopharmacology, 26*, 682–691.

Falleti, M. G., Maruff, P., Collie, A., & Darby, D. G. (2006). Practice effects associated with the repeated assessment of cognitive function using the CogState battery at 10-minute, one week and one month test-retest intervals. *Journal of Clinical and Experimental Neuropsychology, 28* (7), 1095–1112.

Fasotti, L., Kovacs, F., Eling, P., & Brouwer, W. (2000). Time pressure management as a compensatory strategy training after closed head injury. *Neuropsychological Rehabilitation, 10* (1), 47–65.

Fazeli, P. L., Ross, L. A., Vance, D. E., & Ball, K. (2013). The relationship between computer experience and computerized cognitive test performance among older adults. *The Journals of Gerontology Series B: Psychological Sciences and Social Sciences, 68*, 337–346.

Feldstein, S. N., Keller, F. R., Portman, R. E., Durham, R. L., Klebe, K. J., & Davis, H. P. (1999). A comparison of computerized and standard versions of the Wisconsin Card Sorting Test. *The Clinical Neuropsychologist, 13*, 303–313.

Fellows, L. K., & Farah, M. J. (2005). Different underlying impairments in decision making following ventromedial and dorsolateral frontal lobe damage in humans. *Cerebral Cortex, 15* (1), 58–63.

Ferrara, M. S., McCrea, M., Peterson, C. L., & Guskiewicz, K. M. (2001). A survey of practice patterns in concussion assessment and management. *Journal of Athletic Training, 36*(2), 145.

Fish, J., Evans, J. J., Nimmo, M., Martin, E., Kersel, D., et al. (2007). Rehabilitation of executive dysfunction following brain injury: "content-free cueing" improves everyday prospective memory performance. *Neuropsychologia, 45*(6), 1318–30.

Fish, J., Manly, T., Emslie, H., Evans, J. J., & Wilson, B. A. (2008). Compensatory strategies for acquired disorders of memory and planning: Differential effects of a paging system for patients with brain injury of traumatic versus cerebrovascular aetiology. *Journal of Neurology, Neurosurgery and Psychiatry, 79*(8), 930–935.

Flavia, M., Stampatori, C., Zanotti, D., Parrinello, G., & Capra, R. (2010). Effi cacy and specifi city of intensive cognitive rehabilitation of attention and executive functions in multiple sclerosis. *Journal of the Neurological Sciences, 288*(1-2), 101–105.

Fonseca, R. P., Zimmermann, N., Cotrena, C., Cardoso, C., Kristensen, C. H., & Grassi-Oliveira, R. (2012). Neuropsychological assessment of executive functions in traumatic brain injury: Hot and cold components. *Psychology and Neuroscience, 5*, 183–190.

Fornito, A., & Bullmore, E. T. (2014). Connectomics: A new paradigm for understanding brain disease. European Neuropsychopharmacology.

Fortier, M. A., DiLillo, D., Messman-Moore, T., Peugh, J., DeNardi, K. A., & Gaffey, K. J. (2009). Severity of child sexual abuse and revictimization: The mediating role of coping and trauma symptoms. *Psychology of Women Quarterly, 33*(3), 308–320.

Fortin, S., Godbout, L., & Braun, C. M. (2003). Cognitive structure of executive deficits in frontally lesioned head trauma patients performing activities of daily living. *Cortex, 39*, 273–291.

Fortney, J. C., Burgess, J. F, Jr, Bosworth, H. B., Booth, B. M., & Kaboli, P. J. (2011). A reconceptualization of access for 21st century healthcare. *Journal of General Internal Medicine, 26*(Suppl 2), 639–647.

Fortuny, L. I. A., & Heaton, R. K. (1996). Standard versus computerized administration of the Wisconsin Card Sorting Test. *The Clinical Neuropsychologist, 10*(4), 419–424.

Fraga, T., Pichiliani, M., & Louro, D. (2013). Experimental art with brain controlled interface. *Lecture Notes in Computer Science, 8009*, 642–651.

Franzen, M. D., & Wilhelm, K. L. (1996). Conceptual foundations of ecological validity in neuropsychological assessment. In R. J. Sbordone & C. J. Long (Eds.), *Ecological validity of neuropsychological testing* (pp. 91–112). Boca Raton: St Lucie Press.

Franzen, M. D. (2000). *Reliability and validity in neuropsychological assessment*. New York: Springer.

Fray, P. J., Robbins, T. W., & Sahakian, B. J. (1996). Neuropsychological applications of CANTAB. *International Journal of Geriatric Psychiatry, 11*, 329–336.

Fredrickson, J., Maruff, P. P., Woodward, M. M., Moore, L. L., Fredrickson, A. A., Sach, J. J., & Darby, D. D. (2010). Evaluation of the usability of a brief computerized cognitive screening test in older people for epidemiological studies. *Neuroepidemiology, 34*, 65–75.

French, C. C., & Beaumont, J. G. (1987). The reaction of psychiatric patients to computerized assessment. *British Journal of Clinical Psychology, 26*, 267–278.

French, C. C., & Beaumont, J. G. (1990). A clinical study of the automated assessment of intelligence by the Mill Hill vocabulary test and the standard progressive matrices test. *Journal of Clinical Psychology, 46*, 129–140.

Fried, R., Hirshfeld-Becker, D., Petty, C., Batchelder, H., & Biederman, J. (2012). How informative is the CANTAB to assess executive functioning in children with ADHD? A controlled study. *Journal of Attention Disorders*, 1087054712457038.

Garb, H. N., & Schramke, C. J. (1996). Judgment research and neuropsychological assessment: A narrative review and meta-analysis. *Psychological Bulletin, 120*, 140–153.

Gardner, A., Kay-Lambkin, F., Stanwell, P., Donnelly, J., Williams, W. H., Hiles, A., & Jones, D. K. (2012). A systematic review of diffusion tensor imaging findings in sports-related concussion. *Journal of Neurotrauma, 29*(16), 2521-2538.

Gedya, J,L (1967), A teaching machine programme for use as a test of learning ability. In D. Unvyin & J. Leedham (Eds.), *Aspects of Educational Technology*. London: Methuen.

Gedye, J. L. (1968). The development of a general purpose psychological testing system. *Bulletin of The British Psychological Society, 21*, 101–102.

Gedye, J. L., & Miller, E. (1969). The automation of psychological assessment. *International Journal of Man-Machine Studies, 1*, 237–262.

Gentry, T., Wallace, J., Kvarfordt, C., & Lynch, K. B. (2008). Personal digital assistants as cognitive aids for individuals with severe traumatic brain injury: A community-based trial. *Brain Injury, 22*(1), 19–24.

Gershon, R. C., Cella, D., Fox, N. A., Havlik, R. J., Hendrie, H. C., & Wagster, M. V. (2010). Assessment of neurological and behavioral function: The NIH Toolbox. *Lancet Neurology, 9* (2), 138–139.

Gershon, R. C., Wagster, M. V., Hendrie, H. C., Fox, N. A., Cook, K. F., & Nowinski, C. J. (2013). NIH toolbox for assessment of neurological and behavioral function. *Neurology, 80* (11 Supplement 3), S2-S6.

Gibbons, R. D., Weiss, D. J., Kupfer, D. J., Frank, E., Fagiolini, A., & Grochocinski, V. J. (2008). Using computerized adaptive testing to reduce the burden of mental health as-sessment. *Psychiatric Services, 59*(4), 361–368.

Gilberstadt, H., Lushene, R., & Buegel, B. (1976). Automated assessment of intelligence: The TAPAC test battery and computerized report writing. *Perceptual and Motor Skills, 43*(2), 627–635.

Gilboa, Y., Rosenblum, S., Fattal-Valevski, A., Toledano-Alhadef, H., Rizzo, A., & Josman, N. (2011). Using a virtual classroom environment to describe the attention deficits profile of children with Neurofibromatosis Type 1. *Research in Developmental Disabilities, 32*, 2608–2613.

Giles, G. M., & Shore, M. (1989). The effectiveness of an electronic memory aid for a memory-impaired adult of normal intelligence. *American Journal of Occupational Therapy, 43* (6), 409–411.

Gioia, G. A., & Isquith, P. K. (2004). Ecological assessment of executive function in traumatic brain injury. *Developmental Neuropsychology, 25*(1-2), 135–158.

Glotzbach, E., Ewald, H., Andreatta, M., Pauli, P., & Mühlberger, A. (2012). Contextual fear conditioning predicts subsequent avoidance behaviour in a virtual reality environment. *Cognition and Emotion, 26*(7), 1256–1272.

Glotzbach-Schoon, E., Andreatta, M., Reif, A., Ewald, H., Tröger, C., Baumann, C., & Pauli, P. (2013). Contextual fear conditioning in virtual reality is affected by 5HTTLPR and NPSR1 polymorphisms: effects on fear-potentiated startle. *Frontiers in Behavioral Neuroscience, 7*.

Godbout, L., & Doyon, J. (1995). Mental representation of knowledge following frontal-lobe or postrolandic lesions. *Neuropsychologia, 33*, 1671–1696.

Goel, V., Grafman, J., Tajik, J., Gana, S., & Danto, D. (1997). A study of the performance of patients with frontal lobe lesions in a financial planning task. *Brain, 120*, 1805–1822.

Goldberg, E., Podell, K., Harner, R., & Riggio, S. (1994). Cognitive bias, functional cortical geometry, and the frontal lobes: laterality, sex, and handedness. *Journal of Cognitive Neuroscience, 6*, 276–296.

Goldberg, E., Podell, K., & Lovell, M. (1994). Lateralization of frontal lobe functions and cognitive novelty. *The Journal of Neuropsychiatry & Clinical Neurosciences, 6*, 371–378.

Goldberg, E., et al. (1997). Early diagnosis of frontal lobe dementias. Jerusalem: Eighth Congress of International Psychogeriatric Association.

Goldberg, E., & Podell, K. (1999). Adaptive versus veridical decision making and the frontal lobes. *Consciousness and Cognition, 8*, 364–377.

Goldberg, E., & Podell, K. (2000). Adaptive decision making, ecological validity, and the frontal lobes. *Journal of Clinical and Experimental Neuropsychology, 22*(1), 56–68.

Goldberg, E. (2009). *The new executive brain: frontal lobes in a complex world*. New York: Oxford University Press.

Goldberg, E., Funk, B. A., & Podell, K. (2012). How the brain deals with novelty and ambiguity: implications for neuroaesthetics. *Rendiconti Lincei, 23*, 227–238.

Golden, C. J., Hammeke, T. A., & Purisch, A. D. (1980). *Manual for the Luria-Nebraska Neu-ropsychological Battery*. Los Angeles: Western Psychological Services.

Goldenberg, G. (2003). Goldstein and Gelb's Case Schn.: A classic case in neuropsychology? *Classic Cases in Neuropsychology, 2*, 281.

Goldstein, G. (1990). Contributions of Kurt Goldstein to neuropsychology. *The Clinical Neuropsychologist, 4*(1), 3–17.

Goldstein, G. (1996). (1996). Functional considerations in neuropsychology. In R. J. Sbordone & C. J. Long (Eds.), *Ecological validity of neuropsychological testing* (pp. 75–89). Delray Beach, Florida: GR Press/St. Lucie Press.

Goldstein, G., & Shelly, C. H. (1982). A further attempt to cross-validate the Russell, Neuringer, and Goldstein neuropsychological keys. *Journal of Consulting and Clinical Psychology, 50*, 721–726.

Goldstein, K. (1939). *The organism: a holistic approach to biology derived from pathological data in man* (pp. 15–16). New York: American Book Company.

Goldstein, K., & Gelb, A. (1918). Psychologische Analysen hirnpathologischer Fälle auf Grund von Untersuchungen Hirnverletzer. *Zeitschrift für die Gesamte Neurologie und Psychiatrie, 41*, 1–142.

Goldstein, K. (1923). Über die Abhängigkeit der Bewegungen von optischen Vorgängen. Bewegungsstörungen bei Seelenblinden. Monatschrift für Psychiatrie und Neurologie, Festschrift Liepmann.

Goldstein, K. (1931/1971). Über Zeigen und Greifen. In A. Gurwitsch, E. M. Goldstein Haudek, & W. E. Haudek (Eds.), Selected Papers/Ausgewählte Schriften. The Hague: Martinus Nijhoff.

Goldstein, K. (1936). The significance of the frontal lobes for mental performances. *Journal of Neurology and Psychopathology, 17*(65), 27.

Goldstein, K., & Scheerer, M. (1941). Abstract and concrete behavior: An experimental study with special tests. *Psychological Monograph, 43*, 1–151.

Gontkovsky, S. T., McDonald, N. B., Clark, P. G., & Ruwe, W. D. (2002). Current directions in computer-assisted cognitive rehabilitation. *NeuroRehabilitation, 17*(3), 195–200.

Gordon, E. (2003). Integrative neuroscience. *Neuropsychopharmacology, 28*(Suppl. 1), 2–8.

Gordon, E., Cooper, C., Rennie, D., & Williams, L. M. (2005). Integrative neuroscience: The role of a standardized database. *Clinical EEG and Neuroscience, 36*, 64–75.

Gordon, W. A., Zafonte, R., Cicerone, K., Cantor, J., Brown, M., Lombard, L., & Chandna, T. (2006). Traumatic brain injury rehabilitation. *Brain Injury Rehabilitation, 85*, 343-382.

Grafman, J., & Litvan, I. (1999). Importance of deficits in executive functions. *The Lancet, 354*, 1921–1923.

Grafman, J., Schwab, K., Warden, D., Pridgen, A., Grown, H. R., & Salazar, A. M. (1996). Frontal lobe injuries, violence, and aggression: A report of the Vietnam Head Injury Study. *Neurology, 46*, 1231–1238.

Grant, D. A., & Berg, E. (1948). A behavioral analysis of degree of reinforcement and ease of shifting to new responses in a Weigl-type card-sorting problem. *Journal of Experimental Psychology, 38*, 404–411.

Grant, S., Bonson, K. R., Contoreggi, C., & London, E. D. (1999). Activation of the ventromedial prefrontal cortex correlates with gambling task performance: A FDG-PET study. *Society for Neuroscience Abstracts, 25*, 1551.

Gras, D., Gyselinck, V., Perrussel, M., Orriols, E., & Piolino, P. (2013). The role of working memory components and visuospatial abilities in route learning within a virtual environment. *Journal of Cognitive Psychology, 25*(1), 38–50.

Gray, J. M., Robertson, I., Pentland, B., & Anderson, S. (1992). Microcomputer-based attentional retraining after brain damage: A randomised group controlled trial. *Neuropsychological Rehabilitation, 2*(2), 97–115.

Green, M. F. (1996). What are the functional consequences of neurocognitive deficits in schizophrenia? *American Journal of Psychiatry, 153*(3), 321–330.

Green, M. F., Kern, R. S., Braff, D. L., & Mintz, J. (2000). Neurocognitive deficits and functional outcome in schizophrenia: Are we measuring the "right stuff"? *Schizophrenia Bulletin, 26*(1), 119–136.

Green, P. (2003a). Green's word memory test. Green's Pub.
Green, P. (2003b). Welcoming a paradigm shift in neuropsychology. *Archives of Clinical Neuropsychology, 18*, 625–627.
Green, P., & Iverson, G. L. (2001). Validation of the computerized assessment of response bias in litigating patients with head injuries. *The Clinical Neuropsychologist, 15*, 492–497.
Grosch, M. C., Gottlieb, M. C., & Cullum, C. M. (2011). Initial practice recommendations for teleneuropsychology. *The Clinical Neuropsychologist, 25*(7), 1119–1133.
Grosch, M., Weiner, M., Hynan, L. S., Shore, J., & Cullum, C. M. (2015). Video teleconfer-ence-based neurocognitive screening in geropsychiatry. *Psychiatry Research.*
Gualtieri, C. T., & Johnson, L. G. (2005). Neurocognitive testing supports a broader concept of mild cognitive impairment. *The American Journal of Alzheimer's Disease and Other Dementias, 20*, 359–366.
Guilmette, T. J., Faust, D., Hart, K., & Arkes, H. R. (1990). A national survey of psychologists who offer neuropsychological services. *Archives of Clinical Neuropsychology, 5*, 373–392.
Gur, R. C., Ragland, J. D., Moberg, P. J., Turner, T. H., Bilker, W. B., Kohler, C., & Gur, R. E. (2001). Computerized neurocognitive scanning: I. Methodology and validation in healthy people. *Neuropsychopharmacology, 25*(5), 766–776.
Gur, R. C., Ragland, J. D., Moberg, P. J., Bilker, W. B., Kohler, C., Siegel, S. J., & Gur, R. E. (2001). Computerized neurocognitive scanning: II. The profile of schizophrenia. *Neuropsychopharmacology, 25*(5), 777–788.
Gur, R. C., Sara, R., Hagendoorn, M., Marom, O., Hughett, P., Macy, L., et al. (2002). A method for obtaining 3-dimensional facial expressions and its standardization for use in neurocognitive studies. *Journal of Neuroscience Methods, 115*, 137–143.
Gur, R. E., Calkins, M. E., Gur, R. C., Horan, W. P., Nuechterlein, K. H., Seidman, L. J., & Stone, W. S. (2007). The consortium on the genetics of schizophrenia: neurocognitive endophenotypes. *Schizophrenia Bulletin, 33*(1), 49–68.
Gurwitsch, A. (1949). Gelb-Goldstein's concepts of "Concrete" and "categorial" attitude and the phenomenology of idealism. *Philosophy and Phenomenological Research, 10*, 172–196.
Gutierrez-Maldonado, J., Letosa-Porta, A., Rus-Calafell, M., & Penaloza-Salazar, C. (2009). The assessment of Attention Deficit Hyperactivity Disorder in children using continuous performance tasks in virtual environments. *Anuario de Psicologia, 40*, 211–222.
Gyselinck, V., Meneghetti, C., Bormetti, M., Orriols, E., Piolino, P., & De Beni, R. (2013). Considering spatial ability in virtual route learning in early aging. *Cognitive Processing, 14*, 309–316.
Hammers, D., Spurgeon, E., Ryan, K., Persad, C., Barbas, N., Heidebrink, J., & Giordani, B. (2012). Validity of a brief computerized cognitive screening test in dementia. *Journal of Geriatric Psychiatry and Neurology, 25*(2), 89-99.
Halstead, W. C. (1947). *Brain and Intelligence.* Chicago: University of Chicago Press.
Hanfmann, E. (1968). Goldstein and Vygotsky. In M. Simmel (Ed.), *The reach of mind.* New York: Springer.
Hanzevacki, M., Ozegovic, G., Simovic, I., & Bajic, Z. (2011). Proactive approach in detect-ing elderly subjects with cognitive decline in general practitioners' practices. *Dementia and Geriatric Cognitive Disorders Extra, 1*(1), 93.
Happaney, K., Zelazo, P. D., & Stuss, D. T. (2004). Development of orbitofrontal function: current themes and future directions. *Brain and Cognition, 55*, 1–10.
Hardy, K. K., Willard, V. W., & Bonner, M. J. (2011). Computerized cognitive training in survivors of childhood cancer a pilot study. *Journal of Pediatric Oncology Nursing, 28*(1), 27–33.
Harrell, K. M., Wilkins, S. S., Connor, M. K., & Chodosh, J. (2014). Telemedicine and the evaluation of cognitive impairment: The additive value of neuropsychological assessment. *Journal of the American Medical Directors Association, 15*(8), 600–606.
Hart, T., & Hayden, M. E. (1986). The ecological validity of neuropsychological assessment and remediation. In *Clinical neuropsychology of intervention* (pp. 21–50). Springer US.

Hartlage, L. C., & Telzrow, C. F. (1980). The practice of clinical neuropsychology in the US. *Archives of Clinical Neuropsychology, 2*, 200–202.

Heaton, R. (1999). *Wisconsin Card Sorting Test: Computer Version 3 for Windows* (Research ed.). Lutz, Florida: Psychological Assessment Resources.

Heaton, R. K., & Adams, K. M. (1987). Potential versus current reality of automation in neuropsychology: Reply to Kleinmuntz. *Journal of Consulting and Clinical Psychology, 55*, 268–269.

Heaton, R. K., Chelune, G. J., Talley, J. L., Kay, G. G., & Curtiss, G. (1993). *Wisconsin Card Sorting Test manual: Revised and expanded.* Odessa, FL: Psychological Assessment Resources.

Heaton, R. K., Grant, I., Anthony, W. Z., & Lehman, R. A. W. (1981). A comparison of clinical and automated interpretation of the Halstead-Reitan Battery. *Journal of Clinical Neuropsychology, 22*, 121–141.

Heaton, R. K., Grant, I., & Matthews, C. G. (1991). *Comprehensive norms for an expanded Halstead-Reitan Battery: Demographic corrections, research findings, and clinical appli-cations.* Odessa: Psychological Assessment Resources.

Heaton, R. K., & PAR. (2003). Wisconsin Card Sorting Test: Computer Version 4, Research Edition (WCST: CV4). Odessa, FL: Psychological Assessment Resources.

Heaton, R. K., & Pendleton, M. G. (1981). Use of Neuropsychological tests to predict adult patients' everyday functioning. *Journal of Consulting and Clinical Psychology, 49*, 807.

Hebb, D. O., & Penfield, W. (1940). Human behavior after extensive bilateral removal from the frontal lobes. *Archives of Neurology & Psychiatry, 44*(2), 421–438.

Hebb, D. O. (1949). *The organization of behavior.* New York: Wiley.

Hebb, D. O. (1963). Introduction to Dover edition. In K. S. Lashley, Brain mechanisms and intel-ligence.

Hebb, D. O. (1981). Consider mind as a biological problem. *Neuroscience, 6*(12), 2419–2422.

Heeschen, C. (1994). Franz Joseph Gall. *Reader in the History of Aphasia: From Franz Gall to Norman Geschwind, 4*, 1.

Henry, M., Joyal, C. C., & Nolin, P. (2012). Development and initial assessment of a new paradigm for assessing cognitive and motor inhibition: The bimodal virtual-reality Stroop. *Journal of Neuroscience Methods, 210*, 125–131.

Hildebrand, R., Chow, H., Williams, C., Nelson, M., & Wass, P. (2004). Feasibility of neuro-psychological testing of older adults via videoconference: implications for assessing the capacity for independent living. *Journal of Telemedicine and Telecare, 10*(3), 130–134.

Hill, N. J., Häuser, A., & Schalk, G. (2014). A general method for assessing brain-computer interface performance and its limitations. *Journal of Neural Engineering, 11*(2).

Hinson, J. M., Jameson, T. L., & Whitney, P. (2002). Somatic markers, working memory, and decision making. *Cognitive, Affective, & Behavioral Neuroscience, 2*(4), 341–353.

Hinson, J. M., Jameson, T. L., & Whitney, P. (2003). Impulsive decision making and working memory. *Journal of Experimental Psychology: Learning, Memory, and Cognition, 29*(2), 298.

Hoffman, H. G., Chambers, G. T., Meyer III, W. J., Arceneaux, L. L., Russell, W. J., Seibel, E. J., & Patterson, D. R. (2011). Virtual reality as an adjunctive non-pharmacologic analgesic for acute burn pain during medical procedures. *Annals of Behavioral Medicine, 41*(2), 183-191.

Hom, J. (2003). Forensic neuropsychology: Are we there yet? *Archives of Clinical Neuropsychology, 18*, 827–845.

Hoskins, L. L., Binder, L. M., Chaytor, N. S., Williamson, D. J., & Drane, D. L. (2010). Comparison of oral and computerized versions of the Word Memory Test. *Archives of Clinical Neuropsychology, 25*, 591–600.

Huang-Pollock, C. L., Karalunas, S. L., Tam, H., & Moore, A. N. (2012). Evaluating vigilance deficits in ADHD: a meta-analysis of CPT performance. *Journal of Abnormal Psychology, 121* (2), 360.

Hume, D. (1978). A treatise of human nature (LA Selby-Bigge, Ed.). New York: Oxford, 413-418.

Hunt, H. F. (1943). A practical clinical test for organic brain damage. *Journal of Applied Psychology, 27*, 375–86.

Imam, B., & Jarus, T. (2014). Virtual reality rehabilitation from social cognitive and motor learning theoretical perspectives in stroke population. *Rehabilitation Research and Practice.*

Inoue, M., Jinbo, D., Nakamura, Y., Taniguchi, M., & Urakami, K. (2009). Development and evaluation of a computerized test battery for Alzheimer's disease screening in community-based settings. *American Journal of Alzheimer's Disease and other Dementias, 24*, 129–135.

Internet Live Stats. (2015). Internet Users. Retrieved from Internet Live Stats: http://www.internetlivestats.com/internet-users-by-country/.

Inventado, P., Legaspi, R., Suarez, M., & Numao, M. (2011). Predicting student emotions resulting from appraisal of its feedback. *Research and Practice in Technology Enhanced Learning, 6*(2), 107–33.

Irani, F., Brensinger, C. M., Richard, J., Calkins, M. E., Moberg, P. J., Bilker, W., & Gur, R. C. (2012). Computerized neurocognitive test performance in schizophrenia: a lifespan analysis. *The American Journal of Geriatric Psychiatry, 20*(1), 41-52.

Iriate, Y., Diaz-Orueta, U., Cueto, E., Irazustabarrena, P., Banterla, F., & Climent, G. (2012). AULA - advanced virtual reality tool for the assessment of attention: normative study in Spain. *Journal of Attention Disorders, 20*, 1–27.

Iverson, G. L., Lovell, M. R., & Collins, M. W. (2003). Interpreting change on ImPACT following sport concussion. *The Clinical Neuropsychologist, 17*(4), 460–467.

Iverson, G. L., Brooks, B. L., Ashton, V. L., Johnson, L. G., & Gualtieri, C. T. (2009). Does familiarity with computers affect computerized neuropsychological test performance? *Journal of Clinical and Experimental Neuropsychology, 31*(5), 594–604.

Ivins, B. J., Kane, R., & Schwab, K. A. (2009). Performance on the Automated Neuropsychological Assessment Metrics in a nonclinical sample of soldiers screened for mild TBI after returning from Iraq and Afghanistan: a descriptive analysis. *The Journal of Head Trauma Rehabilitation, 24*(1), 24–31.

Jacobsen, S. E., Sprenger, T., Andersson, S., & Krogstad, J. (2003). Neuropsychological as-sessment and telemedicine: a preliminary study examining the reliability of neuropsychol-ogy services performed via telecommunication. *Journal of the International Neuropsycho-logical Society, 9*(03), 472–478.

Jacoby, M., Averbuch, S., Sacher, Y., Katz, N., Weiss, P. L., & Kizony, R. (2013). Effectiveness of executive functions training within a virtual supermarket for adults with traumatic brain injury: a pilot study. *IEEE Transactions on Neural Systems and Rehabilitation Engineering, 21* (2), 182–90.

Jacyna, S. (2004). Bastian's four centres. *Cortex, 40*, 7–8.

Jacyna, S. (2004). Lichtheim's "house". *Cortex, 40*, 413–414.

Jagaroo, V. (2009). *Neuroinformatics for neuropsychology*. US: Springer.

Jansari, A. S., Froggatt, D., Edginton, T., & Dawkins, L. (2013). Investigating the impact of nicotine on executive functions using a novel virtual reality assessment. *Addiction, 108*, 977–984.

Jansari, A. S., Devlin, A., Agnew, R., Akesson, K., Murphy, L., & Leadbetter, T. (2014). Ecological assessment of executive functions: A new virtual reality paradigm. *Brain Impairment, 15*(02), 71–87.

Jatupaiboon, N., Pan-ngum, S., & Israsena, P. (2013). Real-time EEG-based happiness detection system. *The Scientific World Journal*, 618649.

Johansson, B. B., & Tornmalm, M. (2012). Working memory training for patients with acquired brain injury: effects in daily life. *Scandinavian Journal of Occupational Therapy, 19*, 176–183.

Johnson, D. R., Vincent, A. S., Johnson, A. E., Gilliland, K., & Schlegel, R. E. (2008). Reliability and construct validity of the Automated Neuropsychological Assessment Metrics (ANAM) mood scale. *Archives of Clinical Neuropsychology, 1*, 73–85.

Johnson, S. C., Schmitz, T. W., Kawahara-Baccus, T. N., Rowley, H. A., Alexander, A. L., Lee, J., & Davidson, R. J. (2005). The cerebral response during subjective choice with and without self-reference. *Journal of Cognitive Neuroscience, 17*, 1897–1906.

Johnstone, B., & Stonnington, H. H. (Eds.). (2009). *Rehabilitation of neuropsychological disorders: A practical guide for rehabilitation professionals*. Philadelphia: Psychology Press.

Jokel, R., Rochon, E., & Anderson, N. D. (2010). Errorless learning of computer-generated words in a patient with semantic dementia. *Neuropsychological Rehabilitation, 20*, 16–41.

Jones-Gotman, M., Zatorre, R. J., Olivier, A., Andermann, F., Cendes, F., Staunton, H., & Wieser, H. G. (1997). Learning and retention of words and designs following excision from medial or lateral temporal-lobe structures. *Neuropsychologia, 35*(7), 963-973.

Jones, M., & Johnston, D. (2011). Understanding phenomena in the real world: The case for real time data collection in health services research. *Journal of Health Services Research & Policy, 16*, 172–176.

Josman, N., Kizony, R., Hof, E., Goldenberg, K., Weiss, P., & Klinger, E. (2014). Using the Virtual Action Planning-Supermarket for evaluating executive functions in people with stroke. *Journal of Stroke and Cerebrovascular Diseases, 23*, 879–887.

Josman, N., Schenirderman, A. E., Klinger, E., & Shevil, E. (2009). Using virtual reality to evaluate executive functions among persons with schizophrenia: a validity study. *Schizophrenia Research, 115*, 270–277.

Jovanovski, D., Zakzanis, K., Campbell, Z., Erb, S., & Nussbaum, D. (2012). Development of a novel, ecologically oriented virtual reality measure of executive function: The Multitasking in the City Test. *Applied Neuropsychology: Adult, 19*, 171–182.

Jovanovski, D., Zakzanis, K., Ruttan, L., Campbell, Z., Erb, S., & Nussbaum, D. (2012). Ecologically valid assessment of executive dysfunction using a novel virtual reality task in patients with acquired brain injury. *Applied Neuropsychology, 19*, 207–220.

Kandalaft, M., Didehbani, N., Krawczyk, D., Allen, T., & Chapman, S. (2013). Virtual reality social cognition training for young adults with high-functioning autism. *Journal of Autism & Developmental Disorders, 43*(1), 34–44.

Kane, R. L., & Kay, G. G. (1992). Computerized assessment in neuropsychology: A review of tests and test batteries. *Neuropsychology Review, 3*(1), 1–117.

Kane, R. L., & Kay, G. G. (1997). Computer applications in neuropsychological assessment. In *Contemporary approaches to neuropsychological assessment* (pp. 359–392). Springer US.

Kane, R. L., & Reeves, D. L. (1997). Computerized test batteries. *The Neuropsychology Handbook, 1*, 423–467.

Kane, R. L., Roebuck-Spencer, T., Short, P., Kabat, M., & Wilken, J. (2007). Identifying and monitoring cognitive deficits in clinical populations using Automated Neuropsychological Assessment Metrics (ANAM) tests. *Archives of Clinical Neuropsychology, 22*, 115–126.

Kaufmann, T., HOlz, E., & Kubler, A. (2013). Comparison of tactile, auditory, and visual modalityfor brain-computer interface use: A case study with a patient in the locked-in state. *Frontiers in Neuroscience*, *7*, 129.

Kay, G. G., & Starbuck, V. N. (1997). Computerized neuropsychological assessment. Clinical neuropsychology: theoretical foundations for practitioners (pp. 143–161). New Jersey: Lawrence Erlbaum Associates.

Keefe, F. J., Huling, D. A., Coggins, M. J., Keefe, D. F., Rosenthal, M. Z., Herr, N. R., & Hoffman, H. G. (2012). Virtual reality for persistent pain: a new direction for behavioral pain management. *PAIN, 153*(11), 2163–2166.

Kennedy, D. O., & Scholey, A. B. (2000). Glucose administration, heart rate and cognitive performance: Effects of increasing mental effort. *Psychopharmacology, 149*, 63–71.

Kerr, A., & Zelazo, P. D. (2004). Development of "hot" executive function: the children's gambling task. *Brain and Cognition, 55*, 148–157.

Kesler, S. R., Lacayo, N. J., & Jo, B. (2011). A pilot study of an online cognitive rehabilitation program for executive function skills in children with cancer-related brain injury. *Brain Injury, 25*(1), 101–112.

Kingstone, A., Smilek, D., Birmingham, E., Cameraon, D., & Bischof, W. F. (2005). *Cognitive ethology: Giving real life to attention research* (pp. 341–357). Measuring the mind: Speed, control and age.

Kingstone, A., Smilek, D., Ristic, J., Friesen, C. K., & Eastwood, J. D. (2003). Attention, researchers! It is time to take a look at the real world. *Current Directions in Psychological Science, 12*, 176–180.

Kinsella, G. J., Ong, B., & Tucker, J. (2009). Traumatic brain injury and prospective memory in a virtual shopping trip task: Does it matter who generates the prospective memory target? *Brain Impairment, 10*, 45–51.

Kiper, P., Piron, L., Turolla, A., Stozek, J., & Tonin, P. (2011). The effectiveness of reinforced feedback in virtual environment in the first 12 months after stroke. *Neurologia i Neurochirurgia Polska, 45*(5), 436–444.

Kirkwood, K. T., Peck, D. F., & Bennie, L. (2000). The consistency of neuropsychological assessments performed via telecommunication and face to face. *Journal of Telemedicine and Telecare, 6*(3), 147–151.

Kirsch, N. L., Levine, S. P., Fallon-Krueger, M., & Jaros, L. A. (1987). The microcomputer as an "orthotic" device for patients with cognitive deficits. *The Journal of Head Trauma Rehabilitation, 2*, 77–86.

Klingberg, T., Forssberg, H., & Westerberg, H. (2002). Training of working memory in children with ADHD. *Journal of Clinical and Experimental Neuropsychology, 24*, 781–791.

Klingberg, T., Fernell, E., Olesen, P. J., Johnson, M., Gustafsson, P., Dahlstrom, K., Westerberg, H. (2005). Computerized training of working memory in children with ADHD—A randomized, controlled trial. *Journal of the American Academy of Child and Adolescent Psychiatry, 44*, 177–186.

Klinge, V., & Rodziewicz, T. (1976). Automated and manual intelligence testing of the Peabody Picture Vocabulary Test on a psychiatric adolescent population. *International Journal of Man-Machine Studies, 8*, 243–246.

Knight, C., & Alderman, N. (2002). Development of a simplified version of the Multiple Errands Test for use in hospital settings. *Neuropsychological Rehabilitation, 12*(3), 231–255.

Knight, R. G., & Titov, N. (2009). Use of virtual reality tasks to assess prospective memory: Applicability and evidence. *Brain Impairment, 10*, 3–13.

Knights, R, M., Richardson, D, H, & McNarry, L, R, (1973), Automated vs, clinical administration of the Peabody Picture Vocabulary Test and the Coloured Progressive Matrices. *American Journal of Mental Deficiency, 78*, 223–225.

Knouse, L. E., Bagwell, C. L., Barkley, R. A., & Murphy, K. R. (2005). Accuracy of self-evaluation in adults with ADHD: Evidence from a Driving Study. *Journal of Attention Disorders, 8*, 221–234.

Kobayashi, N., Yoshino, A., Takahashi, Y., & Nomura, S. (2007). Autonomic arousal in cognitive conflict resolution. *Autonomic Neuroscience: Basic and Clinical, 132*, 70–75.

Koenig, S. T., Crucian, G. P., Dalrymple-Alford, J. C., & Dünser, A. (2009). Virtual reality rehabilitation of spatial abilities after brain damage. *Studies in Health Technology and Informatics, 144*, 105–107.

Kohler, C. G., Walker, J. B., Martin, E. A., Healey, K. M., & Moberg, P. J. (2010). Facial emotion perception in schizophrenia: A meta-analytic review. *Schizophrenia Bulletin, 36*, 1009–1019.

Koslow, S. H. (2000). Should the neuroscience community make a paradigm shift to sharing primary data? *Nature Neuroscience, 3*(9), 863–865.

Kramer, J. H., Mungas, D., Possin, K. L., Rankin, K. P., Boxer, A. L., Rosen, H. J., & Widmeyer, M. (2014). NIH EXAMINER: conceptualization and development of an executive function battery. *Journal of the International Neuropsychological Society, 20*(01), 11–19.

Kuhn, T. S. (1996). The structure of scientific revolutions (3rd Edn.). Chicago: University of Chicago Press, first published 1962 (The University of Chicago Press).

Kurlychek, R. T. (1983). Use of a digital alarm chronograph as a memory aid in early dementia. *Clinical Gerontologist, 1*, 93–94.

Kwan, R. Y. C., & Lai, C. K. Y. (2013). Can smartphones enhance telephone-based cognitive assessment (TBCA)? *International journal of environmental research and public health, 10* (12), 7110–7125.

Lalonde, G., Henry, M., Drouin-Germain, A., Nolin, P., & Beauchamp, M. H. (2013). Assessment of executive function in adolescence: a comparison of traditional and virtual reality tools. *Journal of Neuroscience Methods, 219*, 76–82.

Lamberts, K., Evans, J., & Spikman, J. (2009). A real-life, ecologically valid test of executive functioning: The executive secretarial task. *Journal of Clinical and Experimental Neuropsychology*, 56-65.

Larose, S., Gagnon, S., Ferland, C., & Pépin, M. (1989). Psychology of computers: XIV. Cognitive rehabilitation through computer games. *Perceptual and Motor Skills, 69*(3 Pt 1), 851-858.

Larrabee, G. J. (2008). Flexible vs. fixed batteries in forensic neuropsychological assessment: Reply to Bigler and Hom. *Archives of Clinical Neuropsychology, 23*(7), 763–776.

Larrabee, G. J., & Crook, T. H. (1996). Computers and memory. In I. Grant & K. M. Adams (Eds.), *Neuropsychological assessment of neuropsychiatric disorders* (2nd ed., pp. 102–117). New York: Oxford University Press.

Larson, E. B., Feigon, M., Gagliardo, P., & Dvorkin, A. Y. (2014). Virtual reality and cognitive rehabilitation: A review of current outcome research. *Neuro Rehabilitation, 34*(4), 759–772.

Lashley, K. S. (1929). *Brain mechanisms and intelligence*. Chicago: University of Chicago Press.

Lashley, K. S. (1950). In search of the engram. In J. F. Danielli & R. Brown (Eds.), *Physiological mechanisms in animal behaviour* (pp. 454–482). New York: Academic Press.

Law, A. S., Trawley, S. L., Brown, L. A., Stephens, A. N., & Logie, R. H. (2013). The impact of working memory load on task execution and online plan adjustment during multitasking in a virtual environment. *The Quarterly Journal of Experimental Psychology, 66*, 1241–1258.

Ledoux, J. (1996). *The emotional brain: The mysterious underpinnings of emotional life*. New York: Touchstone.

Lee, H., Baniqued, P. L., Cosman, J., Mullen, S., McAuley, E., Severson, J., & Kramer, A. F. (2012). Examining cognitive function across the lifespan using a mobile application. *Computers in Human Behavior, 28*(5), 1934–1946.

Lee, H. C., Cameron, D., & Lee, A. G. (2003). Assessing the driving performance of older adult drivers: On-road versus simulated driving. *Accident Analysis and Prevention, 35*, 797–803.

Lee, H. C., Lee, A. H., Cameron, D., & Li-Tsang, C. (2003). Using a driving simulator to identify older drivers at inflated risk of motor vehicle crashes. *Journal of Safety Research, 34*, 453–459.

Lees-Haley, P. R., Smith, H. H., Williams, C. W., & Dunn, J. T. (1996). Forensic neuropsychological test usage: an empirical survey. *Archives of Clinical Neuropsychology, 11*, 45–51.

Legenfelder, J., Schultheis, M. T., Al-Shihabi, T., Mourant, R., & DeLuca, J. (2002). Divided attention and driving: a pilot study using virtual reality technology. *Journal of Head Trauma Rehabilitation, 17*, 26–37.

Levine, B., Dawson, D., Boutet, I., Schwartz, M. L., & Stuss, D. T. (2000). Assessment of strategic self-regulation in traumatic brain injury: Its relationship to injury severity and psychosocial outcome. *Neuropsychology, 14*, 491–500.

Levinson, D., Reeves, D., Watson, J., & Harrison, M. (2005). Automated neuropsychological assessment metrics (ANAM) measures of cognitive effects of Alzheimer's disease. *Archives of Clinical Neuropsychology, 20*(3), 403–408.

Lezak, M. D. (1983). Neuropsychological assessment (pp. 91–97). New York: Oxford.

Lezak, M. (1986). Psychological implications of traumatic brain damage for the patient's family. *Rehabilitation Psychology, 31*(4), 241-250.

Lezak, M. D. (1995). *Neuropsychological Assessment* (3rd ed.). New York: Oxford University Press.

Li, K., Robertson, J., Ramos, J., & Gella, S. (2013). Computer-based cognitive retraining for adults with chronic acquired brain injury: A pilot study. *Occupational Therapy in Health Care, 27*, 333–344.

Lieberman, M. D. (2010). Social cognitive neuroscience. In S. T. Fiske, D. T. Gilbert, & G. Lindzey (Eds.), *Handbook of Social Psychology* (5th ed., pp. 143–193). New York: McGraw-Hill.

Lieberman M. D., Eisenberger N. I. (2005). Conflict and habit: a social cognitive neuroscience approach to the self. In A. Tesser, J. V. Wood, D. A. Stapel (Eds.), *On building, defending and regulating the self: A psychological perspective* (pp. 77–102), New York: Psychology Press.

Liu, L., Miyazaki, M., & Watson, B. (1999). Norms and validity of the DriVR: A virtual reality driving assessment for persons with head injuries. *Cyberpsychology & Behavior, 2*, 53–67.

Logie, R. H., Trawley, S., & Law, A. (2011). Multitasking: multiple, domain-specific cognitive functions in a virtual environment. *Memory & Cognition, 39*, 1561–1574.

Loh, P. K., Ramesh, P., Maher, S., Saligari, J., Flicker, L., & Goldswain, P. (2004). Can pa-tients with dementia be assessed at a distance? The use of Telehealth and standardized as-sessments. *Internal Medicine Journal, 34*(5), 239–242.

Loh, P. K., Donaldson, M., Flicker, L., Maher, S., & Goldswain, P. (2007). Development of a telemedicine protocol for the diagnosis of Alzheimer's disease. *Journal of Telemedicine and Telecare, 13*(2), 90–94.

Long, C. J. (1996). Neuropsychological tests: A look at our past and the impact that ecological issues may have on our future. In R. J. Sbordone & C. J. Long (Eds.), *Ecological Validity of Neuropsychological Testing* (pp. 1–14). Delray Beach: GR Press/St. Lucie Press.

Long, C. J., & Wagner, M. (1986). Computer applications in neuropsychology. In D. Wedding, A. M. Horton, & J. Webster (Eds.), *The neuropsychology handbook* (pp. 548–569). New York: Springer.

Lopez, S. J., Ryan, J. J., Sumerall, S. W., Lichtenberg, J. W., Glasnapp, D., Krieshok, T. S., & Van Fleet, J. N. (2001). Demographic variables and microCog performance: Relationships for VA patients under treatment for substance abuse. *Psychological Reports, 88*, 183–188.

Loring, D. W., & Bauer, R. M. (2010). Testing the limits: Cautions and concerns regarding the new Wechsler IQ and Memory scales. *Neurology, 74*(8), 685–690.

Loring, D. W., & Bowden, S. C. (2014). The STROBE statement and neuropsychology: light-ing the way toward evidence-based practice. *The Clinical Neuropsychologist, 28*(4), 556–574.

Louey, A. G., Cromer, J. A., Schembri, A. J., Darby, D. G., Maruff, P., Makdissi, M., & Mccrory, P. (2014). Detecting cognitive impairment after concussion: sensitivity of change from baseline and normative data methods using the CogSport/Axon cognitive test battery. *Archives of Clinical Neuropsychology, 29*(5), 432–441.

Lovell, M. R., Collins, M. W., Maroon, J. C., Cantu, R., Hawn, M. A., Burke, C. J., & Fu, F. (2002). Inaccuracy of symptom reporting following concussion in athletes. *Medicine & Science in Sports & Exercise, 34*, S298.

Lovell, M., Collins, M., & Bradley, J. (2004). Return to play following sports-related concussion. *Clinics in Sports Medicine, 23*(3), 421–441.

Lovell, M. R. (2013). *Immediate post-concussion assessment testing (ImPACT) test: clinical interpretive manual online ImPACT 2007-2012*. Pittsburgh: ImPACT Applications Inc.

Lubin, B., Larsen, R. M., & Matarazzo, J. D. (1984). Patterns of psychological test usage in the United States: 1935-1982. *American Psychologist, 39*(4), 451.

Lundqvist, A., Grundström, K., Samuelsson, K., & Rönnberg, J. (2010). Computerized training of working memory in a group of patients suffering from acquired brain injury. *Brain Injury, 24*, 1173–1183.

Luria, A. R. (1966/1980). Higher Cortical Functions in Man (2nd ed., rev. and expanded), Basic Books, New York.

Luria, A. R., & Majovski, L. V. (1977). Basic approaches used in American and Soviet clin-ical neuropsychology. *American Psychologist, 32*, 959–968.

Lynch, B. (2002). Historical review of computer-assisted cognitive retraining. *Journal of Head Trauma Rehabilitation, 17*(5), 446–457.

Lysaker, P., Bell, M., & Bean-Goulet, J. (1995). Wisconsin Card Sorting Test and work performance in schizophrenia. *Psychiatry Research, 56*, 45–51.

MacDonald, S., & Wiseman-Hakes, C. (2010). Knowledge translation in ABI rehabilitation: A model for consolidating and applying the evidence for cognitive-communication interventions. *Brain Injury, 24*(3), 486–508.

Maerlender, A., Flashman, L., Kessler, A., Kumbhani, S., Greenwald, R., Tosteson, T., & McAllister, T. (2010). Examination of the construct validity of ImPACT™ computerized test, traditional, and experimental neuropsychological measures. *The Clinical Neuropsychologist, 24*(8), 1309–1325.

Magnussen, S., & Heilstrup, T. (Eds.). (2007). *Everyday memory*. Hove and New York: Psychological Press.

Majovski, L. V., & Jacques, S. (1980). Current neuropsychological approaches in assess-ment, rehabilitation, and clinical research of central nervous system disorders. *Neurosurgery, 7*, 182–186.

Mak, J. N., & Wolpaw, J. R. (2009). Clinical applications of brain-computer interfaces: Current state and future prospects. *IEEE Reviews in Biomedical Engineering, 2*, 187–199.

Makatura, T. J., Lam, C. S., Leahy, B. J., Castillo, M. T., & Kalpakjian, C. Z. (1999). Standardized memory tests and the appraisal of everyday memory. *Brain Injury, 13*, 355–367.

Manchester, D., Priestley, N., & Jackson, H. (2004). The assessment of executive functions: Coming out of the office. *Brain Injury, 18*(11), 1067–1081.

Manes, F., Sahakian, B., Clark, L., Rogers, R., Antoun, N., Aitken, M., et al. (2002). Decision-making processes following damage to the prefrontal cortex. *Brain, 125*, 624–639.

Mapou, R. L. (1988). Testing to detect brain damage: An alternative to what may no longer be useful. *Journal of Clinical and Experimental Neuropsychology, 10*, 271–278.

Marcotte, T. D., & Grant, I. (Eds.). (2009). Neuropsychology of everyday functioning. Guilford Press.

Maringelli, F., Mccarthy, J., Steed, A., Slater, M., & Umiltà, C. (2001). Shifting visuo-spatial attention in a virtual three-dimensional space. *Cognitive Brain Research, 10*, 317–322.

Maroof, D. A. (2012). Assumptions of Statistical Analyses. In *Statistical Methods in Neuropsychology* (pp. 17–22). Springer US.

Marotta, J. J., & Behrmann, M. (2004). Patient Schn: has Goldstein and Gelb's case with-stood the test of time? *Neuropsychologia, 42*(5), 633–638.

Martoni, R. M., Salgari, G., Galimberti, E., Cavallini, M. C., & O'Neill, J. (2015). Effects of gender and executive function on visuospatial working memory in adult obsessive-compulsive disorder. *European Archives of Psychiatry and Clinical Neuroscience*, 1–12.

Maruff, P., Thomas, E., Cysique, L., Brew, B., Collie, A., Snyder, P., & Pietrzak, R. H. (2009). Validity of the CogState brief battery: Relationship to standardized tests and sensitivity to cognitive impairment in mild traumatic brain injury, schizophrenia, and AIDS dementia complex. *Archives of Clinical Neuropsychology, 24*(2), 165–178.

Marusan, M., Kulistak, P., & Zara, J. (2006). Virtual reality in neurorehabilitation: Mental rotation, proceedings of the third central European Multimedia and Virtual Reality Conference (pp. 77–83). Veszprém: Pannonian University Press.

Masmoudi, S., Dai, D. Y., & Naceur, A. (Eds.). (2012). Attention, representation, and human performance: Integration of cognition, emotion, and motivation. Psychology Press.

Mateer, C. A., & Sohlberg, M. M. (1988). A paradigm shift in memory rehabilitation. In Neuropsychological studies of nonfocal brain damage (pp. 202–225). New York: Springer.

Matheis, R. J., Schultheis, M. T., Tiersky, L. A., DeLuca, J., Millis, S. R., & Rizzo, A. (2007). Is learning and memory different in a virtual environment? *Clinical Neuropsychology, 21*, 146–161.

Mathersul, D., Palmer, D. M., Gur, R. C., Gur, R. E., Cooper, N., Gordon, E., & Williams, L. M. (2009). Explicit identification and implicit recognition of facial emotions: II. Core domains and relationships with general cognition. *Journal of Clinical and Experimental Neuropsychology, 31*(3), 278–291.
Mathewson, K. J., Jetha, M. K., Drmic, I. E., Bryson, S. E., Goldberg, J. O., Hall, G. B., et al. (2010). Autonomic predictors of Stroop performance in young and middle-aged adults. *International Journal of Psychophysiology, 76*, 123–129.
McCann, R. A., Armstrong, C. M., Skopp, N. A., Edwards-Stewart, A., Smolenski, D. J., June, J. D., & Reger, G. M. (2014). Virtual reality exposure therapy for the treatment of anxiety disorders: An evaluation of research quality. *Journal of Anxiety Disorders, 28*(6), 625–631.
McDonald, S. (2013). Impairments in social cognition following severe traumatic brain injury. *Journal of the International Neuropsychological Society, 19*, 231–246.
McEachern, W., Kirk, A., Morgan, D. G., Crossley, M., & Henry, C. (2008). Reliability of the MMSE administered in-person and by telehealth. *The Canadian Journal of Neurological Sciences, 35*(05), 643–646.
McGeorge, P., Phillips, L. H., Crawford, J. R., Garden, S. E., Sala, S. D., & Milne, A. B. (2001). Using virtual environments in the assessment of executive dysfunction. *Presence, 10*, 375–383.
McGurk, S., Twamley, E., Sitzer, D., McHugo, G., & Mueser, K. (2007). A meta-analysis of cognitive remediation in schizophrenia. *American Journal of Psychiatry, 164*(12), 1791–1802.
McKeever, J., Schultheis, M., Padmanaban, V., & Blasco, A. (2013). Driver performance while texting: even a little is too much. *Traffic Injury Prevention, 14*, 132–137.
McLean, A., Dowson, J., Toone, B., Young, S., Bazanis, E., Robbins, T. W., & Sahakian, B. J. (2004). Characteristic neurocognitive profile associated with adult attention-deficit/ hyperactivity disorder. *Psychological Medicine, 34*, 681–692.
McMahan, T., Parberry, I., & Parsons, T. D. (2015a). Evaluating Player Task Engagement and Arousal using Electroencephalography. In *Proceedings of the 6th International Conference on Applied Human Factors and Ergonomics*, Las Vegas, USA (July 26-30).
McMahan, T., Parberry, I., & Parsons, T.D. (2015b). Evaluating Electroencephalography Engagement Indices During Video Game Play. Proceedings of the Foundations of Digital Games Conference, June 22-June 25, 2015.
McMahan, T., Parberry, I., & Parsons, T. D. (2015). Modality Specific Assessment of Video Game Player's Experience Using the Emotiv. *Entertainment Computing, 7*, 1–6.
Meacham, J. A. (1982). A note on remembering to execute planned actions. *Journal of Applied Developmental Psychology, 3*, 121–133.
Mead, A. D., & Drasgow, F. (1993). Equivalence of computerized and paper-and-pencil cognitive ability tests: A meta-analysis. *Psychological Bulletin, 114*, 449–458.
Medalia, A., Lim, R., & Erlanger, D. (2005). Psychometric properties of the web-based work-readiness cognitive screen used as a neuropsychological assessment tool for schizophrenia. *Computer Methods and Programs In Biomedicine, 80*(2), 93–102.
Meehan, W. P., 3rd, d'Hemecourt, P., Collins, C. L., Taylor, A. M., & Comstock, R. D. (2012). Computerized neurocognitive testing for the management of sport-related concussions. *Pediatrics, 129*(1), 38-44.
Meehl, P. E. (1987). Foreword. In J. N. Butcher (Ed.), Computerized Psychological Assessment (pp. xv–xvi). New York: Basic Books.
Mehler, B., Reimer, B., Coughlin, J. F., & Dusek, J. A. (2009). Impact of incremental increases in cognitive workload on physiological arousal and performance in young adult drivers. *Journal of the Transportation Research Board, 2138*, 6–12.
Mehta, M. A., Goodyer, I. M., & Sahakian, B. J. (2004). Methylphenidate improves working memory and set-shifting in AD/HD: Relationships to baseline memory capacity. *Journal of Child Psychology and Psychiatry, 45*, 293–305.
Meier, M. J. (1992). Modern clinical neuropsychology in historical perspective. *American Psy-chologist, 47*(4), 550–558.

Menon, A. S., Kondapavalru, P., Krishna, P., Chrismer, J. B., Raskin, A., Hebel, J. R., & Ruskin, P. E. (2001). Evaluation of a portable low cost videophone system in the assess-ment of depressive symptoms and cognitive function in elderly medically ill veterans. *The Journal of Nervous and Mental Disease, 189*(6), 399–401.

Merali, Y., & McKelvey, B. (2006). Using complexity science to effect a paradigm shift in Information Systems for the 21st century. *Journal of Information Technology, 21*, 211–215.

Meyer, V. (1961). Psychological effects of brain damage. In H. J. Eysenck (Ed.), *Handbook of abnormal psychology* (pp. 529–565). New York: Basic Books.

Meyer, R. E. (1996). Neuropsychopharmacology: Are we ready for a paradigm shift? *Neuropsychopharmacology, 14*, 169–179.

Millan, J. D., Rupp, R., Muller-Putz, G. R., Murray-Smith, R., Giugliemma, C., Tangermann, M., & Mattia, D. (2010). Combining brain-computer interfaces and assistive technologies: State-of-the-art and challenges. *Frontiers in Neuroscience, 4*, 10.

Miller, E. (1996). Phrenology, neuropsychology and rehabilitation. *Neuropsychological Rehabilitation, 6*(4), 245–256.

Miller, G. A. (2003). The cognitive revolution: A historical perspective. *Trends in Cognitive Sciences, 7*, 141–144.

Miller, J. B., Schoenberg, M. R., & Bilder, R. M. (2014). Consolidated Standards of Report-ing Trials (CONSORT): Considerations for Neuropsychological Research. *The Clinical Neuropsychologist, 28*(4), 575–599.

Milleville-Pennel, I., Pothier, J., Hoc, J. M., & Mathe, J. F. (2010). Consequences of cognitive impairments following traumatic brain injury: pilot study on visual exploration while driving. *Brain Injury, 24*, 678–691.

Milner, B. (1963). Effects of different brain lesions on card sorting: The role of the frontal lobes. *Archives of Neurology, 9*(1), 90–00.

Mitrushina, M. N., Boone, K. L., & D'Elia, L. (1999). *Handbook of normative data for neu-ropsychological assessment*. New York: Oxford University Press.

Moffat, S. D. (2009). Aging and spatial navigation: what do we know and where do we go? *Neuropsychology Review, 19*(4), 478–489.

Montgomery, C., Ashmore, K., & Jansari, A. (2011). The effects of a modest dose of alcohol on executive functioning and prospective memory. *Human Psychopharmacology: Clinical and Experimental, 26*, 208–215.

Moore, T. M., Reise, S. P., Gur, R. E., Hakonarson, H., & Gur, R. C. (2015). Psychometric properties of the penn computerized neurocognitive battery. *Neuropsychology, 29*(2), 235–246.

Morris, R. G., Kotitsa, M., Bramham, J., Brooks, B. M., & Rose, F. D. (2002). Virtual reality investigation of strategy formation, rule breaking and prospective memory in patients with focal prefrontal neurosurgical lesions. In *Proceedings of the 4th International Conference on Disability*, Virtual Reality & Associated Technologies.

Motraghi, T. E., Seim, R. W., Meyer, E. C., & Morissette, S. B. (2012). Virtual reality exposure therapy for the treatment of PTSD: A systematic review American Psychological Association (APA).

Motraghi, T. E., Seim, R. W., Meyer, E. C., & Morissette, S. B. (2014). Virtual reality exposure therapy for the treatment of posttraumatic stress disorder: A methodological review using CONSORT guidelines. *Journal of Clinical Psychology, 70*(3), 197–208.

Mountain, M. A., & Snow, W. G. (1993). Wisconsin Card Sorting Test as a measure of frontal pathology: A review. *The Clinical Neuropsychologist, 7*, 108–118.

Mueller, C., Luehrs, M., Baecke, S., Adolf, D., Luetzkendorf, R., Luchtmann, M., & Bernarding, J. (2012). Building virtual reality fMRI paradigms: a framework for presenting immersive virtual environments. *Journal of Neuroscience Methods, 209*(2), 290–298.

Mühlberger, A., Bülthoff, H., Wiedemann, G., & Pauli, P. (2007). Virtual reality for the psychophysiological assessment of phobic fear: Responses during virtual tunnel driving. *Psychological Assessment, 19*(3), 340346.

Murray, C. D. (2009). A review of the use of virtual reality in the treatment of phantom limb pain. *Journal of Cybertherapy and Rehabilitation, 2*(2), 105–113.

Nacke, L. E., Stellmach, S., & Lindley, C. A. (2011). Electroencephalographic assessment of player experience a pilot study in affective ludology. *Simulation & Gaming, 42*(5), 632–655.

Nadeau, S. E. (2002). A paradigm shift in neurorehabilitation. *The Lancet Neurology, 1*, 126–130.

Nagamatsu, L., Voss, M., Neider, M., Gaspar, J., Handy, T., Kramer, A., & Liu-Ambrose, T. (2011). Increased cognitive load leads to impaired mobility decisions in seniors at risk for falls. *Psychology and Aging, 26*, 253–259.

Nakao, T., Takezawa, T., Miyatani, M., & Ohira, H. (2009). Medial prefrontal cortex and cognitive regulation. *Psychologia, 52*, 93–109.

Nakao, T., Osumi, T., Ohira, H., Kasuya, Y., Shinoda, J., Yamada, J., & Northoff, G. (2010). Medial prefrontal cortex—dorsal anterior cingulate cortex connectivity during behavior selection without an objective correct answer. *Neuroscience Letters, 482*, 220–224.

Nakao, T., Ohira, H., & Northoff, G. (2012). Distinction between externally vs. internally guided decision-making: operational differences, meta-analytical comparisons and their theoretical implications. *Frontiers in Neuroscience, 6*.

Naugle, R. I., & Chelune, G. J. (1990). Integrating neuropsychological and "real-life" data: A neuropsychological model for assessing everyday functioning. In D. Tupper & K. Cicerone (Eds.), *The neuropsychology of everyday life: Assessment and basic competences* (pp. 57–73). Kluwer Academic Publishers: Boston.

Neigh, G. N., Gillespie, C. F., & Nemeroff, C. B. (2009). The neurobiological toll of child abuse and neglect. *Trauma, Violence, & Abuse, 10*(4), 389–410.

Neisser, U. (1982). Memory: What are the important questions. *Memory Observed: Remembering in Natural Contexts*, 3–19.

Neisser, U. (Ed.). (1987). *Concepts and conceptual development: Ecological and intellectual factors in categorization*. Cambridge: Cambridge University Press.

Newcombe, F. (2002). An overview of neuropsychological rehabilitation: A forgotten past and a challenging future. *Cognitive rehabilitation: A clinical neuropsychological approach*, 23–51.

Nieuwenstein, M. R., Aleman, A., & de Haan, E. H. F. (2001). Relationship between symptom dimensions and neurocognitive functioning in schizophrenia: A meta-analysis of WCST and CPT studies. *Journal of Psychiatric Research, 35*, 119–125.

Nigg, J. T. (2000). On inhibition/Disinhibition in developmental psychopathology: Views from cognitive and personality psychology and a working inhibition taxonomy. *Psychological Bulletin, 126*, 220–246.

Nigg, J. T. (2001). Is ADHD a disinhibitory disorder? *Psychological Bulletin, 127*, 571–598.

Nigg, J. T. (2005). Neuropsychologic theory and findings in attention deficit/hyperactivity disorder: The state of the field and salient challenges for the coming decade. *Biological Psychiatry, 57*, 1424–1435.

Nolin, P., Stipanicic, A., Henry, M., Joyal, C. C., & Allain, P. (2012). Virtual reality as a screening tool for sports concussion in adolescents. *Brain Injury, 26*, 1564–1573.

Notebaert, A. J., & Guskiewicz, K. M. (2005). Current trends in athletic training practice for concussion assessment and management. *Journal of Athletic Training, 40*(4), 320.

Nussbaum, P. D., Goreczny, A., & Haddad, L. (1995). Cognitive correlates of functional capacity in elderly depressed versus patients with probable Alzheimer's disease. *Neuropsychological Rehabilitation, 5*, 333–340.

Nyhus, E., & Barceló, F. (2009). The Wisconsin Card Sorting Test and the cognitive assessment of prefrontal executive functions: A critical update. *Brain and Cognition, 71*(3), 437–451.

Olson, K., Jacobson, K. K., & Van Oot, P. (2013). Ecological validity of pediatric neuropsychological measures: current state and future directions. *Applied Neuropsychology: Child, 2*, 17–23.

Ord, J. S., Greve, K. W., Bianchini, K. J., & Aguerrevere, L. E. (2009). Executive dysfunction in traumatic brain injury: The effects of injury severity and effort on the Wisconsin Card Sorting Test. *Journal of Clinical and Experimental Neuropsychology, 32*(2), 132–140.

Ossher, L., Flegal, K. E., & Lustig, C. (2013). Everyday memory errors in older adults. *Aging, Neuropsychology, and Cognition, 20*(2), 220–242.

Ozonoff, S. (1995). Reliability and validity of the Wisconsin card sorting test in studies of autism. *Neuropsychologia, 9*, 491–500.

Panksepp, J. (1998a). *Affective Neuroscience*. Oxford: Oxford University Press.

Panksepp, J. (1998b). Affective neuroscience: The foundations of human and animal emotions. Oxford University Press.

Panksepp, J. (2009). Primary process affects and brain oxytocin. *Biological Psychiatry, 65*, 725–727.

Panksepp, J. (2010). Affective neuroscience of the emotional BrainMind: evolutionary perspectives and implications for understanding depression. *Dialogues in Clinical Neuroscience, 12*, 389–399.

Parikh, M., Grosch, M. C., Graham, L. L., Hynan, L. S., Weiner, M., Shore, J. H., & Cullum, C. M. (2013). Consumer acceptability of brief videoconference-based neuropsychological assessment in older individuals with and without cognitive impairment. *The Clinical Neuropsychologist, 27*(5), 808–817.

Park, K., Ku, J., Choi, S., Jang, H., Park, J., Kim, S. I., & Kim, J. (2011). A virtual reality application in role-plays of social skills training for schizophrenia: A randomized, controlled trial. *Psychiatry Research, 189*(2), 166–172.

Parsons, T. D. (2011). Neuropsychological assessment using virtual environments: Enhanced assessment technology for improved ecological validity. In *Advanced Computational Intelligence Paradigms in Healthcare 6. Virtual Reality in Psychotherapy, Rehabilitation, and Assessment* (pp. 271–289). Berlin: Springer.

Parsons, T. D., Bowerly, T., Buckwalter, J. G., & Rizzo, A. A. (2007). A controlled clinical comparison of attention performance in children with ADHD in a virtual reality classroom compared to standard neuropsychological methods. *Child Neuropsychology, 13*, 363–381.

Parsons, T. D., & Courtney, C. G. (2011). Neurocognitive and psychophysiological interfaces for adaptive virtual environments. Human Centered Design of E-Health Technologies, 208-233.

Parsons, T. D., & Courtney, C. (2014). An initial validation of the Virtual Reality Paced Auditory Serial Addition Test in a college sample. *Journal of Neuroscience Methods, 222*, 15–23.

Parsons, T. D., Courtney, C. G., Arizmendi, B. J., & Dawson, M. E. (2011). Virtual Reality Stroop Task for neurocognitive assessment. In *MMVR* (pp. 433–439).

Parsons, T. D., Courtney, C. G., & Dawson, M. E. (2013). Virtual reality Stroop task for assessment of supervisory attentional processing. *Journal of Clinical and Experimental Neuropsychology, 35*(8), 812–826.

Parsons, T. D., Courtney, C., Rizzo, A. A., Edwards, J., & Reger, G. (2012). Virtual reality paced serial assessment tests for neuropsychological assessment of a military cohort. *Studies in Health Technology and Informatics, 173*, 331–337.

Parsons, T. D., Cosand, L., Courtney, C., Iyer, A., & Rizzo, A. A. (2009a). Neurocognitive workload assessment using the Virtual Reality Cognitive Performance Assessment Test. *Lecture Notes in Artificial Intelligence, 5639*, 243–252.

Parsons, T. D., Iyer, A., Cosand, L., Courtney, C., & Rizzon, A. (2009b). Neurocognitive and psychophysiological analysis of human performance within virtual reality environments. *Medicine Meets Virtual Reality, 17*, 247–252.

Parsons, T. D., McPherson, S., & Interrante, V. (2013). Enhancing neurocognitive assessment using immersive virtual reality. In Virtual and Augmented Assistive Technology (VAAT), 2013 1st Workshop on (pp. 27–34). IEEE.

Parsons, T. D., & Reinebold, J. (2012). Adaptive virtual environments for neuropsychological assessment in serious games. *IEEE Transactions on Consumer Electronics, 58*, 197–204.

Parsons, T. D., & Rizzo, A. A. (2008). Affective outcomes of virtual reality exposure therapy for anxiety and specific phobias: A meta-analysis. *Journal of Behavior Therapy and Experimental Psychiatry, 39*, 250–261.

Parsons, T. D., & Rizzo, A. A. (2008). Initial validation of a virtual environment for assessment of memory functioning: virtual reality cognitive performance assessment test. *Cyberpsychology and Behavior, 11*, 17–25.

Parsons, T. D., Rizzo, A. A., Rogers, S., & York, P. (2009). Virtual reality in paediatric rehabilitation: A review. *Developmental Neurorehabilitation, 12*(4), 224–238.

Parsons, T. D., Silva, T. M., Pair, J., & Rizzo, A. A. (2008). A virtual environment for assessment of neurocognitive functioning: Virtual reality cognitive performance assessment test. *Studies in Health Technology and Informatics, 132*, 351–356.

Parsons, T. D., & Trost, Z. (2014). Virtual Reality Graded Exposure Therapy as Treatment for Pain-Related Fear and Disability in Chronic Pain. In M. Ma (Ed.), *Virtual and augmented reality in healthcare* (pp. 523–546). Germany: Springer.

Paul, R. H., Lawrence, J., Williams, L. M., RICHARD, C. C., Cooper, N., & Gordon, E. (2005). Preliminary validity of "IntegNeuroTM": A new computerized battery of neu-rocognitive tests. *International Journal of Neuroscience, 115*(11), 1549–1567.

Paulus, M. P., & Frank, L. R. (2006). Anterior cingulate activity modulates nonlinear decision weight function of uncertain prospects. *Neuroimage, 30*, 668–677.

Pedroli, E., Cipresso, P., Serino, S., Pallavicini, F., Albani, G., & Riva, G. (2013). Virtual multiple errands test: Reliability, usability and possible applications. *Annual Review of Cybertherapy and Telemedicine, 191*, 48–52.

Penfield, W., & Evans, J. P. (1935). The frontal lobe in man: a clinical study of maximum removals. *Brain: A Journal of Neurology.*

Pennington, B. F., Bennetto, L., McAleer, O. K., & Roberts, R. J. (1996). Executive functions and working memory: Theoretical and measurement issues. In G. R. Lyon & N. A. Krasnegor (Eds.), *Attention, memory and executive function*. Brookes: Baltimore.

Perry, W. (2009). Beyond the numbers. Expanding the boundaries of neuropsychology. *Archives of Clinical Neuropsychology, 24*, 21–29.

Pessoa, L. (2008). On the relationship between emotion and cognition. *Nature Reviews Neuroscience, 9*(2), 148–158.

Pessoa, L. (2009). How do emotion and motivation direct executive control? *Trends in Cognitive Sciences, 13*(4), 160–166.

Pham, T., & Tran, D. (2012). Emotional recognition using the Emotiv EPOC device. *Neural Information Processing, 7667*, 394–399.

Pineles, S. L., Mostoufi, S. M., Ready, C. B., Street, A. E., Griffin, M. G., & Resick, P. A. (2011). Trauma reactivity, avoidant coping, and PTSD symptoms: A moderating relationship? *Journal of Abnormal Psychology, 120*(1), 240–246.

Plancher, G., Tirard, A., Gyselinck, V., Nicolas, S., & Piolino, P. (2012). Using virtual reality to characterize episodic memory profiles in amnestic mild cognitive impairment and Alzheimer's disease: influence of active/passive encoding. *Neuropsychologia, 50*, 592–602.

Plancher, G., Barra, J., Orriols, E., & Piolino, P. (2013). The influence of action on episodic memory: A virtual reality study. *Quarterly Journal of Experimental Psychology, 66*, 895–909.

Pollak, Y., Shomaly, H. B., Weiss, P. L., Rizzo, A. A., & Gross-Tsur, V. (2010). Methylphenidate effect in children with ADHD can be measured by an ecologically valid continuous performance test embedded in virtual reality. *CNS Spectrums, 15*, 125–130.

Pollak, Y., Weiss, P. L., Rizzo, A. A., Weizer, M., Shriki, L., Shalev, R. S., & Gross-Tsur, V. (2009). The utility of a continuous performance test embedded in virtual reality in measuring ADHD-Related deficits. *Journal of Developmental & Behavioral Pediatrics, 20*, 2–6.

Podell, K., Lovell, M., Zimmerman, M., & Goldberg, E. (1995). The cognitive bias task and lateralized frontal lobe functions in males. *The Journal of Neuropsychiatry & Clinical Neurosciences, 7*, 491–501.

Podzebenko, K., Egan, G. F., & Watson, J. D. G. (2005). Real and imaginary rotary motion processing: functional parcellation of the human parietal lobe revealed by fMRI. *Journal of Cognitive Neuroscience, 17*(1), 24–36.

Popper, K. R. (1962). Conjectures and refutations: The growth of scientific knowledge. New York.

Pribram, K. H. (1971). *Languages of the brain*. Englewood Cliffs: Prentice-Hall.

Prigatano G. P. (1986). Personality and psychosocial consequences of brain injury. In G. P. Prigatano, D. J. Fordyce, H. K. Zeiner & J. R. Roueche (Eds.), *MPepping, BCWood Neuropsychological Rehabilitation after Brain Injury* (pp. 29–50). Baltimore/London: The John Hopkins University Press.

Prigatano, G. P. (Ed.). (1999). *Principles of Neuropsychological Rehabilitation*. Oxford University Press: NewYork.

Prigatano, G. P. (2005). A history of cognitive rehabilitation. In P. W. Halligan & D. T. Wade (Eds.), *The effectiveness of rehabilitation for cognitive deficits* (pp. 3–11). New York: Oxford University Press.

Probosz, K., Wcislo, R., Otfinoski, J., Slota, R., Kitowski, J., Pisula, M., & Sobczyk, A. (2009). A multimedia holistic rehabilitation method for patients after stroke. *Annual Review of Cybertherapy and Telemedicine, 7*, 261–263.

Prouteau, A., Verdoux, H., Briand, C., Alain, L., Lalonde, P., Nicole, L., & Stip, E. (2004). Self-assessed cognitive dysfunction and objective performance in outpatients with schizophrenia participating in a rehabilitation program. *Schizophrenia Research, 69*(1), 85–91.

Pugnetti, L., Mendozzi, L., Attree, E. A., Barbieri, E., Brooks, B. M., Cazzullo, C. L., et al. (1998). Probing memory and executive functions with virtual reality: Past and present studies. *CyberPsychology and Behavior, 1*, 151–161.

Pugnetti, L., Mendozzi, L., Motta, A., Cattaneo, A., Barbieri, E., & Brancotti, S. (1995). Evaluation and retraining of adults' cognitive impairments: Which role for virtual reality technology? *Computers in Biology and Medicine, 25*, 213–227.

Rabbitt, P. (1997). Introduction: Methodologies and models in the study of executive function. In P. Rabbitt (Ed.), *Methodology of frontal executive function* (pp. 1–38). East Sussex, UK: Psychology.

Rabin, L., Barr, W., & Burton, L. (2005). Assessment practices of clinical neuropsychologists in the United States and Canada: A survey of INS, NAN, and APA Division 40 members. *Archives of Clinical Neuropsychology, 20*, 33–65.

Rabin, L. A., Burton, L. A., & Barr, W. B. (2007). Utilization rates of ecologically oriented instruments among clinical neuropsychologists. *The Clinical Neuropsychologist, 5*, 727–743.

Rabin, L. A., Spadaccini, A. T., Brodale, D. L., Grant, K. S., Elbulok-Charcape, M. M., & Barr, W. B. (2014). Utilization rates of computerized tests and test batteries among clinical neuropsychologists in the United States and Canada. *Professional Psychology: Research and Practice, 45*(5), 368.

Raichle, M. E. (2009). A paradigm shift in functional brain imaging. *The Journal of Neuroscience, 29*, 12729–12734.

Ramos-Ríos, R., Mateos, R., Lojo, D., & et al. (2012). Telepsychogeriatrics: A new horizon in the care of mental health problems in the elderly. *International Psychogeriatric, 24*, 1708e1724.

Rand, D., Basha-Abu Rukan, S., Weiss, P. L., & Katz, N. (2009). Validation of the Virtual MET as an assessment tool for executive functions. *Neuropsychological Rehabilitation, 19*(4), 583–602.

Randolph, C. (2011). Baseline neuropsychological testing in managing sport-related concussion: does it modify risk? *Current Sports Medicine Reports, 10*(1), 21–26.

Rajan, R. (2012) The promise of wireless: an overview of a device-to-cloud mHealth solution. *Biomedical Instrumentation & Technology, Suppl*, 26–32.

Raspelli, S., Carelli, L., Morganti, F., Pedroli, E., Cipresso, P., Poletti, B., & Riva, G. (2012). Validating the Neuro VR-Based virtual version of the multiple errands test: Preliminary results. *Presence, 21*, 31–42.

Rauchs, G., Orban, P., Balteau, E., Schmidt, C., Degueldre, C., Luxen, A., & Peigneux, P. (2008). Partially segregated neural networks for spatial and contextual memory in virtual navigation. *Hippocampus, 18*(5), 503–518.

Ray, R. D., & Zald, D. H. (2012). Anatomical insights into the interaction of emotion and cognition in the prefrontal cortex. *Neuroscience and Biobehavioral Reviews, 36*(1), 479–501.

Raymond, P. D., Hinton-Bayre, A. D., Radel, M., Ray, M. J., & Marsh, N. A. (2006). Assessment of statistical change criteria used to define significant change in neuropsychological test performance following cardiac surgery. *European Journal of Cardio-Thoracic Surgery, 29*, 82–88.

Raz, S., Bar-Haim, Y., Sadeh, A., & Dan, O. (2014). Reliability and validity of the online continuous performance test among young adults. *Assessment, 21*(1), 108–118.

Reeves, D. L., Winter, K. P., Bleiberg, J., & Kane, R. L. (2007). ANAM® Genogram: Historical perspectives, description, and current endeavors. *Archives of Clinical Neuropsychology, 22*, 15–37.

Reitan, R. M. (1955). Investigation of the validity of Halstead's measure of biological intelli-gence. *Archives of Neurology, 73*, 28–35.

Reitan, R. M. (1964). Psychological deficits resulting from cerebral lesions in man. In J. M. Warren & A. K. Akert (Eds.), *The frontal granular cortex and behavior* (pp. 295–312). New York: McGraw-Hill.

Reitan, R. M. (1991). The neuropsychological deficit scale for adults computer program, in the Manual from Traumatic Brain Injury Vol. II: Recovery and Rehabilitation. Tucson: Neuropsychology Press.

Renison, B., Ponsford, J., Testa, R., Richardson, B., & Brownfield, K. (2012). The ecological and construct validity of a newly developed measure of executive function: The Virtual Library Task. *Journal of the International Neuropsychological Society, 18*, 440–450.

Resch, J. E., McCrea, M. A., & Cullum, C. M. (2013). Computerized neurocognitive testing in the management of sport-related concussion: An update. *Neuropsychology review, 23*(4), 335–349.

Riccio, C. A., & French, C. L. (2004). The status of empirical support for treatments of attention deficits. *The Clinical Neuropsychologist, 18*, 528–558.

Riva, G. (2009). Virtual reality: an experiential tool for clinical psychology. *British Journal of Guidance & Counselling, 37*(3), 337–345.

Robertson, I. H., Manly, T., Andrade, J., Baddeley, B. T., & Yiend, J. (1997). "Oops!": performance correlates of everyday attentional failures in traumatic brain injured and normal subjects. *Neuropsychologia, 35*, 747–758.

Robertson, I. H., Ward, T., Ridgeway, V., & Nimmo-Smith, I. (1994). *The Test of Everyday Attention. Bury St.* Edmunds: Thames Valley Test Company.

Rock, D. L., & Nolen, P. A. (1982). Comparison of the standard and computerized versions of the Raven Coloured Progressive Matrices Test. *Perceptual and Motor Skills, 54*, 40–42.

Roebuck-Spencer, T. M., Vincent, A. S., Twillie, D. A., Logan, B. W., Lopez, M., Friedl, K. E., & Gilliland, K. (2012). Cognitive change associated with self-reported mild traumatic brain injury sustained during the OEF/OIF conflicts. *The Clinical Neuropsychologist, 26*(3), 473–489.

Rogante, M., Grigioni, M., Cordella, D., & Giacomozzi, C. (2010). Ten years of telerehabilitation: A literature overview of technologies and clinical applications. *Neuro Rehabilitation, 27*, 287–304.

Rogoff, B., & Lave, J. (Eds.). (1984). *Everyday cognition: Its development in social context.* Cambridge: Harvard University Press.

Roiser, J. P., & Sahakian, B. J. (2013). Hot and cold cognition in depression. *CNS spectrums, 18* (03), 139–149.

Ross, S. A., Allen, D. N., & Goldstein, G. (2013). Factor Structure of the Halstead-Reitan Neuropsychological Battery: A Review and Integration. *Applied Neuropsychology: Adult, 20* (2), 120–135.

Ross, S. A., Allen, D. N., & Goldstein, G. (2014). Factor Structure of the Halstead-Reitan Neuropsychological Battery for Children: A Brief Report Supplement. *Applied Neuropsychology: Child, 3*(1), 1–9.

Rosser, J. C, Jr, Gabriel, N., Herman, B., & Murayama, M. (2001). Telementoring and teleproctoring. *World Journal of Surgery, 25*, 1438–1448.

Rourke, B. P. (1982). Central processing deficiencies in children: Toward a developmental neuropsychological model. *Journal of Clinical Neuropsychology, 4*, 1–18.

Rourke, B. P., & Brown, G. G. (1986). Clinical neuropsychology and behavioral neurology: Similarities and differences. *Handbook of Clinical Neuropsychology, 2*, 3–18.

Ruff, R. M. (2003). A friendly critique of neuropsychology: Facing the challenges of our fu-ture. *Archives of Clinical Neuropsychology, 18*, 847–864.

Ruff, R. M., & Hibbard, K. M. (2003). RNBI, Ruff neurobehavioral inventory: Professional manual. Psychological Assessment Resources.

Rupp, R. (2014). Challenges in clinical applications of brain computer interfaces in individuals with spinal cord injury. *Frontiers in Neuroengineering, 7*.

Rus-Calafell, M., Gutierrez-Maldonado, J., & Ribas-Sabate, J. (2014). A virtual reality-integrated program for improving social skills in patients with schizophrenia: A pilot study. *Journal of Behavioral Therapy and Experimental Psychiatry, 45*, 81–89.

Russell, E. W. (1984). Theory and developments of pattern analysis methods related to the Halstead-Reitan Battery. In P. E. Logue & J. M. Shear (Eds.), *Clinical neuropsychology: A multidisciplinary approach* (pp. 50–98). Springfield: Charles C. Thomas.

Russell, E. W. (1995). The accuracy of automated and clinical detection of brain damage and lateralization in neuropsychology. *Neuropsychology Review, 5*(1), 1–68.

Russell, E. W. (1998). In defense of the Halstead-Reitan Battery: A critique of Lezak's re-view. *Archives of Clinical Neuropsychology, 13*, 365–381.

Russell, E. W. (2000). The application of computerized scoring programs to neuropsychological assessment. In R. D. Vanderploeg (Ed.), *Clinician's guide to neuropsychological assessment* (2nd ed.). New Jersey: Lawrence Erlbaum Associates.

Russell, E. W. (2011). The scientific foundation of neuropsychological assessment: With applications to forensic evaluation. Elsevier.

Russell, E. W., Neuringer, C., & Goldstein, G. (1970). *Assessment of brain damage: A neuropsychological key approach*. New York: Wiley Company.

Russell, E. W., & Starkey, R. I. (2001). *Halstead-Russell neuropsychological evaluation system—revised*. Los Angeles: Western Psychological Services.

Saidel-Goley, I., Albiero, E., & Flannery, K. (2012). An evaluation of nonclinical dissociation utilizing a virtual environment shows enhanced working memory and attention. *Cyberpsychology, Behavior, and Social Networking, 15*, 112–116.

Sakoğlu, Ü., Upadhyay, J., Chin, C. L., Chandran, P., Baker, S. J., Cole, T. B., & Luo, F. (2011). Paradigm shift in translational neuroimaging of CNS disorders. *Biochemical Pharmacology, 81* (12), 1374–1387.

Salisbury, D., Driver, S., & Parsons, T. D. (2015). Brain-computer interface targeting non-motor functions after spinal cord injury. *Spinal Cord, 53*, S25–S26.

Sandford, J. A. (2007). *Captain's log computerized cognitive training system*. Richmond: Brain Train.

Salsman, J., La i, J.-S., Hendrie, H., Butt, Z., Zill, N., Pilkonis, P., & Cella, D. (2013). Assessing psychological well-being: Self-report instruments for the NIH Toolbox. *Quality of Life Research, 23*(1), 205–215.

Santayana, G. (1905/2006). The life of reason (Vol. 1). New York: Charles Scribner Publishing.

Sauzéon, H., Arvind Pala, P., Larrue, F., Wallet, G., Déjos, M., Zheng, X., & N'Kaoua, B. (2012). The use of virtual reality for episodic memory assessment: Effects of active navigation. *Experimental Psychology, 59*(2), 99.

Sauzeon, H., N'Kaoua, B., Arvind Pala, P., Taillade, M., Auriacombe, S., & Guitton, P. (2014). Everyday-like memory for objects in ageing and Alzheimer's disease assessed in a visually complex environment: The role of executive functioning and episodic memory. *Journal of Neuropsychology*.

Saxton, J., Morrow, L., Eschman, A., Archer, G., Luther, J., & Zuccolotto, A. (2009). Computer assessment in mild cognitive impairment. *Postgraduate Medicine, 121*, 177–185.

Sbordone, R. J., & Long, C. J. (1996). *Ecological validity of neuropsychological testing* (pp. 91–112). Boca Raton: St Lucie Press.

Sbordone, R. J. (1996). Ecological validity: Some critical issues for neuropsychologist. In R. J. Sbordone & C. J. Long (Eds.), *Ecological validity of neuropsychological testing* (pp. 15–41). Delray Beach: GR Press/St. Lucie Press.

Sbordone, R. J. (2008). Ecological validity of neuropsychological testing: critical issues. *The Neuropsychology Handbook, 367*, 394.

Sbordone, R. J. (2010). Neuropsychological tests are poor at assessing the frontal lobes, executive functions, and neurobehavioral symptoms of traumatically brain-injured patients. *Psychological Injury and Law, 3*, 25–35.

Schacter, D. L. (1983). Amnesia observed: Remembering and forgetting in a natural environment. *Journal of Abnormal Psychology, 92*, 236–242.

Scharre, D. W., Chang, S. I., Nagaraja, H. N., Yager-Schweller, J., & Murden, R. A. (2014). Community cognitive screening using the self-administered gerocognitive examination (SAGE). *The Journal of Neuropsychiatry and Clinical Neurosciences, 26*(4), 369–375.

Schatz, P., & Browndyke, J. (2002). Applications of computer-based neuropsychological assessment. *Journal of Head Trauma Rehabilitation, 17*, 395–410.

Schatz, P., Pardini, J. E., Lovell, M. R., Collins, M. W., & Podell, K. (2006). Sensitivity and specificity of the ImPACT Test Battery for concussion in athletes. *Archives of Clinical Neuropsychology, 21*(1), 91–99.

Schatz, P., & Sandel, N. (2013). Sensitivity and specificity of the online version of ImPACT in high school and collegiate athletes. *The American Journal of Sports Medicine, 41*(2), 321–326.

Schreuder, M., Riccio, A., Risetti, M., Dähne, S., Ramsay, A., Williamson, J., & Tangermann, M. (2013). User-centered design in brain-computer interfaces—A case study. *Artificial Intelligence in Medicine, 59*(2), 71–80.

Schultheis, M. T., & Mourant, R. (2001). Virtual reality and driving: The road to better assessment for cognitively impaired populations. *Presence: Teleoperators and Virtual Environments, 10*, 431–439.

Schultheis, M. T., Himelstein, J., & Rizzo, A. A. (2002). Virtual reality and neuropsychology: upgrading the current tools. *The Journal of Head Trauma Rehabilitation, 17*, 378–394.

Schultheis, M. T., Hillary, F., & Chute, D. L. (2003). The neurocognitive driving test: Applying technology to the assessment of driving ability following brain injury. *Rehabilitation Psychology, 48*, 275–280.

Schultheis, M. T., Rebimbas, J., Mourant, R., & Millis, S. R. (2007). Examining the usability of a virtual reality driving simulator. *Assistive Technologies, 19*, 1–8.

Schuster, R. M., Mermelstein, R. J., & Hedeker, D. (2015). Acceptability and feasibility of a visual working memory task in an ecological momentary assessment paradigm.

Seeley, W. W., Menon, V., Schatzberg, A. F., Keller, J., Glover, G., Kenna, H., & Greicius, M. D. (2007). Dissociable intrinsic connectivity networks for salience processing and executive control. *Journal of Neuroscience, 27*, 2349–2356.

Seguin, J. R., Arseneault, L., & Tremblay, R. E. (2007). The contribution of "cool" and "hot" components of decision-making in adolescence: implications for developmental psychopathology. *Cognitive Development, 22*, 530–543.

Serino, A., Ciaramelli, E., Santantonio, A. D., Malagù, S., Servadei, F., & Làdavas, E. (2007). A pilot study for rehabilitation of central executive deficits after traumatic brain injury. *Brain Injury, 21*(1), 11–19.

Settle, J. R., Robinson, S. A., Kane, R., Maloni, H. W., & Wallin, M. T. (2015). Remote cognitive assessments for patients with multiple sclerosis: A feasibility study. *Multiple Sclerosis Journal*, 1352458514559296.

Shallice, T. I. M., & Burgess, P. W. (1991). Deficits in strategy application following frontal lobe damage in man. *Brain, 114*, 727–741.

Shiffman, S., Stone, A. A., & Hufford, M. R. (2008). Ecological momentary assessment. *Annual Review of Clinical Psychology, 4*, 1–32.

Shih, J. J., Krusienski, D. J., & Wolpaw, J. R. (2012). Brain-computer interfaces in medicine. *Mayo Clinic Proceedings, 87*(3), 268–279.

Shipley, W. C. (1940). A self-administered scale for measuring intellectual impairment and deterioration. *Journal of Psychology, 9*, 371–77.

Silverstein, S. M., Berten, S., Olson, P., Paul, R., Williams, L. M., Cooper, N., & Gordon, E. (2007). Development and validation of a World-Wide-Web-based neurocognitive assess-ment battery: WebNeuro. *Behavior Research Methods, 39*(4), 940–949.

Sinnott, J. D. (Ed.). (1989). *Everyday problem solving: Theory mid applications*. New York: Praeger.

Slate, S. E., Meyer, T. L., Burns, W. J., & Montgomery, D. D. (1998). Computerized cognitive training for severely emotionally disturbed children with ADHD. *Behavior Modification, 22*(3), 415–437.

Slick, D. I., Hopp, G., Strauss, E., & Thompson, G. B. (1997). *Victoria symptom validity test*. Odessa: Psychological Assessment Resources.

Sloan, R. P., Korten, J. B., & Myers, M. M. (1991). Components of heart rate reactivity during mental arithmetic with and without speaking. *Physiology & Behavior, 50*, 1039–1045.

Smith, A. (2014). *Older Adults and Technology Use*. Life Proj: The Pew Research Center's Internet & American.

Smith, L., & Gasser, M. (2005). The development of embodied cognition: six lessons from babies. *Artificial Life, 11*, 13–29.

Snell, D. L., Surgenor, L. J., Hay-Smith, J. C., & Siegert, R. J. (2009). A systematic review of psychological treatments for mild traumatic brain injury: An update on the evidence. *Journal of Clinical and Experimental Neuropsychology, 31*(1), 20–38.

Soares, F. C., & de Oliveira, T. C. G. (2015). CANTAB object recognition and language tests to detect aging cognitive decline: an exploratory comparative study. *Clinical Interventions in Aging, 10*, 37–48.

Sohlberg, M. M., & Mateer, C. A. (1989). *Introduction to cognitive rehabilitation: Theory and practice*. New York, NY: Guilford Press.

Sohlberg, M. M., & Mateer, C. A. (2001). *Cognitive rehabilitation: An integrative approach*. New York: Guilford Press.

Sohlberg, M. M., & Mateer, C. A. (2010). *APT-III: Attention process training: A direct attention training program for persons with acquired brain injury*. Youngville: Lash & Associates.

Sonuga-Barke, E. J. S. (2003). The dual pathway model of AD/HD: An elaboration of neurodevelopmental characteristics. *Neuroscience & Biobehavioral Reviews, 27*, 593–604.

Sonuga-Barke, E. J. S., Sergeant, J. A., Nigg, J., & Willcutt, E. (2008). Executive dysfunction and delay aversion in attention deficit hyperactivity disorder: Nosologic and diagnostic implications. *Child and Adolescent Psychiatric Clinics of North America, 17*, 367–384.

Space, L. G. (1975). A console for the interactive on-line administration of psychological tests. *Behavior Research Methods and Instrumentation, 7*, 191–193.

Space, L. G. (1981). The computer as psychometrician. *Behavior Research Methods and Instrumentation, 13*, 595–606.

Spooner, D. M., & Pachana, N. A. (2006). Ecological validity in neuropsychological assessment: A case for greater consideration in research with neurologically intact populations. *Archives of Clinical Neuropsychology, 21*, 327–337.

Spreen, O., & Strauss, E. (1998). *A compendium of neuropsychological tests: Administration, norms and commentary* (2nd ed.). New York: Oxford University Press.

Spreij, L. A., Visser-Meily, J. M., van Heugten, C. M., & Nijboer, T. C. (2014). Novel insights into the rehabilitation of memory post acquired brain injury: A systematic review. *Frontiers in Human Neuroscience, 8*.

Stern, H., Jeaco, S., & Millar, T. (1999). Computers in neurorehabilitation: What role do they play? Part 1. *British Journal of Occupational Therapy, 62*(12), 549–553.

Stern, R. A., & White, T. (2003). NAB, Neuropsychological Assessment Battery: Attention Module Stimulus Book. Form 2. Psychological Assessment Resources.

Sternberg, R. J. (1997). Intelligence and lifelong learning: What's new and how can we use it? *American Psychologist, 52*, 1134–1139.
Sternberg, R. J., & Wagner, R. K. (Eds.). (1986). *Practical intelligence: Nature and origins of competence in the everyday world*. New York: Cambridge University Press.
Stierwalt, J. A., & Murray, L. L. (2002). Attention impairment following traumatic brain injury. *In Seminars in speech and language, 23*(2), 129–138.
Stone, A. A., Broderick, J. E., Schwartz, J. E., Sfiffman, S., Litcher-Kelly, L., & Calvanese, P. (2003). Intensive momentary reporting of pain with an electronic diary: reactivity, compliance, and patient satisfaction. *Pain., 104*(1-2), 343–351.
Stuss, D. T., Alexander, M. P., Shallice, T., Picton, T. W., Binns, M. A., Macdonald, R., et al. (2005). Multiple frontal systems controlling response speed. *Neuropsychologia, 43*, 396–417.
Stuss, D. T., Benson, D. F., Kaplan, E. F., Weir, W. S., Naeser, M. A., Lieberman, I., et al. (1983). The involvement of orbitofrontal cerebrum in cognitive tasks. *Neuropsychologia, 21*, 235–248.
Stuss, D. T., & Levine, B. (2002). Adult clinical neuropsychology: Lessons from studies of the frontal lobes. *Annual Review of Psychology, 53*(1), 401–433.
Suchy, Y. (2011). Clinical neuropsychology of emotion. Guilford Press.
Sweeney, J. A., Kmiec, J. A., & Kupfer, D. J. (2000). Neuropsychologic impairments in bipolar and unipolar mood disorders on the CANTAB neurocognitive battery. *Biological Psychiatry, 48*(7), 674–684.
Sweeney, J. E., Slade, H. P., Ivins, R. G., Nemeth, D. G., Ranks, D. M., & Sica, R. B. (2007). Scientific investigation of brain-behavior relationships using the Halstead-Reitan Battery. *Applied Neuropsychology, 14*(2), 65–72.
Sweeney, S., Kersel, D., Morris, R., Manly, T., & Evans, J. (2010). The sensitivity of a virtual reality task to planning and prospective memory impairments: Group differences and the efficacy of periodic alerts on performance. *Neuropsychological Rehabilitation, 20*(2), 239–263.
Svoboda, E., Richards, B., Leach, L., & Mertens, V. (2012). PDA and smartphone use by individuals with moderate-to-severe memory impairment: Application of a theory-driven training programme. *Neuropsychological Rehabilitation, 22*(3), 408–427.
Taillade, M., Sauzéon, H., Dejos, M., Arvind Pala, P., Larrue, F., Wallet, G., & N'Kaoua, B. (2013). Executive and memory correlates of age-related differences in wayfinding performances using a virtual reality application. *Aging, Neuropsychology, and Cognition, 20*(3), 298–319.
Tate, D. G., Kalpakjian, C. Z., & Forchheimer, M. B. (2002). Quality of life issues in individuals with spinal cord injury. *Archives of Physical Medicine and Rehabilitation, 83*(12), S18–S25.
Temple, V., Drummond, C., Valiquette, S., & Jozsvai, E. (2010). A comparison of intellectual assessments over video conferencing and in-person for individuals with ID: preliminary data. *Journal of Intellectual Disability Research, 54*(6), 573–577.
Teuber, H. L. (1955). Physiological psychology. *Annual Review of Psychology, 6*, 267–296.
Teuber, H. L. (1966). Kurt Goldstein's role in the development of neuropsychology. *Neuropsychologia, 4*(4), 299–310.
Thayer, J. F., & Lane, R. D. (2000). A model of neurovisceral integration in emotionregulation and dysregulation. *Journal of Affective Disorders, 61*, 201–216.
Thayer, J. F., & Lane, R. D. (2009). Claude Bernard and the heart-brainconnection: Further elaboration of a model of neurovisceral inte-gration. *Neuroscience and Biobehavioral Reviews, 33*(2), 81–88.
Thompson, O., Barrett, S., Patterson, C., & Craig, D. (2012). Examining the neurocognitive validity of commercially available, smartphone-based puzzle games. *Psychology, 3*(07), 525.
Thornton, K. E., & Carmody, D. P. (2008). Efficacy of traumatic brain injury rehabilitation: Interventions of QEEG guided biofeedback, computers, strategies, and medications. *Applied Psychophysiology and Biofeedback, 33*(2), 101–124.
Toet, A., & van Schaik, M. G. (2013). Visual attention for a desktop virtual environment with ambient scent. *Frontiers in Psychology, 4*, 1–11.

Tomb, I., Hauser, M., Deldin, P., & Caramazza, A. (2004). Do Somatic markers mediate decisions on the gambling task? *Nat Neuroscience, 5*, 1103–1104.

Tornatore, J. B., Hill, E., Laboff, J., & McGann, M. E. (2005). Self administered screening for mild cognitive impairment: Initial validation of a computerized test battery. *The Journal of Neuropsychiatry & Clinical Neurosciences, 17*, 98–105.

Tranel, D., (2009). The Iowa-Benton school of neuropsychological assessment. In I. Grant (Ed.), *Neuropsychological assessment of neuropsychiatric and neuromedical disorders* (pp. 66–83). Oxford University Press.

Treder, M. S., & Blankertz, B. (2010). Research Covert attention and visual speller design in an ERP-based brain-computer interface. *Behavioral & Brain Functions, 6*.

Tropp, M., Lundqvist, A., Persson, C., Samuelsson, K., & Levander, S. (2015). Self-ratings of Everyday Memory Problems in Patients with Acquired Brain Injury-A Tool for Rehabilitation. *International Journal of Physical Medicine & Rehabilitation, 3*(258), 2.

Trost, Z., & Parsons, T. D. (2014). Beyond Distraction: Virtual Reality Graded Exposure Therapy as Treatment for Pain-Related Fear and Disability in Chronic Pain. *Journal of Applied Biobehavioral Research, 19*, 106–126.

Troyer, A. K., Rowe, G., Murphy, K. J., Levine, B., Leach, L., & Hasher, L. (2014). Devel-opment and evaluation of a self-administered on-line test of memory and attention for middle-aged and older adults. *Frontiers in Aging Neuroscience, 6*.

Tupper, D. E., & Cicerone, K. D. (1990). *The neuropsychology of everyday life: Assessment and basic competencies*. US: Springer.

Tupper, D. E., & Cicerone, K. D. (Eds.). (1991). *The neuropsychology of everyday life: Issues in development and rehabilitation*. US: Springer.

Turner, T. H., Horner, M. D., VanKirk, K. K., Myrick, H., & Tuerk, P. W. (2012). A pilot trial of neuropsychological evaluations conducted via telemedicine in the Veterans Health Administration. *Telemedicine and e-Health, 18*(9), 662–667.

Turner-Stokes, L., Disler, P. B., Nair, A., & Wade, D. T. (2005). Multi-disciplinary rehabilitation for acquired brain injury in adults of working age. *Cochrane Database of Systematic Reviews, 3*, CD004170.

Unsworth, N., Heitz, R. P., & Engle, R. W. (2005). Working memory capacity in hot and cold cognition. *Cognitive Limitations in Aging and Psychopathology*, 19-43.

Vaughan, C. G., Gerst, E. H., Sady, M. D., Newman, J. B., & Gioia, G. A. (2014). The relation between testing environment and baseline performance in child and adolescent concussion assessment. *The American Journal of Sports Medicine*, 0363546514531732.

Vestal, L., Smith-Olinde, L., Hicks, G., Hutton, T., & Hart, J, Jr. (2006). Efficacy of language assessment in Alzheimer's disease: comparing in-person examination and telemedicine. *Clinical Interventions in Aging, 1*(4), 467.

Vincent, K. R. (1980). Semi-automated full battery. *Journal of Clinical Psychology, 36*, 437–446.

Vincent, A. S., Bleiberg, J., Yan, S., Ivins, B., Reeves, D. L., Schwab, K., & Warden, D. (2008). Reference data from the automated Neuropsychological Assessment Metrics for use in traumatic brain injury in an active duty military sample. *Military Medicine, 173*(9), 836–852.

Vincent, A. S., Roebuck-Spencer, T., Gilliland, K., & Schlegel, R. (2012). Automated neuropsychological assessment metrics (v4) traumatic brain injury battery: military normative data. *Military Medicine, 177*(3), 256–269.

Volz, K. G., Schubotz, R. I., & Von Cramon, D. Y. (2006). Decision-making and the frontal lobes. *Current Opinion in Neurology, 19*, 401–406.

Wald, J., & Liu, L. (2001). Psychometric properties of the driVR: A virtual reality driving assessment. *Studies in Health Technology Information, 81*, 564–566.

Wald, J. L., Liu, L., & Reil, S. (2000). Concurrent validity of a virtual reality driving assessment in persons with brain injury. *Cyberpsychology & Behavior, 3*, 643–652.

Waldstein, S. R., Bachen, E. A., & Manuck, S. B. (1997). Active coping and cardiovascular reactivity: a multiplicity of influences. *Psychosomatic Medicine, 59*, 620–625.

Wang, F. Y. (2007). Toward a paradigm shift in social computing: The ACP approach. *IEEE Intelligent Systems, 22*, 65–67.
Wang, L., LaBar, K. S., Smoski, M., Rosenthal, M. Z., Dolcos, F., Lynch, T. R., & McCarthy, G. (2008). Prefrontal mechanisms for executive control over emotional distraction are altered in major depression. *Psychiatry Research: Neuroimaging, 163(2)*, 143–155.
Waterfall, R. C. (1979). Automating standard intelligence tests. *Journal of Audiovisual Media in Medicine, 2*, 21–24.
Waters, A. J., & Li, Y. (2008). Evaluating the utility of administering a reaction time task in an ecological momentary assessment study. *Psychopharmacology, 197*, 25–35.
Waters, A. J., Szeto, E. H., Wetter, D. W., Cinciripini, P. M., Robinson, J. D., & Li, Y. (2014). Cognition and craving during smoking cessation: An ecological momentary assessments study. *Nicotine & Tobacco Research, 16*(Suppl. 2), S111–S118.
Watson, J. B. (1912). Psychology as the behaviorist views it. *Psychological Review, 20*, 158–177.
Wechsler, D. (1945). A standardized memory scale for clinical use. *Journal of Psychology, 19*, 87–95.
Wechsler, D. (1949). *Manual for the wechsler intelligence scale for children*. New York: Psychological Corporation.
Wechsler, D. (1955). *Manual for the Wechsler Adult Intelligence Scale*. New York: Psychological Corporation.
Wechsler, D. (1958). *The measurement and appraisal of adult intelligence* (4th ed.). Baltimore: Williams & Wilkins.
Wechsler, D. (1967). *Manual for the Wechsler Preschool and Primary School of Intelligence*. New York: Psychological Corporation.
Wechsler, D. (1974). *Wechsler Memory Scale manual*. San Antonio: Psychological Corporation.
Wechsler, D. (1981). *Manual for the Wechsler Adult Intelligence Scale-Revised*. New York: Psychological Corporation.
Wechsler, D. (1987). *Wechsler Memory Scale-Revised manual*. San Antonio: Psychological Corporation.
Wechsler, D. (1989). *Manual for the Wechsler Preschool and Primary Sale of Intelligence Revised (WPPSI-R)*. San Antonio: Psychological Corporation.
Wechsler, D. (1991). *Manual for the Wechsler Intelligence Scale for Children* (3rd ed.). New York: Psychological Corporation.
Wechsler, D. (1992). *Wechsler Individual Achievement Test*. San Antonio: Psychological Corporation.
Wechsler, D. (1997). *Wechsler Adult Intelligence Scale—3rd Edition (WAIS-3) San Antonio*. TX: Harcourt Assessment.
Wechsler, D. (1997). *WAIS-III Administration and Scoring manual*. San Antonio: Psychological Corporation.
Wechsler, D. (1997). *Wechsler Memory Scale: Administration and Scoring manual* (3rd ed.). San Antonio: Psychological Corporation.
Wechsler, D. (2001). *Wechsler Test of Adult Reading*. San Antonio: Psychological Corporation.
Wechsler, D. (2003). *Wechsler Intelligence Scale for Children—4th Edition (WISC-IV)*. San Antonio: Harcourt Assessment.
Wechsler, D. (2008). *Wechsler adult intelligence scale-Fourth Edition (WAIS-IV)*. San Antonio: NCS Pearson.
Wechsler, D. (2009). *Wechsler Memory Scale-(WMS-IV)*. New York: The Psychological Corporation.
Wedding, D. (1983a). Clinical and statistical prediction. *Clinical Neuropsychology, 5*, 49–55.
Wedding, D. (1983b). Comparison of statistical and actuarial models for predicting lateralization of brain damage. *Clinical Neuropsychology, 4*, 15–20.
Weigl, E. (1927). Zur Psychologie sogenannter Abstraktionsprozesse. *Zeitschrift fur Psychologie, 103*, 2–45. (Translated by M. Rioch (1948) and reprinted as: On the psychology of so-called processes of abstraction. *Journal of Abnormal and Social Psychology, 36*, 3–33).

Weiss, D. (2004). Computerized adaptive testing for effective and efficient measurement in counseling and education. *Measurement and Evaluation in Counseling and Development, 37* (2), 70–84.

Weintraub, S., Dikmen, S. S., Heaton, R. K., Tulsky, D. S., Zelazo, P. D., Bauer, P. J., y Gershon, R. C. (2013). Cognition assessment using the NIH Toolbox. *Neurology, 80*(11 Suppl 3), S54–S64.

Wells, F. L., & Ruesch, J. (1942). *Mental Examiner's Handbook*. New York: Psychological Corporation.

Welsh, M. C., & Pennington, B. F. (1988). Assessing frontal lobe functioning in children: Views from developmental psychology. *Developmental Neuropsychology, 4*, 199–230.

Welsh, M. C., Pennington, B. F., & Grossier, D. B. (1991). A normative-developmental study of executive function: A window on prefrontal function in children. *Developmental Neuropsychology, 7*, 131–149.

Wender, R., Hoffman, H. G., Hunner, H. H., Seibel, E. J., Patterson, D. R., & Sharar, S. R. (2009). Interactivity influences the magnitude of virtual reality analgesia. *Journal of Cyber Therapy and Rehabilitation, 2*(1), 27.

Werner, P., Rabinowitz, S., Klinger, E., Korczyn, A., & Josman, N. (2009). Use of the virtual action planning supermarket for the diagnosis of mild cognitive impairment. *Dementia and Geriatric Cognitive Disorders*, 301–309.

Wernicke, C. (1874). *Der Aphasische Symptomkomplex*. Breslau: Cohn & Weigart.

Westerberg, H., Jacobaeus, H., Hirvikoski, T., Clevberger, P., Ostensson, M. L., Bartfai, A., & Klingberg, T. (2007). Computerized working memory training after stroke-a pilot study. *Brain Injury, 21*(1), 21–29.

Widmann, C. N., Beinhoff, U., & Riepe, M. W. (2012). Everyday memory deficits in very mild Alzheimer's disease. *Neurobiology of Aging, 33*(2), 297–303.

Wilkins, R. H., & Classic-XVII, N. (1964). The Edwin Smith surgical papyrus. *Journal of Neurosurgery, 5*(1), 240–244.

Willcutt, E. G., Doyle, A., Nigg, J. T., Faraone, S. V., & Pennington, B. F. (2005). Validity of the executive function theory of attention-deficit/hyperactivity disorder: A meta-analytic review. *Biological Psychiatry, 57*, 1336–1346.

Williams, J. M. (1988). Everyday cognition and the ecological validity of intellectual and neuropsychological tests. In J. M. Williams & C. J. Long (Eds.), *Cognitive approaches to neuropsychology* (pp. 123–141). New York: Plenum.

Williams, W. H., Evans, J. J., & Wilson, B. A. (2003). Neurorehabilitation for two cases of post-traumatic stress disorder following traumatic brain injury. *Cognitive Neuropsychiatry, 8*, 1–18.

Williams, J. E., & McCord, D. M. (2006). Equivalence of standard and computerized versions of the Raven progressive matrices test. *Computers in Human Behavior, 22*, 791–800.

Williams, L. M., Mathersul, D., Palmer, D. M., Gur, R. C., Gur, R. E., & Gordon, E. (2009). Explicit identification and implicit recognition of facial emotions: I. Age effects in males and females across 10 decades. *Journal of Clinical and Experimental Neuropsychology, 31*(3), 257–277.

Wilson, B. A. (1993). Ecological validity of neuropsychological assessment: Do neuropsychological indexes predict performance in everyday activities? *Applied & Preventive Psychology, 2*, 209–215.

Wilson, B. A. (2011). Cutting edge developments in neuropsychological rehabilitation and possible future directions. *Brain Impairment, 12*, 33–42.

Wilson, B. A. (2013). Neuropsychological rehabilitation: State of the science. *South African Journal of Psychology, 43*(3), 267–277.

Wilson, B. A., Alderman, N., Burgess, P. W., Emslie, H., & Evans, J. J. (1996). *Behavioral Assessment of the Dysexecutive Syndrome. Bury St.* Edmunds: Thames Valley Test Company.

Wilson, B. A., Clare, L., Cockburn, J. M., Baddeley, A. D., Tate, R., & Watson, P. (1999). The Rivermead Behavioral Memory Test—Extended Version. Bury St. Edmunds: Thames Valley Test Company.

Wilson, B., Cockburn, J., & Baddeley, A. (1991). *The Rivermead behavioural memory test manual. Bury St.* Edmunds: Thames Valley Test Corporation.

Wilson, B. A., Cockburn, J., Baddeley, A., & Hiorns, R. (1989). The development and validation of a test battery for detecting and monitoring everyday memory problems. *Journal of Clinical and Experimental Neuropsychology, 11*, 855–870.

Wilson, B. A., Emslie, H. C., Quirk, K., & Evans, J. J. (2001). Reducing everyday memory and planning problems by means of a paging system: a randomised control crossover study. *The Journal of Neurology, Neurosurgery, and Psychiatry, 70*, 477–82.

Wilson, B. A., Evans, J. J., Brentnall, S., Bremner, S., Keohane, C., & Williams, H. (2000). The Oliver Zangwill Centre for Neuropsychological Rehabilitation: a partnership between health care and rehabilitation research. In A.-L. Christensen & B. P. Uzzell (Eds.), *International Handbook of Neuropsychological Rehabilitation* (pp. 231–46). New York: Kluwer Academic/Plenum.

Wilson, B. A., Shiel, A., Foley, J., Emslie, H., Groot, Y., Hawkins, K., et al. (2004). *Cambridge Test of Prospective Memory. Bury St.* Edmunds: Thames Valley Test Company.

Windmann, S., Kirsch, P., Mier, D., Stark, R., Walter, B., Gunturkun, O., et al. (2006). On framing effects in decision making: linking lateral versus medial orbitofrontal cortex activation to choice outcome processing. *Journal of Cognitive Neuroscience, 18*(7), 1198–1211.

Witsken, D. E., D'Amato, R. C., & Hartlage, L. C. (2008). Understanding the past, present, and future of clinical neuropsychology. In R. C. D'Amato & L. C. Hartlage (Eds.), *Essentials of neuropsychological assessment, second edition: Treatment planning for rehabilitation* (pp. 3–29). New York: Springer Publishing Company.

Witt, J. A., Alpherts, W., & Helmstaedter, C. (2013). Computerized neuropsychological testing in epilepsy: Overview of available tools. *Seizure, 22*(6), 416–423.

Wolbers, T., & Hegarty, M. (2010). What determines our navigational abilities? *Trends in Cognitive Sciences, 14*(3), 138–146.

Woo, E. (2008). Computerized neuropsychological assessments. *CNS Spectrums, 13*(10 Suppl 16), 14–17.

Woods, S. P., Weinborn, M., & Lovejoy, D. W. (2003). Are classification accuracy statistics underused in neuropsychological research? *Journal of Clinical and Experimental Neuropsychology, 25*(3), 431–439.

Wright, C. E., O'Donnell, K., Brydon, L., Wardle, J., & Steptoe, A. (2007). Family history of cardiovascular disease is associated with cardiovascular responses to stress in healthy young men and women. *International Journal of Psychophysiology, 63*, 275–282.

Wu, D., Courtney, C., Lance, B., Narayanan, S. S., Dawson, M., Oie, K., & Parsons, T. D. (2010). Optimal Arousal Identification and Classification for Affective Computing: Virtual Reality Stroop Task. *IEEE Transactions on Affective Computing, 1*, 109–118.

Wu, D., Lance, B., & Parsons, T. D. (2013). Collaborative filtering for brain-computer interaction using transfer learning and active class selection. *PLOS ONE*, 1–18.

Yellowlees, P. M., Shore, J., & Roberts, L. (2010). Practice Guidelines for Videoconferencing-Based Tele-mental Health—October 2009. *Telemed e-Health., 16*, 1074–1089.

Yerkes, R. M. (1917). Behaviorism and genetic psychology. *Journal of Philosophy, Psycholo-gy, and Scientific Methods, 14*, 154–160.

Yoakum, C. S., & Yerkes, R. M. (1920). *Army mental tests*. New York: Holt.

Zackariasson, P., & Wilson, T. L. (2010). Paradigm shifts in the video game industry. *Competitiveness Review, 20*, 139–151.

Zakzanis, K. K. (1998). Brain is related to behavior ($p < 0.05$). *Journal of Clinical and Experimental Neuropsychology, 20*(3), 419–427.

Zakzanis, K. K. (2001). Statistics to tell the truth, the whole truth, and nothing but the truth: formulae, illustrative numerical examples, and heuristic interpretation of effect size anal-yses for neuropsychological researchers. *Archives of Clinical Neuropsychology, 16*(7), 653–667.

Zakzanis, K. K., & Azarbehi, R. (2014). Introducing BRAIN screen: Web-Based Real-Time Examination and Interpretation of Cognitive Function. *Applied Neuropsychology: Adult, 21*(2), 77–86.

Zald, D. H., & Andreotti, C. (2010). Neuropsychological assessment of the orbital and ventromedial prefrontal cortex. *Neuropsychologia, 48*(12), 3377–3391.

Zangwill, O. L. (1947). Psychological aspects of rehabilitation in cases of brain injury. *British Journal of Psychology, 37*(2), 60–69.

Zelazo, P. D., Müller, U., Frye, D., Marcovitch, S., Argitis, G., Boseovski, J., & Carlson, S. M. (2003). The development of executive function in early childhood. Monographs of the society for research in child development, i–151.

Zygouris, S., & Tsolaki, M. (2015). Computerized Cognitive Testing for Older Adults A review. *American Journal of Alzheimer's Disease and other Dementias, 30*(1), 13–28.

Index

T.D. Parsons, *Clinical Neuropsychology and Technology*,
DOI 10.1007/978-3-319-31075-6

FSC
www.fsc.org
MIX
Papier | Fördert
gute Waldnutzung
FSC® C083411

Kolibri 360 GmbH
Ferdinand-Jühlke-Straße 7
99095 Erfurt, Deutschland
produktsicherheit@kolibri360.de